BULLETS
and
BREAD

BULLETS and BREAD

The Story of the Sacrifice in American Homes to Feed Troops in World War II

Kent Whitaker

History Publishing Company
Palisades, New York

Copyright ©2013 by Kent Whitaker

Whitaker, Kent, 1965-

Bullets and bread : the WWII story of feeeding americans at home and on
the battlefield / Kent Whitaker. -- 1st ed. -- Palisades, NY :
History Pub. Co., c2013.

p. ; cm.

ISBN: 978-1-933909-75-2 (cloth) ;
978-1-933909-76-9 (ebk.)
Includes bibliographical references and index.
Summary: Examines the foods, food supplies, and the transformation of
the food industry needed to supply a military that grew from one to ten
million over night, as well as the menus and the difficulties on the home-
front. Includes examples of menus from heads of state, princesses and
generals; as well as recipes for, and comments from, the fighting men and
women.--Publisher.

1. World War, 1939-1945--Food supply--United States. 2. Cooking,
American--History--20th century. 3. War and society--United States--
History--20th century. 4. Food supply--United States--History--20th
century. 5. Food conservation--United States--History--20th century.
6. Rationing--United States--History--20th century. 7. Menus--United
States--History--20th century. 8. Agriculture--Economic aspects--United
States--History--20th century. I. Title.

TX357 .W45 2013
641.5973/09044--dc23   1302

SAN: 850-5942

Published in the United States by
History Publishing Company LLC
Palisades, NY
www.historypublishingco.com

Printed in the United States on acid free paper

9 8 7 6 5 4 3 2 1

First Edition

Dedicated to my wife Ally.
Also to our son Georgia National Army Strong son
Macee and our parents, Arleta and Eli M. Whitaker,
Joan and Henry Joseph "Bruce" Nagem.
Also to our brothers and sisters, family and friends.
I would also like to dedicate and thank all of the veterans
and families who shared their memories and stories

TABLE OF CONTENTS

SPECIAL NOTES FROM THE AUTHOR

My wife Ally and I were visiting our son Macee (Macy) at North Georgia College and State University which is one of six senior military colleges in the United States. He had already finished basic training and was now a North Georgia cadet. We were in town at a shop looking over cookbooks when Macee mentioned my barbecue book to a gentleman standing near us. The three of us started talking about BBQ, a favorite Southern pastime.

When I mentioned a possible book on Civil War cooking our new BBQ buddy instantly told a story about military chow when he served in the 1980's. Another veteran overheard us and mentioned the food he had in the Navy. He was followed with a story about the worst food in the Army from another veteran in the shop. Several veterans wandered into the conversation over the next several minutes. It was pretty cool to listen in. The conversation was a strange mix of memories of the best and worst chow served up with a helmet full of respect.

I started taking mental, and a few real, notes. I thought I could somehow work the stories into the Civil War book or magazine article. Over several months the project grew from grub served in the Civil War to present day MRE's. It was getting overwhelming.

Thankfully, Don Bracken, at History Publishing, suggested that the focus should be on "The Greatest Generation." World War Two veterans, their stories and how food played a defining factor in the Allied War Effort.

I hope this mixture of information, humor, stories and pictures honors the "Chow" memories of all of the veterans who served during the war while not diminishing the combined hard work of ration developers, researchers, growers, packagers, citizens and of course the cooks, bakers, mess sergeants, mess men, quartermasters and more who served up meals during World War Two.

About the Memories & *"submitted by anonymous."*

Many of the memories in the book are followed by a name of a person while some are credited to "anonymous," or just with initials. I respect those who wanted to share a story with their names attached, and respectfully honor the request of those who wish to remain anonymous.

The memories shared in this book are reprinted as they were shared with me in person, phone, mail or by email. Only minor editing was performed on these wonderful stories in order to keep the "voice" of the person. The memories come from World War Two veterans, from people submitting stories in honor of a loved one who served or lived during the WWII years. Other recipes and stories are submitted from various organizations and museums which are listed in the back of the book.

About the Recipes

All of the recipes, tips and cooking advice in this book are reproduced from World War Two era material such as training manuals, propaganda flyers, news sources and more. Some recipes are designed for serving 100 plus men while others are geared towards family cooking during the war. Some ingredients are spelled wrong. Some recipes may use terms associated with the times and may call for ingredients that may not be on the market or use cooking methods that are not typical today. I included recipes that I thought a reader could easily adapt using modern cooking methods and ingredients.

That being said, the recipes printed in this book are for historical purposes. Any reader trying to use these recipes should only do so at their own risk and attempt to do so only when using modern ingredients, cooking methods, safety measures and proper cleaning materials. Hope you enjoy these stories and memories as much as I enjoyed them.

About the Author

From left to right: The author-Matthew Kent Whitaker (in his diaper) along with his older brothers Scot Campbell Whitaker and Eli "Ty" Meredith Whitaker III. According to my mom this photo was probably taken in 1967 during one of our family trips to the Gulf Coast and our first visit to the USS Alabama. The picture brought back memories from my brothers when told of its use in this book. Ty claims to have hit Scot with the ukulele shortly after the picture was taken. And Scot proudly exclaimed with a grin. "I bet nobody on that ship has ever found where I hid your pacifiers." I vaguely remember losing one. Scot puts the total number of pacifiers he hid on board as three.
Photo provided by Eli and Arleta Whitaker.

Kent Whitaker is a culinary writer and cookbook author with a deep love for family, friends, food, history, tailgates, beaches and things cooked on a smoker or a grill. You can often find Kent enjoying a motorcycle ride, visiting a historic battlefield or just hanging out with his Golden Retriever. But, as his wife and son will tell you, he is bound to take some notes or pictures for a new project at any time. Kent is also a member of the United States Coast Guard Auxiliary. He and his wife Ally and son Macee live in East Ridge Tennessee.

Gearing Up
Food Production for War

The United States industrial build up for World War II was a vital part of the Allied victory. America transformed industries, factories and a massive workforce focused on the downsizing of numerous consumer goods to a combination of limited consumer items while creating a multitude of items needed for war. Factories turning out household items now were producing bullets, tents, PT boats, tanks, planes and various items service men needed during war. A large number of nontraditional workers were recruited, hired and trained. America went through an industrial, economic and lifestyle revolution.

This massive buildup and transformation was so impressive that an equally amazing change in another American industry is somewhat overlooked. This second transformation occurred in the food production industry. On the simplest level, the United States was a rural, farm based society where outlying farms and producers fed and supplied nearby thriving urban areas. National brands of consumer goods were beginning to show up on rural shelves but once you left the city, things in the area of food production, farming, transportations needs were fairly limited. Cross country travel and transportations of goods was limited to a number of railways and a growing airline business with limited capacity or by sea. All of this would change in a relatively short time.

The manner in which farmers worked, food was harvested, shipped, processed and moved from one farm to production plants, ramped up in a manner that rivaled the growth of industrial production. The two processes were linked together. Both required better management, records, facilities and safeguards. Food production, packaging, ration development, and distribution systems similar to the one in place after World War I, was quickly changing for both civilians and the military. By contrast, while amazing changes were taking place, a heavy reliance on old fashioned home gardening and canning for home front consumption ensured that more food went to the troops.

Before America officially entered the war over $50 Billion dollars in various types of support was given to Allied nations. This aid was part of a buildup of industrial strength and laid the foundation for an increased effort when the US entered the conflict. Everything pertaining to war production and supply needed to be brought up to date. This included food for the troops. By the late 1930's the various service branches saw a planned increase in manpower in case war came to the states. At the start of 1939, around 174,000 men were enlisted in the army. The navy had 126,400 men with 19,700 in the Marine Corps. Around 26,000 men were in the Army Air Corps and the smallest service branch, the Coast Guard, had 10,000 men in its ranks. These pre-war numbers grew steadily as more bases were built and more military manufacturing capabilities were brought into service. The build up, which began after Pearl Harbor, was actually underway years before.

By 1945, the United States Army numbered upwards of 6,000,000 men compared to the 1941 numbers of 174,000. Other service branches also swelled when compared to pre war numbers. The Navy had over 3,400,000 men and 484,000 men in the Marine Corps. The Army Air Forces grew to 2,400,000 men and the Coast Guard had about 170,000 men. Don't forget to then add in the women who served in various services such as WACS, WASPS, WAVES, SPARS and Army and Navy nurses.

All of those additional people, men and women, had to be trained, clothed, transported and housed. They also had to be fed three times a day on base, in the field, on the battlefield front lines, on ships, in planes and anywhere else they visited, rested, camped, marched or sought medical help. After World War I many military leaders realized that properly being able to feed and supply troops was an issue that needed to be addressed. In fact, feeding armies has always been a source of frustration for military leaders. Napoleon's oft-quoted note that "an army travels on its stomach," is a reflection of that reality.

The opening of the new Quartermaster Subsistence Research and Development Laboratory ensured that better rations could be developed in a more scientific manner. This combined with the improved training of cooks and bakers helped feed Allied Armies better than its AXIS foes. By 1938 working prototypes of some new rations had been developed and cooks and bakers schools were being vastly improved for all military branches. The Quartermaster Corps focused on developing ways to serve the troops in the field in every area from food to clothing.

The early development of modern rations included the Combat ration and the Individual ration, and when first shown to the General Staff were well received and orders were given to proceed with more development. Budget planners noting that "The Great War" was over, slashed budgets but development continued with little funding. Some progress was made as new rations and packaging solutions developed before Pearl Harbor. Further development continued throughout the course of the war.

Field testing rations.
Photo Courtesy of the Fort Lee United States Army Quartermaster Museum

But only a few rations had been developed to an operational point and put into service when the war started. Soldiers often held ration cans and items in their hands with dates printed on them from years prior. During the first few hectic months a "grab what you can get" and " work with what you got" attitude was used to take advantage of available stocks. This was mundane for men fighting in the field who tired of the never ending flow of similar ration bars and canned items three times a day. But the use of these items, of limited variety, allowed for a quick way to get food to the troops while new solutions were sought.

The D bar was one such item. The D Bar was a seemingly indestructible block of a chocolate developed by Colonel Paul Logan and the Hershey Candy Company. Logan and Hershey apparently decided that the D Ration should not be too tasty. If it tasted too good, troops would eat it before it was needed in an emergency. His effort to develop a ration bar that lacked taste and appeal worked. In fact many troops threw the D rations away for fear of breaking a tooth or were convinced the thing was not edible. The block was so hard that pieces had to be shaved off with a knife and it resisted melting up to temps of 140 degrees.

Many years after the war ended Colonel Alvin Hulsey recalled the efforts men went through to eat the D ration bar. He remembered trying to eat a D bar with his teeth, attempting to break it in small pieces, tried using a knife, and ended up scraping it apart with a bayonet, all with little success. His next effort at making the bar edible was even more extreme; he tried to melt the bar against a hot tank engine. It didn't work.

Despite the supply situation at the outset of the war, the initial training of service men, including the Quartermaster Corps, was an impressive statement as to how American forces would perform, even in the face of disaster.

The Quartermasters (QMs) who fought and defended the Philippines were a perfect example of how Quartermasters were able to use their improved training to adapt to the situation. The QM's under attack had a limited store of goods, mostly dated armor style rations, combined with limited numbers of the newly developed D ration bars and some C rations. This was supplemented with a dwindling supply of local foods.

Once the fighting started the QM's had already put into action a buildup of supplies that they maintained and began to stretch. The idea was based on limited waste and recycling anything that could be used. If a farm animal or military mule died, or was no longer needed, it probably became food. If a vehicle broke down it became parts to keep other trucks and jeeps moving. Nothing was wasted.

Early fighting proved that the industrial build up and the food production improvements would have to work towards the same goal. American companies such as canners, food producers and packagers had to be brought into the system as quickly as possible. Then these companies had to get production going, produce the supplies which in turn had to make it into the hands of the troops that needed them. The same effort that was used to convert plants into military production facilities was duplicated for food producers and packagers. The Rosie the riveter mind set worked in shipyards, factories, and the entire food production industry of the United States from farms to transportation.

The message to provide the best for the troops that was put into use for both military and civilians. On the home front, hard work, sacrifice, and a "can do" attitude pushed civilians. The same "can do" attitude applied to the military. Several civilian researchers and scientists were hired in order to move ration development forward. These new people came from the private sector and civilian scientific ranks and were able to think outside of the military box even with the lack of proper funding. One such person was Dr. Ancel Keys, developer of the K ration.

Keys and his coworkers would make impromptu trips to the local Piggly Wiggly grocery store to buy assorted items in order to test a new idea for a ration when time and funding did not allow for other options. A description requirement for one of the projects Dr. Keys was working on, included a line that the ration "should not disrupt normal elimination from the bowel or derange the chemistry of the body!" While the new K Ration started out with lackluster reviews Key's ability to combine items ranging from biscuits and reduced sized ration bars combined with a few other items in a small package made it a successful ration to use and build on.

Para K Ration
In this undated Signal Corps photo, provided by the Quartermaster Museum at Fort Lee, several paratroopers are grabbing a quick meal consisting of the Emergency "K" ration.
Photo Courtesy of the Fort Lee United States Army Quartermaster Museum

This led to the development and continued improvements in the C-Ration and other rations. Keys and other researchers quickly learned to make the best out of what they had. When something worked or showed promise, they kept it and improved it. When something didn't work, they shelved it. All while continuing to develop new ideas.

As the war progressed Dr. Keys became a factor in every area and even led the efforts to study methods in which starved POW's could be returned to health. He tapped an under-utilized resource of overlooked conscientious objectors who wanted to help in some way with the war effort without using a weapon. These volunteers dropped an average of 25% of their body weight to replicate the effects of a starved POW. They were then nursed back to health under the watchful eye of researchers. The safest methods were quickly transferred to the field.

While ration development and food production, packaging, and distribution, were a huge effort, the other side of the food equation was developing the normalcy of the super-abundance of hot food served directly to troops. The issue of properly training enough cooks and bakers to prepare hot meals on bases, ships, airstrips and other military locations which eventually spanned the globe had to be tackled. Finding the personnel was primary and WACS and SPARS were among the first candidates.

Two cartoon postcards depicting the readiness, in a humorous way, of WACS. In fact, these highly trained women served a variety of duties during the war effort.
From the collection of the 6th Calvary Museum, Fort Oglethorpe, Georgia

There are countless stories of men standing in line who elected to be, or were selected to be a cook simply because they knew a few recipes from their mom or family cookbook. When asked if anyone had experience in a kitchen these guys raised their hands. Some former World War Two cooks will tell you that they had no idea how they became a military cook. Thousands and thousands attended Cooks and Bakers schools in order to learn about healthy cooking, sanitation, recipes, food safety and more. Many African American men started to break down racial walls during the war. Like other Americans they served in combat units across the globe, as tankers, pilots, truck drivers as well as cooks, bakers and in countless other roles often while under enemy fire. Regardless of race or background "cookies" were doing their jobs while still being a soldier who was expected to pick up a rifle or man a gun when needed. Stateside, many POW's served as cooks and bakers.

William Wamsley was the principal of the American Institute of Baking which was vital to the war effort. He served with the AIB for over thirty years. Wamsley, picture to the far left, watches as two military officers and another observer, examine one of the field ovens that were set up on the front lawn of the American Institute of Baking in Chicago as part of the training "campus" for the U.S. Army Training School for Advanced Bakers.
Photo courtesy of the Harold M. Freund American Baking Museum - WWII Collection. Original photo United States Signal Corps.

A class full of United States Army officers, non-commissioned officers and privates are pictured attending a baking class at the U.S. Army Training School for Advanced Baking Instructors in Chicago during World War Two.
Photo courtesy of the Harold M. Freund American Baking Museum - WWII Collection. Original photo United States Signal Corps.

Cooks and bakers were being trained and sent across the globe by land and sea but they still needed a mind numbing assortment of equipment items, supplies and of course food. This required people working in supply, transportation, storage, procurement, development and more. This led to the marriage of industrial military output, safer food production, and more efficient packaging and transportation, all of which eventually ended back in the hands of the mom and pop and commercial farmers and ranchers on the home front.

After World War II, American troops would never be fed the same way again… unless you ask a Korean War veteran.

CHAPTER ONE

Famous Names in the Chow Line

During World War II there was an enormous strain on the people, resources and militaries of many countries. Shortages and rationing were common place. England was not spared the hardship as the island nation was targeted by Hitler in order to cut off as much trade and support as possible. The attempted blockade, combined with the difficulties involved with supply during a war, made many consumer items scarce, even for a royal family. As the war raged a small group of workers loyal to the Queen Mother were assigned a task. When the word was given they fanned out across the country side in order to carry out their mission.

Sometimes these missions were secret and relied on a network of spies, codes and clandestine events. But this mission was culinary in nature. According to the McIlhenny Co., the search was on for one of the Queen Mother's favorite kitchen pantry items, *Tabasco Sauce*. In fact, Tabasco brand pepper sauce has achieved the ultimate Royal seal of approval from Her Majesty Queen Elizabeth II.

The famous pepper sauce, a product of the United States and the McIhenney Company since 1870, had been an item in the royal pantry for years and became a staple in rations for many allied soldiers. The product is now sold in over 160 countries with labels printed with over twenty two different languages.

The Queen mother and the King made an effort to keep a public face despite the issues facing the country. As a family the royals had many decisions to make, as did their people. All suggestions to send their children, Princess Elizabeth and Princess Margaret, to the safety of Canada were rejected. "The children won't go without me. I won't leave without the King. And the King will never leave," stated the Queen of England about her daughters. The Royal Family felt that it was important the people to see them as being united. The King and Queen became a visible symbol of the resilience and steadfastness of the British people. They did this by visiting troops in the field, wounded soldiers and civilians in hospitals and by touring plants and shaking hands with everyday people despite the obvious dangers.

The Vulcan Foundry in England is famous for locomotive production. During World War II and WWI the foundry produced tanks, and other war related items, instead of trains. King George and the Queen tour the factory in 1941.
From the private collection of Graeme Pilkington.
www.enuii.org/vulcan_foundry

Like everyone in England the royal family changed the way they lived. On many occasions they were hurried into bomb shelters just as were civilians. The King and his family appeared to endure the same hardships that the people were going through, such as simplified and rationed based meals as well as bombings. The Royal family became a national symbol of hope for many because they suffered through the war the same as everyday people were doing.

2

Princes Elizabeth is shown in this photo improving her skills as a mechanic
during the later years of the war.
Photo from the collection of the Author

Princess Elizabeth, later to become Queen Elizabeth, faced the same problems the people of the country faced. Despite efforts to have she and her sister Margaret sent to Canada during the fighting, she did not sit at home and wait out the war. She joined the war effort by becoming a member of the uniformed W.A.T.S. which as the Women's Auxiliary Territorial Service. Princess Elizabeth trained as a mechanic and truck driver. She had shown that, while being part of royalty, she also understood what it was like to work and serve your country.

Many years after the war had ended the Queen once again showed her "everyday person" side to a United States president. As a simple offering between two people she gave a rather simplistic scone recipe to President Eisenhower. The recipe, which could easily be made in a private residence kitchen with limited ingredients, is now in the Eisenhower Library collection.

Her Father, King George, was a veteran of World War I and served as a member of the Royal Navy on the HMS Collingwood. He later served in the Royal Air Force. His duty on the HMS Collingwood during World War I helped keep him safe during the Second World War. He traveled under the allied codename "General Collingwood" in order to help hide his activities.

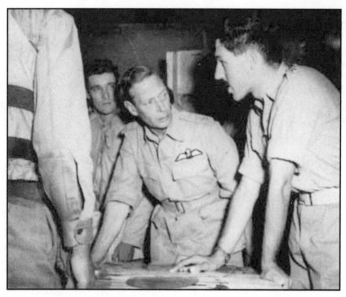

King George shown under his code name "General Collingwood."
From the private collection of Graeme Pilkington
www.enuii.org/vulcan_foundry

During a visit to the United States in 1939 the King and Queen had several social and official meetings with President Roosevelt and the First Lady. During one visit of the Royal couple to the United States the president's mother, Sara Roosevelt, objected to the President making of a pitcher of martinis to be served to the King and Queen. According to Philip Cantelon, in his article for *American Heritage*, the president's mother suggested that tea would be a better choice. When King George was offered the martini by F.D.R. the president voiced his mother's concerns. "My mother thinks you should have a cup of tea-she doesn't approve of cocktails." George VI answered, "Neither does my mother," the King took the martini.

This photo was taken by an unknown photographer on May 14, 1943 and shows
Franklin D. Roosevelt with Winston Churchill
at the presidential retreat Shangri, La.
From the collection of Franklin D. Roosevelt Library.

Roosevelt had down home preferences when it came to food.
According to the FDR Library, Henrietta Nesbitt - a White House house-
keeper, said that FDR had very simple American style tastes in food. He
liked things that "he could dig into." His favorite dishes ranged from
scrambled eggs and fish chowder to a simple grilled cheese sandwich, hot
dogs, and fruitcake. According to the Franklin D. Roosevelt Presidential

5

Library, Franklin Roosevelt also had a fondness for fish chowders and kedgeree, a concoction of fish, rice and hard-boiled eggs.

In a 1958 article from *Reader's Digest* author Crosby Gaige commented on some of the thrifty dinning ideas of the president and the First lady.

"During Franklin D. Roosevelt's administration I was a guest at a dinner at the White House. Mrs. Roosevelt sat at one side of a long table and her husband sat facing her. After the soup a huge boiled salmon was brought in on an enormous silver platter. When it appeared Mr. Roosevelt remarked to his wife, "Who gave us that magnificent fish?"

"Why are you so sure somebody gave it to us?" she asked him.

"Because nobody in his senses would go out and actually buy a fish as big as that," said the President."

Roosevelt loved scrambled eggs. They were served every Sunday night whether dining alone or entertaining important guests. Mrs. Roosevelt would often prepare them herself in a chafing dish.

Eleanor Roosevelt, known for her globetrotting visits to troops,
is greeted by sailors during a 1943 visit to Bora Bora.
From the Collection of the Franklin D. Roosevelt Library & Museum

The First Lady was a perfect food fit for the president. Eleanor Roosevelt brought her free willed, respectful style and caring attitude to the White House. During the war she traveled, visited troops, hospitals & wounded, attended rallies, fought for causes she believed in and even wanted to learn how to fly by taking lessons from Amelia Earhart. The president talked her out of it. Her outspoken style prompted her to be the first of the First Ladies to hold regular press conferences. Others had granted interviews, or spoken to the press on a limited basis. Eleanor took it a step further and embraced the media to further her voice and the projects and causes she was interested in. Before, during and after World War Two Eleanor would travel the world to visit injured solders, champion a cause or lend her voice to a charity and made visits to her four sons who all served in the military.

Like the president Eleanor had a wide variety of food tastes ranging from scrambled eggs to more sophisticated fare. Her fondness for what could be considered low brow food even made its way onto the official menu for a picnic honoring the King and Queen of England's 1939 visit. Once again the president's mother, Sara, was stunned when she found out what the planned menu was for an upcoming picnic to be held in honor of the King and Queen during their first ever Royal visit to the United States. The menu included traditional American picnic classics such as hotdogs - weather permitting, shortcake, sodas and cold beer along with some additional dishes. Despite the concerns of the President's mother, and some outcries in the press, the President and First Lady stuck by their chosen menu of plain and simple fare for a picnic. And by all accounts the Royal couple loved the event.

When President Franklin D. Roosevelt died in office Vice President Truman was sworn in President in time to guide the free world towards the end of the Second World War. During his brief time as vice president Truman rarely saw President Roosevelt and was not fully aware of many topics that the president was privilege to. It was not until after Roosevelt's death that Truman was fully briefed on issues including the development of the Atomic Bomb. He told reporters, "I felt like the moon, the stars, and all the planets had fallen on me."

President Truman dines with Chief Petty Officers on the USS Augusta in 1945
Official US Navy photo, National Archives

Before entering politics Truman served during World War I and was stationed in France with the artillery. His unit launched some of the final artillery rounds into German positions towards the end of the war. As a civilian Truman started his own business with a friend named *Truman's Haberdashery*. Business was not very good and the store shut its doors after a few years. Truman then entered politics as a Judge and later served as a Senator where he led an oversight committee focused on overspending that saved the government millions of tax dollars. He served only a few months as Vice President before he was sworn in as President upon the death of Roosevelt.

Truman was known for his love of fried chicken, roast, chocolate cake and dumplings. He also enjoyed a good steak cooked up Kansas City Style. According to the Truman library President Truman sometimes tried to cook, but was not good at it and really had no desire to try to learn. Truman was not a picky eater and seemed to prefer traditional farm style food. When pushed to comment on his food preferences he one time stated: "Never notice what's put before me. Learned in the army to eat what could be obtained and like it. In my outfit when a man kicked about the food, he was given a chance to improve it. That soon cured the kickers and they took what was put before them and liked it." Truman did have a fondness for his aunt's pound cake which is said to have been in the Truman family for 200 years.

One famous World War II leader that had a strong fondness for food was Winston Leonard Spencer Churchill. The British statesman rallied the people of Great Britain against the Germans and was a steadfast symbol of defiance against Axis aggressions. He was a soldier, orator, war correspondent and author as well as twice a prime minister serving first from 1940 to 1945 and later from 1951 to 1955.

Churchill Roosevelt and Stalin pose for a photo opportunity during a conference in Yalta in 1945.
Photo from the National Archives

Churchill and his wife accepted the offer of chef Georgina Landemare to be their cook during the war. Landemare later wrote a cookbook titled *Recipes from Number 10* which included some of Churchill's favorites. Landemare was well known at the time as a wonderful cook and she catered to large parties and formal affairs. The Prime Minister kept Mrs. Landemare busy. He often worked late and asked for late night snacks.

Sometimes she would prepare a meal for a dinner, a meeting or even to be delivered to a bomb shelter. Once after Churchill tried to hurry her to a shelter fearing a bombing raid, Landemare refused due to concerns her soufflé was not done.

According to the Churchill Centre and Museum, the Prime Minister enjoyed fowl, roast beef & Yorkshire pudding, clear soups, raw oysters & other shellfish, underdone beef and Irish stew. All of which Georgina Landemare was able to provide despite rations and lack of proper ingredients. And sometimes while being bombed by the Nazis. As the war progressed the various leaders adapted to life as did their people.

On the other end of the cooking spectrum was General Dwight D Eisenhower who loved outdoor activities ranging from sports to cooking wild game. He enjoyed hunting and fishing. As a high school student he excelled in athletics and eventually received an appointment to West Point.

President Eisenhower, in his later years, grilling a steak.
Photo from The Eisenhower Archives

In November of 1942 Eisenhower commanded the Allied Forces landing in North Africa. On D-Day, Eisenhower was named Supreme Commander of the troops invading France. After the war he served as the president of Columbia University before he was called back into action in 1951 as supreme command over NATO forces before being elected president.

President Eisenhower suffered from many health problems which actually helped raise awareness about public health issues. Despite the health problems Eisenhower still loved activities such as hunting, fishing and cooking wild game and fresh fish whenever he could. Eisenhower believed that if you are going to hunt and fish you need to learn how to cook! His love for hunting, fishing and cooking wild game suffered in his later years as he suffered from Crohn's disease which caused him to suffer several problems with his intestines.

Always at his side was Mamie Geneva Doud Eisenhower who was born on November 14, 1896 in Boone Iowa. She was raised with a down-home, penny saving style. As a young lady in high school her family already knew she had a keen mind for budgeting and finance. Not considered to be poor in her youth, nor her early years of marriage, Mamie was well aware of the tight budgets that many everyday families and military wives worked with. Her ability to budget, save money and "penny pinch" became one of her trademarks.

Mamie Eisenhower, known for her reputation for everything from budgets to kitchen tips, accepts a Thanksgiving Turkey for the White House as a gift from the Poultry Growers Association. Also pictured is the 35lb live turkey that was raised by Mr. Trevor L. Jones, President of the National Turkey Federation from Springfield Illinois. The live turkey was taken away after the presentation and large frozen turkey left in its place. *Courtesy of The Eisenhower Archives*

11

She enjoyed fancy cakes for many occasions in the White house, including workers birthdays. This made her a favorite First lady with the staff. Many recipes have been credited to Mamie Eisenhower. One such is a simple recipe that has variations and is often called White House Fudge, Mamie's Fudge, Mrs. Eisenhower's Fudge, Million dollar fudge among just a few. According to the National First Ladies Library, on occasion Mamie also enjoyed a Fruit Old Fashioned, a cocktail. She was not a heavy drinker despite rumors. She often stumbled but these bouts of being unsteady came from her battle with Meniere's disease which is an inner ear disorder.

Mamie was known for her fudge recipe but she was not the only person who had a sweet tooth. General Douglas MacArthur was born on January 26, 1880 in Little Rock, Arkansas and enjoyed sweets as well. During his many years of military service he ascended through the ranks of the Army, became Army Chief of Staff, went on to command the Southwest Pacific Theatre in World War II, and was assigned to be the administer of postwar Japan.

General Douglas MacArthur (center) with Vice Admiral Thomas C. Kinkaid (left center) standing on the flag bridge of USS Phoenix during action at Los Negros Island on February 28, 1944. At right is Colonel Lloyd Labrbas, acting aide to General MacArthur.
Photograph from the Army Signal Corps Collection in the U.S. National Archives.

According to the MacArthur Memorial Museum, General Doulas MacArthur was very fond of chocolates and one particular dessert; Spanish Cream. During the war his departure from the Philippines highlighted the work that had to be done in the areas of ration development, improving the supply chain and provided the first real test of what modern trained Quartermasters could do under fire.

In the European Theater, General George Patton was known for his words as well as his actions. In an address to his men in 1944 Patton stated several reasons that he believed would make the American forces victorious. *"We have the finest food, the finest equipment, the best spirit, and the best men in the world. Why, by God, I actually pity those poor sons-of-bitches we're going up against. By God, I do."* This attitude helped make Patton a commander that was both respected and feared by his men as well as his enemies.

Lt. Gen. George S. Patton and Lt. Col. Lyle Bernard, CO, 30th Infantry Regiment, a prominent figure in the second daring amphibious landing behind enemy lines on Sicily's north coast, discus strategy in 1943.
From the collection of the National Archives

13

In1960 his daughter, Ruth Patton Totten, wrote a cookbook titled *The Rolling Kitchen* which was inspired by the rolling kitchens she saw being used in the military. Totten featured many recipes that she collected, not only as the daughter of the famous General, but also as an Army wife. In the book she featured two recipes attributed to General Patton. She also noted some kitchen habits of the famed General in stating that he "was not one to lurk around the kitchen and bother the cook." She did point out that the general was a great shot and enjoyed dove and quail when "it was not overcooked and treated like Spam."

Another famous military figure during World War II was Britain's Field Marshall Montgomery, called "Monty" by members of the press, his solders and his peers. Born in 1887 to a Bishop, Bernard Montgomery stayed away from many vices including drinking, smoking and excess. In 1908 he was commissioned with the Royal Warwickshire Regiment. During World War I, Montgomery served on the Western Front and eventually was wounded which caused him to serve for the remainder of the conflict as a staff officer. After the war Montgomery found that the military life fit him well and by 1938 he had risen to the rank of Major General.

General Bernard L. Montgomery watches his tanks in action in North Africa during November of 1942. *From the collection of the National Archives*

Montgomery was also known for his love of a traditional English breakfast, or a "full breakfast." Many attribute the term "Full Monty" as being based on the Field Marshall's love of the full breakfast that comes with just about everything. The traditional full breakfast varies somewhat from village and shire and from England, Ireland and Scotland but the basic theme is the same. The breakfast includes just about everything from bacon, eggs and grilled tomatoes to mushrooms, beans and toast. But others say the phrase, Full Monty, has roots related to clothing. Montague Maurice Burton (1885-1952), was a men's tailor, and the term "Full Monty" is often referred to the purchase of a complete, or full, three-piece suit.

A "Full Breakfast" was often hard to come by in many places during the war and this included the Pacific theatre. Food in the Pacific, as it was in other combat areas, was sometimes in short supply. Despite all efforts supply could quickly be outpaced by demand. And battle conditions often disrupted the flow of supplies, proper storage facilities, and refrigeration as troops moved across the globe. Such was the case when Admiral "Bull" Halsey arrived at Guadalcanal to have a look at the overall battle situation

Admiral "Bull" Halsey dines with the crew of the USS New Jersey in 1944 during Thanksgiving. Halsey is seated left center.
Official Navy Photograph from the collection of the National Archives

15

in a region he knew had limited prospects for seeing any decent chow. Guadalcanal had been the recent scene of horrific battles and it was still under fire. A good meal was and not a priority for him during the visit.

In the book *Bull Halsey*, author E.B. Potter, notes that after arriving by B-17 Halsey rode in a waiting jeep which whisked him away to a meeting with General Alexander A. Vandegrift who had lead the Marines on Guadalcanal and many other Pacific campaigns. He would later become Commandant of the Marine Corps. Along the way to meet Vandegrift, Halsey came across various marines and made a point to try and stop and talk to a few. Vandegrift, knowing that Halsey was due later in the day, sent some of his men out on a mission to commandeer and gather items for a good meal for the visiting Admiral and his staff. The staff traded and made deals for the best food they could find from supply ships in the area. Apparently they were successful.

After a meeting everyone was seated for dinner. The group dined on an amazing feast of steaks, assorted side dishes and even fresh baked apple pie. Knowing that the good food was an issue because of many factors Halsey was very impressed by the spread since he had really not expected anything. He eventually asked to meet the cook that could make such a meal with so little to choose from.

The kitchen door opened and a scruffy red headed man named Sergeant Butch Morgan appeared. Sergeant Morgan was wearing his khaki pants, skivvy shirt and sported a bright red mustache. Halsey praised the dinner, the cook, and staff, for the meal. The admiral kept talking about the meal and the how good the pie was. "A man can serve his country with a skillet as well as a gun," Halsey proclaimed. Beginning to feel a bit embarrassed about the lavish praise Morgan suddenly blurted out "Aw HORSE-SHIT Admiral, thwarn't nothing!"

The red mustached sergeant quickly turned and walked away disappearing into the kitchen leaving General Vandegrift in stunned silence sitting next to an Admiral who just had a sergeant say the word "horseshit." Halsey began chuckling breaking the tension and the room filled with laughter.

As Halsey boarded an airplane to leave he left and turned to General Vandegrift and stated, "Vandegrift…don't you do a thing with that cook!"

In Europe, after the Allied breakout from the beaches of France, the main source of supply delivery came by air-landed shipments. Or items were delivered across the English Channel by ship and then hauled to drop off points by an ever growing number of supply trucks. Sometimes things don't go as planned. At some points, troops moved faster than supplies could catch up with them. Some items were running short and the ravages of war made it near impossible for some supplies to be delivered.

Men from the 101st watch as planes drop supplies to troops defending Bastogne in December of 1944.
From the collection of the US Army Center of Military History

This was the case at Bastogne, when Brigadier General Anthony McAuliffe's 101st Airborne Division was completely surrounded by German forces, traditional forms of supply delivery were cut off. The Germans met with a group of officers representing McAuliffe and his men and demanded the surrender of the Allied Troops. McAuliffe was reported to have responded… "NUTS."

When the German officers asked what "Nuts" meant the response by Col. Harper, who was delivering the message stated… "If you don't understand what 'Nuts' means, in plain English it is the same as 'Go to hell.'"

17

But, the problem remained, how to re-supply the men? The answer was the C-47 "Sky trains" of the U.S. Troop Carrier Command and their "flying Quartermaster" cargo crews. The planes flew fast and low enough to drop enough supplies to keep the trapped troops alive. Over 850 tons of supplies including medial material, ammo, food and assorted equipment were delivered by air. The supply drops worked. The fighting men were able to hold out, although hungry and with heavy casualties, until they were re-enforced by tanks from General Patton.

The hard fighting of McAuliffe's men, combined with the ability of the Pathfinder's who parachuted in to set up drop zone points, the Quartermaster Corps and aircrews who worked together in getting supplies to the beleaguered troops, made it possible for them to survive. It also issued in a new era of supplying troops with the items they need.

When the call of duty rang out across the United States many people answered the call. This included many Hollywood stars and many people that after the war would go on to become famous. This includes people such as Burt Lancaster, James Whitmore, TV's Judge Wapner who was saved from a snipers bullet when it hit a can of tuna he had in his pocket. Others were David Niven, Tyrone Power, Lee Marvin, Brian Keith, William Holden, Gene Autry, Eddie Albert, Don Adams, Ernest Borgnine and Alan Hale who was the Skipper on Gilligan's Island, Benny Hill, legendary golfer Bobby Jones, and even Mel Brooks. Audrey Hepburn was a child courier for resistance fighters in Holland during the war. The list of people that went on to be actors, writers, politicians and more is almost endless.

Actor James "Jimmy" Stewart served during World War II and through the Vietnam War. When World War II came to the states Jimmy Stewart was already on his way to having a successful movie career and he was also a trained pilot. At the outbreak of the war Stewart signed up with the draft but he was rejected for not weighing enough. Despite this Stewart still felt he could be of use and decided to start eating more and bulking up while working as an actor. He tried to sign up again and this time he weighed enough. Because of his pilot training he joined the Army Air Corps in hopes of heading overseas to fight. Instead of being shipped overseas as he had hoped, Stewart spent about two years stateside. During this time he rose in rank and became a trainer of twin-engine crews that flew B-17's and the B-24.

Col Jimmy Stewart is awarded the Croix De Guerre with Palm by Lt. Gen. Valin, Chief of Staff of the French Air Force for exceptional services in the liberation.
Photos from the collection of the National Museum of the U.S. Air Force

Eventually, after heavy lobbying on his part, he was shipped overseas in 1943. Stewart, now a Captain and Operations officer for the 703rd Squadron, 445th Bombardment Group of the Eighth Air Force, arrived in Europe with a heavy amount of logged hours and a massive amount of experience due to the work he did training other crews. Stewart's combat record included 20 dangerous combat missions while he served as command pilot, wing commander or squadron commander. He was awarded the Distinguished Flying Cross with two Oak Leaf Clusters, The Air Medal with three Oak Leaf Clusters, and the French Croix de Guerre with Palm. After the war he remained with the US Air Force Reserves and was eventually promoted to Brigadier General in 1959.

Stewart disliked too much publicity over his service and kept his work with the USAF reserves as low key as possible. His last combat mission was actually flown over Vietnam in a B52 in 1966. In an article by Warren Thompson titled *Mr. Stewart Goes to Vietnam* Captain Bob Amos recalled the last mission. While doing paperwork Captain Bob Amos found out an additional pilot was lined up to make the flight and that it would be Stewart.

19

He assumed it was simply a visiting General but was informed it was the famous actor and general. Captain Amos sent one of his crew to the commissary to pick out some extra supplies including fresh eggs, bacon, bread and cheese. Because bombing flights were so long the crews could cook small meals using an electric stove. Once underway the familiar voice of the famous star echoed in the crew's headsets as the checklists were run down.

During the long flight the small stove was fired up and the elaborate dinner, by in-flight standards, was served. Amos recalled Stewart's comments. "You all really know how to top off a successful bomb run," Stewart and the rest of the crew enjoyed scrambled eggs, bacon and grilled cheese sandwiches. But the flight was not over. A problem with the bomber, later found out to be a faulty gauge, could have resulted in a forced landing and possibly a bailout by the crew, which of course included Stewart. The plane landed safely. Jimmy Stewart had flown his last bombing run, as an observer, over twenty years after receiving his first Distinguish Flying Cross.

Another familiar face to movie goers and TV viewers is Charles Durning. Pvt. Charles Durning went on to become one of Hollywood's most versatile actors. Before becoming famous as a Hollywood actor, appearing in films such as the *Best Little Whorehouse in Texas* and *The Sting*, Charles Durning landed on Omaha Beach during the initial wave of the invasion force on D-Day. He later suffered wounds while taking out a machine gun nest and after recovering was stabbed several times by a German soldier wielding a bayonet. Durning fought back in hand to hand combat and eventually killed his attacker with a rock. While speaking to a small veterans group Durning recounted in a low voice that they had both lost their rifles, they ended up fighting, and when it was over he cried thinking that if there was no war the two could have been friends.

During the Battle of the Bulge he was taken prisoner. Durning, like so many others, lived the life of a POW surviving on limited rations and prison camp food. He was one of only three survivors of the massacre of American prisoners of war at Malmedy, Belgium. He and two others escaped as the rest of the prisoners were murdered. After being re-united with Allied troops Durning was asked by the military to return to the site of the massacre to help identify the bodies of his fellow prisoners and friends.

Durning again returned to combat but after suffering a chest wound was sent back to the states where he remained until he was discharged in

1946 after being awarded the Silver Star and three Purple Hearts. For his actions Burning received the Combat Infantryman's Badge, Silver Star, Bronze Star, and three Purple Hearts.

During one of his first pubic talks about being a veteran, Durning began to open up to a group of veterans during a speech to the American Legion in Woodland Hills, California. The event was organized by a small group of veterans and pilots named *Wings over Wendy's*. The small, loosely formed, organization meets every week at their local Wendy's Hamburger restaurant to talk about the war and planes while dinning on value menu items and coffee.

While Durning had yet to become a well known actor, Clark Gable was already a rising star when the war started. Gable signed up to serve in the military shortly after the attack on Pearl Harbor. He attended officer's training school and eventually was sent overseas to Europe where he flew with a crew that included a camera man, sound man and script writer. Gable was assigned to a United States war time documentary film crew that focused on B17 crews specifically gunners and their training.

While stationed in England Clark Gable takes a moment for a quick picture with the crew of the "Eight Ball" in 1943. Gable was seen as one of the guys even though he was a famous movie star.
From the collection of the National Archives.

The duties included flying alongside bomber's on missions, and shooting film as the action progressed. In the end Gable ended up flying five combat missions, one of which ended up with his bomber being damaged by antiaircraft fire. The blast was so close to Gable that the sole and heal of his boot were torn away. Hitler knew of Gables presence in the war and even is said to have offered a bounty for him to be captured and brought in as a POW.

After the war Gable, like other celebrities turned service men, wanted to continue his career in both the military and show business but he realized his age would make this difficult, not to mention his ever growing schedule. In 1947 Gable resigned his commission and returned fully to civilian life.

Gable was known to enjoy Chocolate cake and a good glass of lemonade as well as some other favorites. In the book *Clark Gable*, by Chrystopher J. Spicer, it is noted that the silver screen star also liked a good steak served up with potato salad, dill pickles, knockwurst and sauerkraut. Spicer also wrote that Gable enjoyed a rather strong, in the aroma sense, snack. The actor would eat thick slices of raw onion... whole.

Unlike Gable, Audie Murphy was as far away from being a Hollywood star as one could possibly imagine. He ended up a legend in World War II, a Hollywood movie star, songwriter and author. But Audie Murphy almost did not make it into the military. After the attack on Pearl Harbor, he tried to enlist but was found to be underage and rejected.

In this 1945 Army Signal Corps photo Audie Murphy is shown being awarded the Distinguished Service Cross and Silver Star from Major General John O'Daniel in Nancy France.
Original photo Army Signal Corps, National Archives

Audie was very mature for his young age. He helped support his family after his father had left them. He spent much of his time honing his shooting and hunting abilities in order to put food on the dinner table and he also worked several odd jobs. The family included his eleven siblings and mother who soon died leaving Audie to raise his brothers and sisters. Murphy again tried to enlist. This time with the Marines but was denied for being too short. The Navy also turned him down for being too small. Finally Murphy was able to enlist in the Army. Before leaving, he faced another heart breaking event as he was forced to place three of his youngest siblings in an orphanage. Audie promised them that when he returned from the war, he would find them and bring them home.

Now in the Army the young Audie passed out during a drill and his company commander tried to have him transferred to cooking school. Audie persisted and completed basic training and advanced infantry training. He was soon sent overseas where he became the most decorated soldier in history.

After the war Audie did become a famous actor but his Hollywood success was not instant. Like many aspiring actors he struggled with landing significant roles. He was remembered by a neighbor as being a young man who was trying to work and save enough money to send to his family. After finding a recipe for extending meat with assorted filler, a kind neighbor made several meatloaves and took an extra one over to Audie. Soon Audie was knocking on the neighbors door and with much thanks returned the dish saying that it reminded him too much of Spam which he had his fill of during the war. As the saying goes… there never will be another Audie Murphy. But there may always be SPAM.

On the Axis side of the war many of the more famous names also had a love for food or a related chow story. During the war in Africa General Irwin Rommel was a Hitler favorite and had proved himself time and time again at being able to perform often with less supplies and men than his Allied foes.

Field Marshall Irwin Rommel
From the collection of the
Camp Gordon Johnston Museum

While serving in Africa Rommel was known to treat his prisoners with as much respect as possible. He did his best, even if his forces were running low on supplies, to make sure prisoners had food and supplies along with needed medical attention. Hitler later would turn on Rommel as he was associated with a group of people seeking to assassinate the Nazi Leader. Rommel's car was strafed by an Allied fighter plane causing the death of his driver and a wreck that caused a severe head injury to him. He was sent home to heal his wounds. During this time the assassination attempt was carried out on Hitler. Implicated in the plot because of his loose acquaintances with the people who carried out the plan, Rommel was given the choice of a show trial or a vial of poison.

Fearing attacks on his family Rommel accepted a promise from Hitler that if he took the poison he would receive a full state funeral and his family would be spared. According to Rommel's son Manfred, who was fifteen at the time, two generals came to visit his father in a very courteous and respectful manner. Faced with his options, Rommel told his son and family of his decision. Rommel later drove off with the two generals. Soon after news was announced to the German people that one of its hero's had died of his wounds from the attack on his car.

Admiral Isoroku Yamamoto of the Japanese Navy is one of the most recognizable symbols of Japanese fighting forces. In several movies Yamamoto's character says famous lines such as, ""I fear all we have done is to awaken a sleeping giant and fill him with a terrible resolve." While it has yet to be proven that Yamamoto ever said this, he did believe that a protracted war with the United States was not winnable.

Imperial Japanese Navy Combined Fleet commander Admiral Isoroku Yamamoto (left) at Rabaul in April 1943, shortly before Yamamoto's death. *Photo from the collection of the U.S. Naval History and Heritage Command*

24

He believed that his forces would achieve early victories in a war with the United States but would not have long term success. On September 27, 1940, as Japan signed the Tripartite Pact with Germany and Italy, Admiral Yamamoto warned Premier Konoye Fumimaro "If I am told to fight regardless of the consequences, I shall run wild for the first six months or a year, but I have utterly no confidence for the second or third year. The Tripartite Pact has been concluded and we cannot help it. Now that the situation has come to this pass, I hope you will endeavor to avoid a Japanese-American war."

Yamamoto was born Takano Isoroku but later he was adopted by the Yamamoto family as a young adult. This practice was fairly common in Japan if a family had lost male heirs. He joined the naval academy at the age of 16 and fought during WW I losing two fingers and sustaining other injuries. During the years of 1919 and 1920 he attended Harvard University and studied the Oil business learning the ins and outs of the life blood of any modern day navy.

Yamamoto was known to enjoy visits with ladies of the night despite being married and having four children. But his visits to Geisha houses included things other than sex and drinking which he shied away from. Instead he loved playing cards including poker, bridge, other games and various forms of gambling. Another side of Yamamoto showed his concentration and memory skills as he was an accomplished calligrapher. He even noted that his ability to memorize so many characters in calligraphy made it easy to keep track of fifty two cards in a deck.

He was also fond of attending dinner parties. But as Japan entered the war they two felt the effects of food shortages as the majority of non-staple foods were imported. The diet during the time relied heavily on rice and fish dishes as the natural landscape of Japan did not lend itself to cattle or other types of herd animals.

Adolf Hitler is often reported to have been a vegetarian. But that image of the Nazi Leader may have been nothing but a PR stunt in order to make him appear to be more intellectual. In an article by Rynn Berry, noted vegetarian writer, Berry found the evidence she needed to label Hitler as a meat eater. She wrote that it was "as plain as the Chapinesque mustache on the Fuhrer's face," a reference to the small mustache that Charlie Chaplin often sported. Hitler had a deep hatred for the comedian and film maker and even included him on a hit list which also included Albert Einstein and many others. Chaplin spoofed the Nazi leader in the 1940 motion picture the Great Dictator.

Adolf Hitler
From the collection of S. Westley

Berry's evidence of Hitler not being a vegetarian was located in a book titled *The Gourmet Cooking School Cookbook* by Dione Lucas. Berry noted a reference to Hitler's favorite recipe written by a chef who worked at a hotel restaurant that the Fuhrer frequented. The recipe was anything but vegetarian as it was for stuffed squab. In her 1964 cookbook Dione Lucas noted that Hitler frequently visited the hotel where she was chef in Hamburg before the war. "I learned this recipe when I worked as a chef before World War II, in one of the large hotels in Hamburg, Germany. I do not mean to spoil your appetite for stuffed squab, but you might be interested to know that it was a great favorite with Mr. Hitler, who dined at the hotel often. Let us not hold that against a fine recipe though."

Berry also notes the fact that Hitler biographer Robert Payne says that Hitler's diet was anything but vegetarian. Payne wrote, "Hitler's asceticism played an important part in the image he projected over Germany. According to the widely believed legend, he neither smoked nor drank, nor

26

did he eat meat or have anything to do with women. Only the first was true. He drank beer and diluted wine frequently, had a special fondness for Bavarian sausages and kept a mistress, Eva Braun, who lived with him quietly in the Berghof." Another reference to Hitler's diet by Payne gave even greater insight to the Axis leader's favorite foods.

"Although Hitler had no fondness for meat except in the form of sausages, and never ate fish, he enjoyed caviar. He was a connoisseur of sweets, crystallized fruit and cream cakes, which he consumed in astonishing quantities. He drank tea and coffee drowned in cream and sugar. No dictator ever had a sweeter tooth."

One of the most popular figures during the war for many workers did not actually exist although she represented millions of workers across the country and in other Allied nations. For a society coming out of a depression, the idea of a stream of women heading to production lines and factories to join a traditionally male dominated workforce was a new concept. The old school thoughts of women at home and the man at work were seemingly challenged. Women had long been in the workforce. The role was just expanded massively and quickly. Suddenly large numbers of women were working alongside burly construction and steel workers in boatyards, factories and more.

One of the most iconic images of "Rosie" on the famous poster created by J. Howard Miller.
From the collection of the National Park Service from the US National Archives.

A real "Rosie!" This pictured shows a female riveter at the Lockheed Aircraft
Corporation in Burbank, California during the war years.
From the collection of the National Archives

With World War II coming to the United States, the government realized as did many businesses, that women were the answer to any labor
shortage coming as men were called to the armed services. A large propaganda and media campaign to lure women to the workforce, and to help
the war effort, included a *Saturday Evening Post* cover painting by famed
artist Norman Rockwell of a "Rosie" with a flag in the background.
Rockwell's painting showed a female worker perched atop a construction
beam with a rivet gun in her lap, her feet resting on a copy of Hitler's book
Mein Kampf, a lunch box with the name Rosie on it.

The Rockwell image was copyrighted so use of it was slow to reach the
masses after appearing on the *Saturday Evening Post* cover. An earlier
poster painting with a woman rolling up her sleeve titled "We Can Do It!"
was produced by Westinghouse War Production artist J. Howard Miller.
This poster which was mass produced has become an iconic image of what

28

"Rosie" looked like. A popular song titled *Rosie the Riveter* was written by Redd Evans and John Jacob Loeb and recorded by big band leader Kay Kyser. The song, combined with the Norman Rockwell painting of the riveter with the "Rosie" lunchbox eventually fused with the Howard Miller poster in the conscience of Americans. The image of hard working women helping the war effort now had a face, a name and even a song.

Women not only streamed into plants, offices, production lines and shipyards across the United States. They also joined the war effort in uniform serving as nurses, WACS, WAVES, SPARS and more. The result was a continued massive build up of wartime production and the cementing of the idea that women could perform alongside men. Many women with real variations of the name Rose, or Rosie, appeared in the news as being a real life "Rosie." Some even made media tours. After the war many women returned to the home front but many remained in the workforce. The amount of women in the workforce would never drop below pre-war levels.

As for food, Rockwell's famous lunch time pose as a worker, shows that Rosie seems to enjoy a good sandwich which was common lunch time meal of workers powering the war effort.

United States Coast Guard SPARS in action.
From the collection of the United States Coast Guard Museum

29

WACS at Fort Oglethorpe Georgia were trained in a
variety of skills including baking.
From the collection of the 6th Calvary Museum, Fort Oglethorpe, Georgia

Bing Crosby does his best to entertain WAC troops during World War Two.
Many Hollywood stars worked the war effort by fighting low morale.
From the collection of the 6th Calvary Museum, Fort Olgethorpe, Georgia.

CHAPTER TWO

Canned Chow
United States Rations of
World War Two

Photo Courtesy of the Fort Lee United States Army Quartermaster Museum

It is necessary to review the history of the United States Quartermaster Corps to understand the way troops were fed and supplied during World War II. The process of feeding and supplying troops was addressed and undertaken on a national scale during the early years of the Revolutionary War. George Washington realized that feeding the troops would be a major concern. The appointment of the first Quartermaster General, Major General Thomas Mifflin, set the initial steps into place for an orderly way to supply and feed fighting men. Before the appointment of Mifflin, state militias had fed their own men. Some did a good job, others not so, and the process was not uniform. The problem for Washington

was that the supply chain was not in place, it started from scratch and the need in which to feed and supply troops did not match up with the technology, or delivery systems of the time. This was a problem that would be addressed by Quartermaster Generals all the way to WWII and the issue is still addressed today.

Photo Courtesy of the Fort Lee United States Army Quartermaster Museum

Some of the major issues that have troubled quartermasters have included packaging, development, storage, shipping, waste and spoilage. It appears that Revolutionary troops were essentially left to feed themselves despite the efforts of the new Quartermaster General. Revolutionary troops had some basic rations and supplies, but as the war progressed supply issues were overwhelming. The basic rations included meat, peas, flour, rice, soap, milk, a candle and even beer.

Ration list for American Revolutionary War Soldier
    l6 oz; beef
    6.8 oz.peas
    18 oz. flour
    1.4 oz. rice
    16 oz. milk
    .1830 oz. Soap
    1 qt. spruce beer
    .0686 oz. candle
    November 4, 1775
    Source: Fort Lee Quartermaster Museum

One of the problems the young country faced was the way meat was supplied to troops. The way to cure beef at the time was with salt which was imported. With salt shortages becoming common place. the ability to cure beef was limited resulting in the movement of live cattle and butchers with the troops..

In addition to official means the young government turned to private industry in the form of sutlers and contracts.. If a certain item or product was not obtainable by contract then a commanding officer could approve items to be purchased at fair market rates and brought to any fort or garrison by vendors called sutlers. The sutlers could be considered a forerunner to the PX and commissary system and were commonplace on every installation. Their official use was abolished in 1866 after the Civil War. Many of the items sutlers sold were now to be made available to troops under the official guidance of the Subsistence Department.

During the Civil War the modern ration was beginning to take shape but was still very similar to Revolutionary War and Mexican War rations. One major difference, the everyday use of commercial items such as Bordons canned milk and Tabasco bottled hot sauce. While these goods were not official parts of soldier's daily ration they were available to consumers and in camps. Both sides of the conflict hoped to supply and feed their troops a set menu of items designed to be filling and nutritious.. Advancements in packaging, mostly in the northern states, allowed for a few canned items that stood up better to shipping. But advancements were limited.

The Noncommissioned officers' mess of Co. D, 93d New York Infantry.
This picture was taken in August of 1863 in Bealeton, Virginia
by Timothy H. O'Sullivan.
Civil War photographs, 1861-1865 / compiled by Hirst D. Milhollen and Donald H.
Mugridge, Washington, D.C. : Library of Congress, 1977. No. 0214

Supplies of rations to troops were often unreliable or spoiled by the time they arrived. Units were often left to cook and eat what they could find to supplement the few supplies that did make it to them. Despite improvements, the Civil War official rations were not very far advanced from what soldiers had during the Revolutionary War. In general Civil War rations had a short shelf life; meats were salted, cured or handed out raw. Fruits and vegetables were limited or canned and hard tack became legendary. The daily ration was handed to the soldier and how he cooked it was often left up to him. Sometimes a small group would pool their rations in order to make a meal and they were termed messmates. While the official list of items in a daily ration had increased on paper many instances of soldiers relying on improvised coffee and hardtack abounded. When items were not available the "grab as you go" mentality was put into place in order to feed hungry troops.

As happened during the outset of the Revolutionary War, Civil War armies were often followed by a herd of livestock and butchers. Supply lines from both armies and assorted groups of vendors that sold items to soldiers on both sides, were nearby as well. The sutler camps were a fixture at many Civil War battles prior to fighting. Sometimes the vendors list of offerings included everything from food and spirits to seamstresses and brothels.

Ration list for U.S. Mexican War Soldier
  20 dz. beef
  .64 oz. salt
  18 oz. flour
  .0686 oz. candle
  2.4 oz. dried beans
  .183 oz. soap
  .16 gill vinegar
  .96 oz. green coffee
  1.92 oz. sugar
  Source: Fort Lee Quartermaster Museum

Ration list for U.S. Civil War Soldier

20 oz. beef

2.4 oz. sugar

22 oz. flour

.32 gill vinegar

7 oz. potatoes

.64 oz. salt

.045 oz. yeast

.04 oz. pepper

2.65 oz. dried beans

.64 oz. soap

1.6 oz. green coffee

.24 oz. candle

Source: Fort Lee Quartermaster Museum

Officially the development of proper rations was progressing slowly. Advancements in canning and food preservation were beginning to move forward for commercial use. There were many canned and bottled items increasingly available to the public and the soldier in the field. As more items became available, the list of things a solider could see issued to him could grow if they were not damaged, stolen or spoiled on the way.

And the items in rations would change with time. The beer in the rations for Union troops had been replaced by rum, then the rum was replaced by other items including sugar. Just as happened in the Revolutionary War, spoiled food and unreliable supply lines caused many problems for the everyday Civil War foot soldier despite advancements in packaging and transportation. Food and proper rations became a Civil War commodity for both sides. Many guerilla-fighting attacks were aimed at stealing the other side's meat and other supplies.

Some progress was made with ration development for the Spanish American War. The list of items increased slightly and some were shuffled a bit such as the replacement of yeast by baking powder. But again, supply lines and packaging caused many issues. A pattern was developing for military planners and leaders in the United States.

As America entered conflicts, the procurement of food seemed to become a priority again. But as conflicts ended, so did much of the development, often due to budget cutting. At the outbreak of the Spanish-American War, the troops shipped from the states to tropical Cuba had been issued heavy wool style uniforms for colder climates along with little or no medical supplies and, all too often, the issue of rotting meat and other food items. A large number of American casualties actually resulted from food poisoning. After the war stricter laws and methods of obtaining, inspecting and packaging food for shipment to soldiers in the field were beginning to be seriously developed and put into place.

Before World War I, the overall majority of food supplied to fighting troops was cooked on the spot from materials shipped overseas or obtained locally. The military cooks did their best to feed hungry troops but often supplies were limited and sometimes spoiled, as was the case in the Spanish- American War. Food to be provided to foot soldiers was to be cooked daily, even though the methods of keeping things fresh and refrigerated that were becoming available had yet to be translated to field use. These cooked meals were served in conjunction with the use of better developed pre-packed and canned ration items.

On the ration side of the equation the modern day field ration was beginning to see some vast improvements as America's Dough Boys were heading overseas. The list or items included in a ration were increased and a wide variety of foods were becoming available to the United States soldier. Thought was given to variety, size, ease of use and more as developers began to realize that certain rations could be developed for certain uses. Items ranging from ration bars to assorted canned goods, to snacks and more, were utilized. But once again, spoilage issues and other problems still existed with rations, but was becoming less commonplace as in previous wars. Progress was being made.

The legendary Iron Ration was in use during World War I. It was put into use in 1907, and is often considered the first modern attempt to provide an individual ration for use of soldiers in forward positions. It contained 3 three ounce "cakes" made from beef bouillon and parched and cooked wheat as well as 3 bars of sweetened chocolate and some seasoning such as salt. The ration weighed about one pound and was packed in a sealed tin container. Eventually the Iron Ration was phased out as the newer Trench Ration and later the Reserve Rations were developed. These rations better addressed the daily needs of the soldier but lessons learned from the development of the Iron Ration were put to use later when better emergency rations were developed.

During the ending stages of World War I, military leaders realized that there was a need for diversification in both specialized rations and ration menu items. Planners better understood the fact that rations developed for one use, such as marching and camping, would not be suited for fighting or during emergencies. Several types of rations were put into place including the four major rations of the 1920's and 1930's. These included the Garrison, Travel, Field and Reserve rations. All were combinations of assorted canned and prepackaged items which could be combined with food stuffs cooked in the field from available stores. An emergency ration was developed with the thinking that the ration needed to be limited in weight and bulk but still provide needed nourishments similar to the dried meat and dried grain Mexican soldiers and American Indians had used years prior in states with drier climates. This ration included evaporated beef, parched wheat, salt, pepper and a bit of sweet chocolate all packaged in a vacuum sealed container weighing less than a pound.

In addition to the development of rations for different needs many military planners began to realize that the U.S. would be somehow involved in the growing conflict of the late 1930's that would eventually become World War II. However, most development of safer foods and rations was slowed as budgets tightened after World I ended. Even though budgets were tight, leaders knew that new specialized rations had to be developed and put into production in order to overcome the shortcomings of the supply system. The age old problem of keeping fresh food fresh for soldiers in the field, and often on the other side of the globe, would always seem to be an issue. Leaders knew that a safe and reliable food source that met certain dietary and operational guidelines would have to be ready.

The Second World War was already underway in Europe and Asia before the United States entered the fight. But efforts were already put forward by the various service branches to improve food and cooking. The leap seen from World War I era military cooking and rations to the methods used in the Second World War were astronomical. This was true mainly on larger bases and on larger naval ships but many of the improvements did begin to be put into field use. The improved cooking methods were backed by an explosion of cooks and bakers schools that were opened at bases across the country as the United States entered the war.

From the collection of the 6th Calvary Museum, Fort Olgethorpe, Georgia
Photo by Kent Whitaker

On the pre-packed ration side of feeding troops the start of the Quartermaster Subsistence Research and Development Laboratory ensured that proper ration development would move forward as the facility opened in 1939. The Quartermaster Subsistence Research and Development had an overall goal which was to evaluate older rations, improve them or develop new ones. These new rations were to be field-tested, taste-tested and developed using set operational and dietary guidelines. The new, or improved rations, needed to use the best available modern technology in order to provide the most suitable end product for the deployed soldier. The mission also included developing new packaging that suited for the rations and how they would be used, stored and shipped. In addition the Quartermaster Corps continued to make incredible strides in developing methods for field cooking and food preparation. The efforts were matched in the Navy, Marines and Coast Guard. Menu books from the various service branches combining a vast number of recipes and cooking methods took advantage of new cooking appliances, technology, an improved supply chain and packaging.

The Marine Master Menu in a cartoon version from 1944. The Master menu was published monthly with a theme cover designed to represent the season.
Courtesy of the Historical Reference Branch, Marine Corps History Division, Quantico, VA

Food quality and service in World War II for American troops was starting at a new high as huge numbers of trained cooks, bread bakers and food specialists flowed into the military ranks. Despite problems along the way that any fighting force faces the American service men from the Army to the Marines, Air Corps and Navy had the most modern cooking, most varied menus and safest food supply chain of any of the militaries involved in World War II. The U.S. quickly became the leader in ration and food development and an improved safer supply line.

When a service branch perceived the need for a new ration the new specs were sent to the developers and researchers who would start work on producing the ration according to the specs. The process was a fairly straightforward one. As a need was identified the process would begin. Rations were developed and tested according to specifications and guidelines sent in from military services. The newly developed ration also went through a series of tests. Sometimes the ration would require the development of specialized packaging. At the very least it might require a rethinking of an existing packaging that could be adapted. After the item was tested and approved it was procured, contacted out to suppliers, produced and finally put into the supply line for troops. While this sounds easy it was actually a far more complicated process. In fact, it was a huge undertaking. This is where the revamping of commercial food production paid off.

The new item might require the manufacturer to have, develop or invest in equipment, and train a workforce or retrain workers. Specialized packaging might require additional adjustments in existing equipment or new equipment needed to be purchased and installed. The next hurdle was that the producers of rations were spread across the country as well as their suppliers. The logistics needed, and everything else involved in mass food production from harvest to final product, was staggering. The numbers of companies involved in ration producing and packaging was enormous.

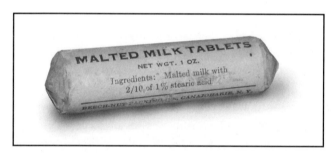

A roll of malted milk tablets from WWII.
The collection of the 6th Calvary Museum, Fort Olgethorpe, Georgia
Photo by Kent Whitaker

On the confection side virtually every chocolate and candy manufacturer in the country had some sort of contract to supply portions of rations, or complete rations, to the government Just about every food producer or packager had, or bid for, some of the business. Farms across the country produced goods and meat producers contracted beef, chicken, pork and more. Every aspect of food production was affected by the war. This included shipping and transportation.

This massive effort was not just for food items. Suppliers of all goods were part of the ration development and food process. As development progressed during the war many ration packs also included items such as

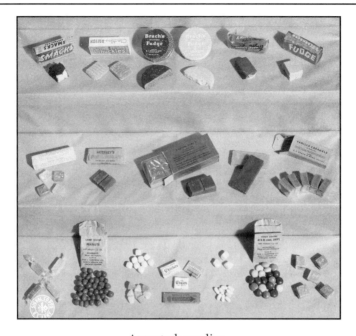

Assorted candies.
Photo Courtesy of the Fort Lee United States Army Quartermaster Museum

matches, needle, thread, drink powders, can openers and of course tobacco products. The list of items developers inserted into rations was almost endless. There are many movies with soldiers passing out ration pack cigarettes, candy and trading items for something else. Cigarettes were a favorite item. But consider that there were many different brands of cigarettes utilized. And, they were not just packing cigarettes. Some ration packs included rolling papers and pouches of tobacco or cigars and even chewing tobacco. The simple finger sized can opener proved to be one of the greatest inventions of the war. It served as a can opener, toothpick, knife, fingernail cleaner, screw driver and could be used for countless other needs. It was commonly called the P-38 or the John Wayne since the actor was seen using one in a training film. The small can opener was a ration pack hit.

Once the specs and contracts were finished the varied manufactures began to produce the items specific to their contract. It could be a single ration bar, a canned item, a button or almost anything. Depending on

41

what was produced, and where, the Quartermasters had a job to do. Production facilities that won a contract had a quartermaster on hand. These QM's oversaw the production quality to ensure the items produced fit the specs and needs of the contracts. They also worked as liaisons. Once the item was produced it was either shipped into the supply chain or shipped to another producer in order for them to include the item in a ration they were producing or packing. The food items in rations required a tremendous amount of food producers to fall into a standardized method for producing, handling and packaging food. A high degree of standardization and uniformity had to be maintained.

Once the supply chain was advanced enough ration developers and planners had the ability to re-utilize proven items into new configurations. Using the lessons learned from Dr. Keys in earlier stages of development new ration needs could possibly be quickly developed by using proven items that worked while discarding those that didn't. Proven canned rations could be repacked as needed and as new items came on line. Many items could be made smaller, packed in different numbers for different needs and the selections could be changed as the need arouse or if something was in short supply.

If one candy manufacture ran short on supplies a similar sized item from a different producer could be used. If one cigarette manufacture ran behind a different brand could be used. At the beginning of the war rations were simple, plan, and offered little variety. By the end of the war over twenty different styles of rations that could be repacked or bundled in many ways were developed.

Variations of the multi use—multi item, rations were essentially unlimited because the canned meals, breads, candy, condiments and snacks could easily be switched around in packaging and number. And everything food related in the ration was selected to provide life sustaining sustenance, on any level, to the troops. Or provide a needed item such as a can opener or matches. Even a small condiment or pack of candy would provide some calories even if it was just a handful of peanuts dipped in chocolate or candy coated chocolate pieces called M&M's. The famous candy that was designed to melt in your mouth and not in your hand was introduced in 1941 as a candy item for American GI's. M&M's went on to become a post war favorite. Many complaints about rations stem from the fact that all too often the same rations were given out over and over again. People got sick of the same foods. Packaging and progress made it easy to rearrange items in a style of ration and change menu items around from main courses to the smallest candies. This way a soldier was hopefully not going to get the same meal every day. While many rations overall are not remembered fondly by GI's many of the individual items included in them, such as the variety of candy, were highly regarded. The small can opener can still be purchased today and is often used by emergency relief organizations.

Of course, when items needed to be developed for extreme conditions such as heat or cold, the research and development process was fully utilized. But not before rations that were already in use were tested to see if something already developed would fit the new specs. Why re-invent the wheel? Something may already be in production that could be altered or repacked without causing too much of a delay before being used in the field.

Basic Rations of World War II

This listing of rations briefly touches on the major types developed during the years leading up to and during World War II by the Quartermaster Subsistence Research and Development Laboratory. The information comes from many sources, such as the Fort Lee Quartermaster Museum, but please note that it is not a complete list. Many variations and different types of rations were developed, tried and tested but only the major rations that were produced and put into use are listed here. Many others never made it from the planning stages to mass production, or out of field testing.

In the field, under real life use, pre-packed and canned rations of all types could be repacked and shipped as needed. A great example of this could be found in many remote depots simply because after shipping the boxes rations were shipped in often came apart or labels came off. A great way to unload a load of materials could be as simple as pushing it off the back of the truck. Quartermasters and supply officers were left with piles of assorted cans spilled from shipping containers. Sometimes they guessed right about what was in the cans... sometimes they didn't and some unlucky unit could get a load of the same items day after day. Or, the supply officer and quartermaster could repack items to fit the needs of a certain situation in the field which in essence meant that they had developed a new ration pack.

In other cases a developed ration could be officially reused in other ration packs. For instance when some item was found to work for one ration pack and could possibly fit the needs and specification of another ration, the item would be incorporated into the new pack as needed without having to develop something new. This saved time and money.

Great effort was put into reducing the monotony of menu items in pre-packed C rations even though many stories exist about soldiers eating the same canned meal for days on end. This complaint was common. Often the problem was that troops may have been issued C rations for single use that also were included in B Ration supplies for larger facilities that had structured mess halls and kitchens. A soldier eating can after can of C Ration meat stew or hash in a forward position would rotate back to the larger facility only to find large pots and pans filled with the same meat stew and hashes repacked as B Rations. But as supply chains improved the general mess situation improved dramatically for the military and the variety of food increased as a whole.

A few exceptions to the problem with monotony in menu items and food quality could be found by troops stationed, or training at, larger permanent bases in the States and overseas. Often these troops were amazed at the variety and quality of food being prepared. These facilities could make better use of local supplies, storage, refrigeration and properly trained cooks and bakers.

Also, the quality of food served on many larger Navy Vessels was exceptional compared to that of foot soldiers and forward units. This was due to several similar factors of larger facilities found on shore including onboard storage, freezers and refrigeration. Even medium sized ships had decent facilities even if small in square footage. But not all Navy crews fell into this perception of the "well fed Navy" category. Smaller vessels such as escorts and even PT boats seemed to sometimes fall into the cracks of the supply chain. One PT boat crewman commented that often *"it seemed that the Navy forgot that they (the PT crews) needed food."*

In the May-June 1946 *Quartermaster Review* Colonel James C. Longino, Q.M.C. stated the following. *"We have heard from very high sources that the American Army was the best fed army in the world. We know exhaustive research and development were conducted to make it so. We know that the product of that research and development was a ration superior to that supplied the troops of any other nation. But we also know that the end-product—namely, the food eaten by the soldier in the front lines in the combat zone at times fell far short of what it should have been."* Improvements in research, supply, packaging, development and procurement was combined with huge improvements in cooking, training and menus by all of the military services during World War Two but after the war planners knew that more could be done.

The D Ration.
Photo Courtesy of the Fort Lee United States Army Quartermaster Museum

The D Ration: The D Ration follows in the footsteps of the emergency rations of the First World War. A similar L-Ration, named for Col. Paul Logan head of the subsistence school was also tested. The D ration bar was made from ingredients including chocolate, sugar and peanut butter. The initial product did not store well and often caused people that tested early versions of it to be too thirsty. The L-Ration included three bars made of chocolate, sugar, oat flour, cacao fat, skim milk powder, and artificial flavoring. Three smaller bars were then wrapped in aluminum foil and over-wrapped in parchment paper. The D ration was often misused because of a lack of education on it being an emergency ration, not a ration for everyday use for regular meals. It was simply designed to stave off hunger and provide minimum dietary needs, not to be a repeated meal. One of the early trains of thought for the D rations was that they should not taste too good so that troops would not eat them before they truly needed them.

The D and L rations were developed as emergency style rations for short term use. Eventually a large D Ration bar would be made smaller as a supplement for other rations. At one point the D Ration was so overstock piled that thought was given to sending them back to the manufactures to see if they could be recycled for other use. Despite the heavy disdain for the D ration it was an incredible emergency ration though often miss used.

The C Ration.
Photo Courtesy of the Fort Lee United States Army Quartermaster Museum

The C Ration: The roots of the C ration date back as far as ration development goes. The idea has always been the same... get the food to the soldier in the field with some variety to fit their needs. Quartermasters of all eras sought to develop a full ration that could be packed, delivered and served with as little effort as possible. Technology in manufacturing a ration like this simply was not available on a large scale prior to World War Two. The modern C ration was developed over the course of several years and is similar to early developments started by Major W.R. McReynolds who was the first director of the Sustenance Research and Development Laboratory. Earlier attempts to produce rations in cans had taken place years before and canning items for soldiers goes as far back as the Civil War. But McReynold's idea was to develop a wider variety of meals such as beef stew, beef with noodles and even and Irish stew which were packaged in 12 ounce cans. These cans utilized improved canning methods. They lasted longer and were safer for units in the field.

The idea was well received and the OK was given to further develop the idea. But there was a slight problem. Only $300 was awarded to the

Laboratory for continuing research on McReynold's new ration ideas. The C-Ration continued to evolve and the 12-ounce rectangular can was replaced by 16-ounce round cans. Field trials in 1940 raised concerns that the larger cans were too bulky and that the meat lacked variety. Other complaints suggested that the meals contained too many beans. Because of the concerns raised from field trials several changes took place.

These early field trials with the D ration and C ration proved to be valuable part of every successful ration development. The 12-ounce can was brought back as the standard size for the ration, improvement were made in the meat production, chocolate and coffee were added and eventually hard candies. Early in the war heavy emphasis on using meats that could be obtained in large quantities quickly made for a lack of variety but this improved as the war progressed. The C ration as a whole continued to improve as additional items were added including biscuits, cereal, candy-coated peanuts and raisins, sugar, flavored juice powder, jam, cocoa powder, caramels, cigarettes, water-purification tablets, matches, toilet paper, chewing gum, and a can opener.

The B-Ration was simply a larger version of many of the canned food items found in the C Ration. It was designed for use in larger field kitchens and messes. The B ration contained much of the same canned items as the C ration. The B-Ration should not be confused with the B unit which was part of the C ration but contained the bread or desert items found in the C Ration. A breakfast version also named the B unit was issued that was geared towards breakfast foods in 1944.

The K Ration supper version.
Photo Courtesy of the Fort Lee United States Army Quartermaster Museum

The K ration: The initial idea for the K ration was that it would be" developed for use with paratroopers, flight crews and other troops in mind that may be in need of a smaller size ration. This reduced size was better suited for an individual soldier on the move. This was something the C Ration could not easily provide. The K ration eventually developed into a 3 meal system which included a breakfast, dinner and supper ration and contained items including canned meat, biscuits, bouillon, gum, candy, coffee, sugar, cigarettes, can opener and other items as they were developed. The K ration was deemed a success as developers and end users seemed to be very pleased with the product. Even with the success the K Ration continued to be developed for more uses and operational situations. This development did include changes in menu items but much of the continued development was aimed at packaging. This included waxed packaging, plastic coating and even color coding to distinguish between the breakfast, dinner and supper meals. A pull string package was tested and even packaging that could withstand 20 degrees below zero or 135 degrees was tested.

In 1944 more than 105 million rations were procured. While the K ration was more popular when it was first introduced the ration did fall from popularity in a fashion similar to the unpopularity of the C ration. Overuse and use for days and weeks on end caused some dislike due to monotony. It's over use as a ration came from the fact that it was a good ration, packaged to serve a variety of uses, was easy to distribute and was easy to plan into an operational situation. After the war it was recommended that the majority of K rations left in depot stocks be used for the overseas civilian feeding programs during rebuilding and humanitarian efforts.

The Mountain ration.
Photo Courtesy of the Fort Lee United States Army Quartermaster Museum

Mountain ration: The Mountain ration was developed for troops that were fighting in higher altitudes. The ration was developed to better withstand the climates found in these areas. Both the Mountain and the Jungle ration were a result of the realization that battles would be fought in a wide variety of places instead of what could be called the traditional battlefields of prior conflicts. Planners realized that different foods and packaging would be needed. While the needs for these specialized rations were fundamental the overall guidelines were very loose. Developers warned that the Mountain and the Jungle rations should not be rushed into use before proper research was done as other rations could possibly fill the need.

The basic specifications were that the ration could not weigh more than 40 ounces, could be cooked at high altitudes, had compact packaging, had 4800 calories and required slow digestion. The Mountain ration was packed to serve four men for one day. It contained various items including Carter's spread (a butter substitute), coffee, dry milk, biscuits, hard candy, a variety of cereal, dehydrated cheese, D ration bars, fruit bars, gum, lemon-juice powder, dehydrated soup, salt, sugar and tea. It also included cigarettes and toilet paper. Although the Mountain ration served its initial purpose of providing food in a high altitude environment the Quartermaster Subsistence Research and Development Laboratory warned that proper testing and development was not fully finished before shipping was started. Almost one and a half million Mountain rations were purchased and shipped in 1943 before production was halted. The developers at the Quartermaster Subsistence Research and Development Laboratory were right, other rations could better fill the need.

The Jungle ration: The Jungle ration is similar to the Mountain ration, in the sense that it was developed for a certain climate and region, the Jungle ration was quickly put together as it was realized that a large portion of the war would be fought in the Pacific region. Once again the Jungle ration was hurried and the Quartermaster Subsistence Research and Development Laboratory cautioned that more development should be done before the items were completely satisfactory for the intended use. The need for a specialized ration was apparent but specific guidelines to fully develop a working jungle ration were lacking. Because of this the Jungle ration followed a food for four men for one day style similar to the Mountain ration. What made the Jungle ration and Mountain Ration work for their limited production spans was that the Quartermaster Subsistence Research and Development Laboratory's workers were able to design better packaging and containers more suited for the Pacific or mountain environment. Both the mountain and the jungle ration were phased out as improvements were made to K rations, C rations and of course on site cooking. During the whole time the Mountain and Jungle rations were in use the Quartermaster Subsistence Research and Development Laboratory noted that the K ration was already developed, in production, and ready to use in both situations with minor adjustments in packaging. The Mountain Ration and Jungle Ration were also similar to the 5 in 1 ration which was used to feed five men for one day as the Mountain and Jungle rations both were designed to feed four men for one day.

A version of the 5-in-1 ration.
Photo Courtesy of the Fort Lee United States Army Quartermaster Museum

5-in-1 ration: The 5-in-1 ration was introduced in 1942 with the purpose of providing a ration solution for motorized combat groups operating in desert areas. The thought process was similar to the Mountain Ration and the Jungle Ration. The name actually describes the ration perfectly. It was a ration that could provide meals for five men for one day. The 5-in1 could be used by the smaller groups on the move with minimal cooking equipment and even without somebody in the unit that could cook. The ration, like many others during the war, was a combination of new developed items and items that were proven. These items were similar to the K ration but were combined and packed for the specific use of the 5-in-1. The packaging included canned items and condiment items consisted of spreads, vegetables, meat, evaporated milk, juice, fruits soups, cereal, biscuits, salt, sugar toilet paper and hard candy. The 5-in-1 ration

50

varied from menu item to menu item as different meal combinations were developed and procured. The 5-in-1 ration also included a helpful menu and guide to help portion out meals properly. At the end of the war the 5-in-1 had been replaced by the 10 in 1 but many 5-in-1 items were still pulled from stock to supply the larger 10 in 1 ration.

The 10 in 1 ration.
Photo Courtesy of the Fort Lee United States Army Quartermaster Museum

The 10-in-1 ration: Doubling up was an easy solution to any problems with 5-in-1 rations as far as larger use was concerned. The 10-in-1 was phased in as the 5-in1 was phased out during 1943 but stock piles of the 5-in-1 kept it in use for many years during the war. The 10-in-1 was loosely based on the success of a British ration used in the desert war which was a 14-in-1 type. The ration would feed ten men for one day. It could be shipped and packed easily via truck or animal or even broken down for single man use. The 10-in-1 was developed fairly fast by combining two 5-in1 rations but with added variety. With the added variety the menus could be diverse enough to break some of the monotony men found in repetitive meals.

The 10-in-1 came packed with the familiar 5-in1 items including soap and toilet paper but was better organized to allow for a breakfast, dinner and super meal. The mid-day dinner meals were often of the snack variety with quick bag packaging. Over 300 million 10-in-1 rations were procured from 1943 until the end of the war. The 10-in-1 was the only group ration in procurement from 1943 to the end of the war making it the official last United States small group ration of World War Two.

The Assault Lunch and X ration: The Assault lunch was a ration developed for the sole purpose of feeding Allied assault soldiers hitting the beaches of Europe and the Pacific. The Assault lunch had a very specific list of requirements. The Assault Lunch ration had to be light weight, packed for ease of use, supply suitable calories and sustain a soldier in case their advancement outpaced normal supply chains. These requirements were for use in Europe and the Pacific. The Pacific theater was a major factor in the development of the Assault Lunch as any foods would have to survive a wide range of conditions. Specifications stated that the ration would have to withstand temperatures between -60 degrees to 130 degrees.

One interesting property in the packaging for the Assault lunch was the use of a water-proof bag. The ration contained some standard food items as well as specially developed chocolate bars, caramels, dried fruit (prunes and raisins), chewing gum, peanuts, salt tablets, cigarettes, matches, and water-purification tablets. The packaging was designed to resist mold, moisture and rough handling. Before the Assault ration was developed another ration simply titled the X-ration was in the planning and testing stages. It was called the X ration. Because of its secretive nature not much is known about the development or specifications of the X ration.

What is known is that it was to be made and packed completely without any markings that could identify its purpose. One possible reason for this could have been to simply keep secret any possible invasion plans. A variation of the ration was actually tested for a short time and included items such as biscuits, chocolate, bouillon powder, coffee, fruit bars, sugar, gum, hard candy, canned meat, and even a vitamin tablet. The X ration used a specialty wax dipped packaging designed to survive varied conditions and shared similarities to the Assault Lunch. In 1943 over 600,000 X rations were ordered and in 1944 an additional 250,000 units were ordered. The X ration after that simply disappeared.

The Aircrew Lunch: Another specialty ration developed during the war was one for aircrews. Early on aircrews simply created their own meals for their specific needs. This included individuals making sandwiches, bringing along commercial candies, thermoses of coffee, juice and other easy to carry items. But it was soon realized that a variety of rations were needed for aircrews consisting of single pilots to whole bomber crews. There were four basic uses that were eventually settled upon by the Army

Air Force and the Quartermaster Corps. These were as follows.

1- For pilots in single-seater or combat planes.

2- For bail-out (parachute) emergency purposes.

3- For crews and passengers in large planes equipped with heating devices for cooking.

4- For survivors in crash landings 60

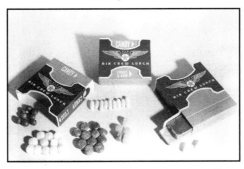

A version of the Air Crew ration that mostly utilized small containers of candy.
Photo Courtesy of the Fort Lee United States Army Quartermaster Museum

One easy solution for several uses was to utilize pre-pack assorted candies in easy to open and close pocket sized packs for aircrews of any size. This "candy" version was in use by 1942 and developed into a series of Aircrew lunches ranging from simple candy packets and ration bars to smaller meals developed from the K ration line. All versions of the "Pocket" style meals were based on ease of use, quick storage and almost nothing to dispose of or carry. For larger crews a wide variety of variations of ration solutions were utilized. In the early days of the war crews simply used any ration they could find, grabbed assorted fruits, foods, candies and made self rations from their own stores as well as the standard K ration, the 5-in-1, 10-in-1 and even C rations. Sometimes an inflight lunch was a simple as a quick sandwich when available.

The Aircrew Combat Lunch: As bombing runs and other missions increased in length the crews often were hungry as the simple rations and pocket candies did not fill the needs of the pilot or crews on a satisfaction level or on a proper nutritional level. The combat lunch was developed to fill this void and put into place by 1944 slowly phasing out procurement of the original Aircrew lunch although it the original Aircrew lunch available throughout the war. The major difference between the two was that the Combat lunch consisted of items that the crews could cook on board during flights based on a 3 man crew number but packed on a plane as needed to feed larger crews. The solution offered greater variety and better foods but in the long run it was too much to ask for a crew to stop and cook a meal during a mission when they should be concentrating on other things. In addition many planes were simply not large enough or well enough equipped to handle the cooking requirements of the Combat lunch. The Combat Lunch consisted mainly of items including assorted unprepared dehydrated foods, dry milk, chili powder or tomato paste, bouillon cubes, hard candy, gum, precooked rice, salt, tea tablets, and can opener. The Aircrew Combat Lunch was phased out by 1945. After the ration was phased out research showed that aircrews saw that the food was not worth the effort in trying to prepare it, a simple sandwich, piece of fruit and a can of soup would have been preferred with coffee in a jug. The only part of the ration that was well liked was the candy.

The Sandwich Pack: At the beginning of the war aircrews often relied on bringing their own lunch. This thought process often reappeared during the entire war. Most of the rations developed early for in flight use were simply too cumbersome or bulky to use. So crews adapted them for their use, or simply made their own filling a few thermoses with coffee or soup, packing some sandwiches, some candy and whatever they could easily get and store. Crews tossing a bag of handmade sandwiches or snacks instead of, or in addition to, normal rations before a mission did not go unnoticed and the development of a Sandwich pack was underway. The idea was based on the idea of a ration that could provide a few items to quickly make a sandwich and also provide a beverage. Due to the end of the war development was stopped on the Sandwich ration in 1945 but research would appear in later years that was similar in the form of prepared in flight meals called the in flight food packet.

The Bail-out and Parachute Emergency Ration: The bailout ration was developed and quickly procured in 1942. It had a very simple purpose. It was developed to be small in size but rich enough in calories and sustenance to sustain a downed pilot, or even an airborne troop, in an emergency survival situation. The Bailout ration consisted of a combination of D bars, fruit bars, hard candy, lemon-juice powder, and biscuits. This quick solution of packing proven smaller items together was a good start but was replaced in 1943 by the development of the Parachute-emergency ration. This ration was designed to fit in the pocket of an emergency vest. The new ration pack included sweet chocolate, hard candy, dehydrated cheese and crackers, bouillon cubes, sugar, cigarettes, water-purification tablets, soluble coffee and chewing gum. Developers also took into consideration the fact that once opened a downed pilot, or soldier dropping from a parachute in an emergency situation, had nothing to store unused rations for later use. So a small cellophane bag to contain uneaten food and other items until needed was included storage.

Lifeboat and Life Raft Rations: The duties of the Coast Guard and Merchant Marine required that a specialty ration be developed for lifeboat and life raft use. It was seen a good idea for any vessel. The special ration was developed and procured starting in 1942. Items included C biscuits, pemmican, chocolate tablets, and milk tablets which were packed in airtight containers. Another "at sea" ration was one developed in 1944 and was designed to be stowed in life rafts dropped from an airplane to survivors of a ditched plane, parachute drop over water and possibly survivors of a sunken ship. The ration was small, contained items such as a breakfast and supper unit and varied items from the C ration. These were often canned soup or meat food combination along with matches, toilet paper. The ration was designed to feed two men for one meal. Procurement was halted for this ration in 1944. A commercial aircraft version of the Life Raft ration was also developed which weighed over four pounds during the early years of the war. Because of its size and bulky packaging the commercial version was not adapted for military use. Instead the Quartermaster Corps developed a version consisting of confections ranging from fruit flavored hard candies to gum and even vitamin tablets. This ration was packed in a sealed tin container and included instructions for use.

Hospital Rations & Aid Station Rations: Several rations were developed under the hospital and aid station theme. The idea was to supply injured patients, or evacuees, being treated at forward bases with a quick source of nutrients as well as a hot meal if possible. Considered supplementary in nature theses rations included varied items as development progressed throughout the war. An early version shipped at the onset of the war ran into packaging problems. This prompted the Sustenance

The Hospital ration.
Photo Courtesy of the Fort Lee United States Army Quartermaster Museum

The Aid Station Ration.
Photo Courtesy of the Fort Lee United States Army Quartermaster Museum

Laboratory to develop an improved version and improved packaging. They settled on a more standardized list of items which were packed in more industrial sized cans or in many smaller cans and dehydrated items. Items often included canned fruit, cans of orange juice, cans of evaporated milk, tins of coffee, soup, sugar, premixed cereal, cocoa beverage powder, malted milk tablets, tea, tomato juice toilet paper and more. Versions of the ration were perfect for everything from small aid-stations and field hospitals to larger medical facilities.

A weeks menu on German rations and a Canadian Red X Parcel.				
	Breakfast.	Lunch.	Tea.	Dinner.
Monday.	Biscuit Por. Tea.	Pea Soup	Tea Biscuit.	Bully & pots. ersatz Coffee.
Tuesday.	Sardines. Tea.	Cheese Boil. pots	Tea	Salmon and Potatoes.
Wednesday.	Prunes Tea	Millet	Tea Biscuit.	German Stew Ersatz coffee.
Thursday.	Bis.Porr. Tea	Salmon	Tea Biscuit	Meat roll and Boiled pots.
Friday.	Sardines Tea.	Barley soup.	Tea Biscuit	Bully and pots
Sat.day.	Prunes Tea	Cheese Potatoes	Tea Biscuit.	German Stew Ersatz coffee
Sunday.	Bis.Porr. Tea	Boil.Pots	Tea Biscuit.	Meat Roll and Potatoes
The raisins usually were used to make a very potent wine .				

A weekly menu of POW war ration meals from the POW diary of RASC
Sergeant Ian Henry Duncan.
Submitted by Henry Duncan in honor of his father Ian Henry Duncan.

Red Cross Ration: The Red Cross approached the Quartermaster Corps for help and expertise in packaging a ration for prisoners of war. The Red Cross had very specific ideas for what the ration should contain and the majority of these items were already developed for military use. In short the Quartermaster Corps filled the shopping list of items for the Red Cross. The finished ration, which was only produced during the last five months of the war, was packed in a large can. Each can contained a wide variety of items for prisoners including Army spread, canned bacon, luncheon meat, salmon, dehydrated corned beef, canned cheese product, coffee, powdered milk, chocolate D bars, toilet paper, soap, paper towels, can openers and more. The other items included buttons; needles, thread, and patching cloth, vitamin capsules, salt, and tobacco were also packed in the sundry can. As the war ended so did the need for a ration for a prisoner of war.

This collection of labels is from the POW diary of RASC Sergeant Ian Henry Duncan. The diary contains illustrations, cartoons, scrapbook style items and information about the daily life of a POW. Duncan was a POW from 1942 to 1945 in various camps. According to his son, Henry, these labels are from various items contained in POW rations from relief organizations.
Submitted by Henry Duncan in honor of his father Ian Henry Duncan.

The Kitchen Spice Pack: While not an actual ration, the development of the Kitchen Spice Pack was a welcome improvement for military cooks. Using the technology, expertise of the ration developers and the Quartermaster Corps growing base of knowledge a special Kitchen Spice Pack was developed and packaged for use. It contained a wide variety of spices, flavorings, condiments and more. It could be packaged for kitchens of any size and situation. The spices and condiments could be utilized in ration style cooking or in kitchens where fresher meals were prepared.

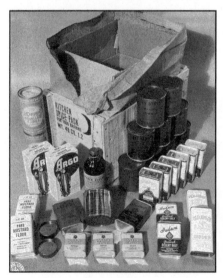

The specialty spice pack that helped cooks add flavor to meals in kitchens, galleys and mess halls of all sizes.
Photo Courtesy of the Fort Lee United States Army Quartermaster Museum

CHAPTER THREE

A Look at Allied and Axis Rations

SECTION 1

INTRODUCTION

1. One of the primary duties of an officer, no matter to whatever arm of the Service he may belong, is to ensure that those under his command are properly fed. Good feeding is one of the main factors which attribute to a soldier's health and fighting fitness. The indication of the importance attached to catering, which is recognized as a highly skilled profession, is the existence of the Army Catering Corps.

2. C~~atering~~ ~~trade~~

This one paragraph introduction from the British 1945 Manual of Army Catering Services speaks volumes about the serious attitude taken towards feeding troops.
From the collection of Hugh Beamish.

World War Two forced many countries to modernize the way they prepared for war. It also forced them to develop better methods to supply and feed their troops. Because of its industrial might and capabilities the United States would eventually lead the world in ration development and ration output. The United States started off a bit slow and hit a few bumps in the road, but by the end of World War Two the U.S. was the leader in ration development, production and shipping. American produced rations were used to feed the troops of many Allied nations, Axis troops held as P.O.W.s as well tens of thousands of people seeking humanitarian relief across the globe due to the ravages of the war.

59

The United States effort in feeding troops equaled the effort used to turn factories and shipyards into production facilities for the industrial war machine. The ability to develop, procure, produce, package and ship food and rations during the war can easily be argued as one of the reasons Allied troops were successful. This effort was seen in many countries, including Axis ones. In the United States the effort developed new foods, packaging, packaging methods, production methods, standards for food items and more. These huge steps forward in ration development were spread out to other nations. Many increased their own wealth of knowledge and the information and methods coming from the United States added to their own programs.

Many American troops actually dinned on rations provided by other countries including Great Britain and some procured from countries such as Australia and New Zealand. Some U.S. troops were known to make a "Baaaaa" sound when they were issued rations from New Zealand because of a heavy use of Mutton. Despite the initial lack of enthusiasm for these rations, many of the troops fed in the Pacific were done so with rations procured from sources in Australia and New Zealand. The rations were essentially the same; the major differences would be in food choices. American produced rations were based on 39 different food items while the Australian and New Zealand versions were based on a 21 food item list. Other differences include the types of vegetables used.

The British military saw a need for improvement in their rations after World War One. They realized several shortcomings and set out to improve the rations that were provided to troops. During the First World War the combined practice of supplying troops with canned tin and pre-packed rations and shipping cooked food to front line soldiers by hand was not acceptable as a common practice during the Second World War. Many soldiers were killed, on all sides, while in the process of carting food containers back and forth from front line positions to rear mess areas. Planners agreed that a better method for feeding troops in the field at forward positions or those on the move needed to be addressed. Allied packaged rations during the First World War lacked variety, had inadequate packaging and were not very popular with troops.

Another reason for change and updating they way British troops, and other countries, were fed was the fact that the German forces had introduced the idea of a Blitz style offensive maneuvers. It was obvious that troops would possibly be moving faster and further than in wars past. Troops had to be fed in a new way.

At the outset of the Second World War British troops were already at a disadvantage as far as food and rations were concerned. While there were a variety of rations available to troops the effectiveness of Nazi plans to block supplies from reaching Britain, and just about any part of the common wealth, eventually put a heavy strain on ration production. Despite the limitations and shortages the British put out a wide variety of rations for several uses much like their American Allies. The British armed forces also made heavy use of American rations of all types and sizes but also were able to adapt packaging and storage concepts from the Americans to their own needs.

Members of the Army Catering Corps during class.
Picture submitted by The RLC Museum, Surrey England

In 1941 the British Army Catering Corps was formed with a simple mission… feed the troops. They did. From the beginning of the war and the formation of the official Army Catering Corps to the war's end over 70,000 soldiers were trained to help feed and support the British Army. The Catering Corps cooked cleaned, developed recipes as well as served many other duties. Before the formation of the Army Catering Corps the daily cooking duties fell on the Royal Army Service Corps which handled just about everything dealing with supplies, storage, transportation and more. A cooking school had been set up in the small town of Aldershot prior to World War I. This cooking school was the basis for the new version of the Army Catering Corps which is part of the Royal Logistics Corps. Cooks were cross trained and when the new ACC was formed many crossed over to join the new Corps.

The British also faced similar problems that their United States Allies faced as far as older rations being used until newer versions were produced. Ration development was under way as the war began to rumble but an early reliance on proven rations and available items were needed. British rations ranged from the small emergency style and airdrop and field rations. They contained similar items to American versions but with British tastes in mind. Here is a great quote from the 1944 January- February Quartermaster Review in a report by Major General Robert Littlejohn.

"DIFFERENT peoples have different tastes. Methods of living are also affected by environment. That is why the British Army and the United States Army have different types of rations. The British ration is a good ration, but the average American does not like the high levels of tea, bread, potatoes, and mutton, the limited quantity of coffee, and the limited variety of fruits and vegetables. Furthermore, the American is a heavy meat-eater. The average Briton is more frugal in this respect."

The British Composite Ration, or Compo14 man ration - similar to the American 5 in 1 and the 10 in 1 rations, contained enough food for fourteen men for one day. Menu items included canned tins of meat, such as stewed lamb, salmon, oxtail, beef as well as canned combo items such as steak and vegetable, pork and vegetable, kidney and beef with gravy and the dreaded mystery meat and vegetable. In many countries soldiers said that it was anyone's guess as to what meat was used if the packaging could not even describe it or list it. These canned meats and meals were complemented by other items and condiments including bacons, sardines, assorted soups, vegetables, fruit, fruit cocktails, puddings, teas, margarine, candies, biscuits, toilet items, matches and more.

The 14 in 1 rations could be broken down to smaller portions or cooked for the larger group. By combining several 14 in 1 boxes even larger numbers of troops could be fed. Cooking in the field was done mostly using camp methods ranging from issued stoves, pots, pans and such to old fashioned campfire cooking.

One of the more interesting rations used by the British was actually a combination of items used in other rations. It was called a Brew Up Kit. This package contained a wide assortment of items needed for British soldiers to "brew up" a cup of tea. Items varied as supplies changed but for the most part the Brew Up Kit contained teas, sugar, matches, biscuits, candies and other items. The Brew up Kit helped fill the need for a more traditional beverage as well as a feeling of normalcy to British troops as coffee did for many American troops.

The British were able to improve their rations for use in the field as well as develop new technology vastly superior to versions used during World War One. They also were able to heavily supplement their own stock piles of rations with rations developed and produced by the Americans.

General Food Items of the Japanese Forces

These items were found in the downed planes of Japanese pilots involved in the raid on Pearl Harbor. Besides propaganda leaflets, supplies of food including bottle of whiskey, cider drink, candy, chocolate, hardtack, tooth powder and chop sticks.
Photo, National Archives

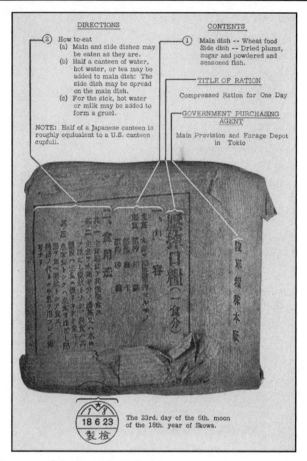

Photo Courtesy of the Fort Lee United States Army Quartermaster Museum

By the time the United States had entered the war Japan had been involved with the growing armed conflict since the early 1930's. While much had been done in Japan to try and modernize the fighting methods and equipment used little had been done to improve the overall food, cooking and ration situation. However, the methods used to cook in a military kitchen in a set place served as a model of catering efficiency in many areas such as space, menu and more.

In general, despite a very adaptive messing system, Japan eventually relied on a makeshift method of delivering food and prepared rations to its troops. A large part of the effort to feed Japanese forces was based on trying to prepare hot meals for fighting men using a system of centralized cooking areas. These cooking centers could be for only a few men or for many. Regardless of the size the meals generally tended to be centered based on ingredients familiar to the troops.

The Japanese soldier, during some time periods of the war, seemed too lived on rice alone while trying to add items found locally. At larger bases Japanese forces would live on the opposite end of the spectrum. They sometimes have a very wide variety of food choices as compared to duty in the field. At a well supplied outpost or garrison a foot soldier often would eat much more that he would have had at home. At home the average Japanese citizen was suffering from shortages caused by the lengthy war they were involved in. Households grew even more dependent on the staples of rice, vegetables and seafood.

Daily meals were not the only thing the troops had available. Like the Allied solider, the Japanese military often set up civilian type stores for their troops in order to let them purchase extra items that they desired. The list of goods ranged from store to store, and area of operation to area of operation. For the most part these stores carried consumer items such as an assortment of books and magazines, newspapers, various snack foods, toilet and personal items and even a favorite among many soldiers on both sides of the conflict... beer.

The Japanese commanders, planners and leaders did their best to provide a home style diet to both soldiers and sailors. These meals prepared by cooks at the centralized location consisted of fish, fowl or some type of meat, soup, traditional seasonings rice, fruit, vegetables, tea, sake or beer, and assorted other items. They tried to supplement the standard rations with local fruits and vegetables whenever possible. But when these were not available then canned items were served up on chow lines as was done with many forces. As mentioned before, since the armed forces of Japan were already fighting a prolonged war they were facing many supply issues by the time the United States entered.

The fighting men of Japan relied on a variety of pre-packed rations that were designed to be similar to their traditional fare when away from a facility with a central kitchen or a central kitchen in the field. As with other countries the kitchens were staffed with cooks and men trying their best to serve up hot meals under less than ideal conditions. Similar to the meals prepared and served from central kitchens the Japanese rations also were developed to appeal to the tastes of the soldier. Often pre-packed rations were based on rice with fish or fowl but they also contained many other items that the Japanese soldier could relate to. Rice came in a paper container along with a tin of packed fish or other meat. Rations also included available seasonings, bread such as crackers, sugar and other items in order to provide some diversity. Smaller versions included tightly packed rice, dried fish or meat, hard crackers, vitamins, teas and a variety of items as they were available. Other emergency style rations for the Japanese consisted of hard candy and ration bars made of items such as peanuts or sesame. These small rations were designed to carry a huge amount of calories in a small size.

Overall the Japanese tried their best to provide a pre-packed ration meal similar in concept to other armies. The meal had to be in durable packaging, provide nutrients; it had to be easy to carry and take little effort to prepare. Packaging changed often during the war as different materials were used and as different providers were contracted. This quickly limited what could be used as a ration. As bombing hit industrial areas the packing designs would be altered to fit whatever manufacturing process could be utilized no matter how small. Rations were packed in paper, cans or tins; wax coated and packed in a variety of sizes. Towards the end of the war Allied bombing had so damage the production capacity of ration manufactures that a large cottage industry of small home based packers began to develop. These small home based packagers provided rations of all sorts and sizes.

As the war progressed more and more Japanese rations came into the possession of Allied troops. As with U.S. style rations Allied troops found that the Japanese rations were developed for certain use ranging from standard field rations to combat and air rations. These rations provided a welcome addition to normal U.S. Rations and many Allied forces supplemented their own diets with captured stores because many of the items in the rations were already familiar to the Allied troops. For safety it was urged that any rations be inspected before consuming. And once opened the entire ration should be consumed because any waste during the war was discouraged, even if it was wasting the rations of the enemy.

After the war the divide that existed between what urban and rural citizens of Japan enjoyed on a daily basis was largely erased. The majority of the everyday diet was heavy in any vegetable that could be grown in just about any space. Like the Victory Gardens in wartime Allied Countries, AXIS countries depended on Post War gardens of all sizes to help narrow the food gap. In addition, the war introduced many people living in Japan and it's occupied countries, to various Westernized foods because of the use of military rations and stored item used for relief.

Australian Army Catering Corps

An impressive spread of Australian military food from the booklet
Soldiering On—The Australian Army At Home and Overseas from 1942 by
Halstead Press Pty Ltd, Sydney, it is a collection of stories, jokes, photos and
drawings from Aussie Soldiers serving overseas at the time.
From the collection of Michael Hallinan

Heading into World War Two the Australian Army, like many other nations, found that it was somewhat ill prepared to properly feed its fighting forces on such a large scale. What worked in previous conflicts were now outdated for the World War that was building. While some basic rations were in production, and many units had their own cooks, the overall picture left much to be desired. Various forms of canned rations containing assorted items along with other dried and prepared foods were given to troops at the outset of the war and for several years. But these rations often proved to be bulky, did not stand up to the wear and battering of a soldier's everyday life and above all did not properly address nutritional needs. Added problems with supply issues did not do anything to relieve problems soldiers found with food.

By the end of the war Australia had improved its ability to feed its troops in both the field kitchen area and with improved rations. Australia eventually became supplier and producer of pre-packed rations for Allied troops. Production capability had improved to the point that many of the rations that troops fighting in the Pacific came from Australia and even New Zealand. American troops seemed to prefer rations from the states produced using flavors they were more accustomed to.

The Australian military suffered from problems relating to wide variations in training and outdated equipment that was available to cooks when World War Two started. This is not to say the cooks did not try to do their best or properly feed Australian troops, there was just not enough standardization of training, supplies and proper equipment to get the job done despite a cooks best efforts. Many of the methods for cooking, menus and training for cooks that were in place for World War One were still practiced when Australia entering the Second World War. Improvements were slow in coming between the two conflicts. In a sense, Australia did not have its own identity when it came to feeding troops in any branch of the military. According to the Australian Naval Historical Society the mainstay for Naval cooking was based mainly on traditional British Naval methods including the use of British manuals and recipe information. The cooks from down under were using methods, equipment, recipes and training that were completely outdated.

One person that understood the issue, and worked towards a solution, was Sir Stanton Hicks who not only was highly educated but he also had an incredible understanding of nutritional needs and food management. Prior to the joining the military Hicks took a leading role in examining the everyday diets of the Australian people as well as looking at the lifestyle of native aborigines. In 1939 Hicks joined the Army as a captain and was quickly able to apply his knowledge to the War effort. He was assigned part time duty as a catering supervisor. He quickly began to realize the need for taking a more standardized and scientific approach to the way the military fed its troops. He began to push for reform in many areas including development of better rations, proper methods or preparing food efficiently, better cooking equipment for field use and better education of cooks. Hicks was soon named Chief Inspector of Catering. He began to apply his ideas to areas he saw that needed improvement. Due largely to his efforts the Australian Army Catering Corps was formed in 1943. Hicks was promoted to a Lt. Colonel and appointed the first Director of the new corps.

Under his guidance the Corps dramatically improved and standardized many of the methods used in procuring, developing and preparing food. Huge advancements were also made in the training of cooks as specialized schools and training were put in place. Nutritional value of prepared foods, storage, packing and ration development were also moving forward. One side effect of the improvements made by Hicks was a dramatic drop in waste and spoilage. All of this led to better nourished troops, less food borne illness, better supply lines and guidelines for properly feeding Australian forces during the war.

Better pre-repacked rations were also developed under the guidance of Hicks who quickly realized older versions were not designed for the way they were being used. As with other countries some of the problem was because of available technology. World War One style rations, and food packaging, was not up to World War Two needs. A stop gap measure that many Allied countries relied on was the use of a growing number of available American military rations to bolster their own stores. Australia was able to take advantage of this while improving several of their rations at the same time and, as mentioned before, supplying many of the Allied Pacific troops with rations. Under Hicks the Corps developed and improved its line of rations, water purification kits and developed of two specialty rations named the Jungle Emergency Ration and the Air Drop Ration.

Both of these rations took advantage of better packaging and food preparation technology. The packaging was designed to better protect items from the elements to prevent damage, spoilage, to be less bulky and weigh less. The Jungle emergency ration contained items for three meals which were each packed in its own inner carton. Items, which varied somewhat over production, such as carrot biscuits fruit & nut blocks, meat & vegetable stew or hash, meat & beans, peanut butter, barley sugar rolls, caramel bar, skim milk powder, sugar, tea, salt tablets, cheese, chocolate, spreads and assorted personal items. The Australian Airdrop ration was small in size and contents. It was designed to meet specific short-term needs. This ration could be used in a variety of situations such as combat flights, bail-outs, parachute, emergency drops and more when no other ration was available. It contained the bare essentials ranging from powdered flavorings to salt tablets.

As for field cooking for Hicks realized vast improvements were needed in all manners of preparing food for Australian soldiers and placed emphasis on field cooking. During the First World War the Wiles Army Steam Cooker, a horse drawn cooking wagon, was developed by James (Jim) Fletcher Wiles of Victoria, Australia who was also an Army veteran and cook. The unit combined a boiler, roasting oven, hot and cold water tanks and other features. The wagon could also be adjusted in height and withstood hard use.

Over 300 cookers were produced and used under active service conditions in Australia, Egypt and France. But after the war a move was put in place to better align Australian Army cooking with British methods and the Wiles Cooker was taken out of service. Discouraged that his well performing invention was no longer used Jim Wiles sold his workshops and purchased an irrigated fruit growing business with property of over 100 acres. Unfortunately the dried fruit industry collapsed and just prior to the Great Depression Wiles, now broke, abandoned the business and settle with his family in Adelaide Australia in 1926. Not being one to sit around Wiles started a new Electroplating business with the help of his sons and soon was considered a leader in these growing industry.

Over the years Wiles often commented to his sons about the success of the Wiles Cooker and the important role it had in preparing and keeping men suited for battle by feeding them in a proper manner. As Wiles grew older he understood that war was once again looming and despite health problems began to convince his sons, Ken, Richard, Ivor, Jack and Ray, that an updated version of his cooker could still be used to help the Army. Jim Wiles died in August of 1939 before he could resume work on his cooker but his sons, led by Ken, decided that their father was right and the Wiles Cooker could be brought back. They were able to make working models from descriptions and photos of the original units. They advanced the technology and tested many aspects of the design and adjusted things quickly. After working day and night for months the Wiles brothers had a working updated oven that modernized the way meals could be prepared for troops.

Wiles Cookers ready for transport to front line positions during World War Two.
Photo courtesy of Hugh Williams, Nephew of the Wiles Brothers.

Kenneth Wiles, one of the four sons of Jim Wiles who developed the versatile Wiles Cooker patterned after their fathers 1914 unique design, is shown pictured with Sir Stanton Hicks. Hicks is widely regarded as being the force behind moving the Australian Catering Corps forward with safer, more reliable and nutritious foods.
Photo courtesy of Hugh Williams, Nephew of the Wiles Brothers.

71

At the same time Australian military leaders were rethinking the move to align themselves with the British standards for cooking and realized that an approach that better suited their methods was needed. After field testing with the Garrison Battalion at Keswick word spread about the advantages of the new steam cookers ease of use, its safety and consistency. But as with many military related topics official acceptance was slow to catch on despite approving reports from individual units during testing. During one test the cooker took the place of 20 plus smaller field fires and cooking equipment pieces. It was also shown to work as a mobile and static item. The reduction of field fire cooking reduced the amount of fuel, equipment and cooks needed to feed troops.

Eventually the person who was working on parallel efforts to improve things, Colonel Hicks, was alerted to the new piece of equipment. During a live demonstration Hicks was amazed of the performance of the cooker and noted the amount of fuel savings compared to output of finished food. One cooker could feed over 500 men twice a day with hot food and hot water. Hicks later noted in his own writing this about the Wiles prototype cooker. "Soup, stews and vegetables steamed so that 'troops will eat them and return for more', as the Commanding Officer said. He continued, 'There must be something important about this, and you are just the one to find out'.

But once again progress towards a full implementation of the cooker for the Army as a whole was slowed. Almost eight months went by before the brothers heard any word about the cooker but they continued to improve it and make prototypes all at their own company's expense. As stated by one of the Wiles sons, no one was willing to change in the Army despite Hicks call for improvements. "Most Army Officials were keen to use the cooker but no one would make the forward step."

As the war expanded so did the size of bases and camps. This meant that the older, often unsanitary, methods of cooking for troops were expanded to fill the needs. It was not until Hicks made a trip to one of the larger camps located near the Wiles plant that progress towards full implementation of the Wiles cooker was made. The camp cooking area was a mess and the thick smoke from fires clogged the air. Hicks was so horrified about the poor cooking conditions that he rushed plans forward in order to begin work with the Wiles brothers to make a larger version of the Wiles cooker for base use. Once the Wiles units began to be installed Hicks pressed for more units for use on other bases in order to replace the old pot and cooking fire methods forever. A double version was developed and in place within three weeks which could cook 3 course meals for over 500 men or a two course meal for over 1000 men.

The new versions also could be fueled by wood, coal or oil. Hicks pressed to have the Wiles Cooker placed into service throughout the Army stating that it would revolutionize the way the Australian Army fed its troops. Hick's correct feelings about the future of Army cooking combine and the persistence and ingenuity of the Wiles brothers paid off. By the end of the World War Two the Wiles cooker came in mobile and stationary units designed to fit a wide variety of needs. The units could be found attached to train cars, built with jeep like configurations for cooking on the move. They could be dropped by parachute, set up at hospitals, forward areas and even strapped to rail cars as part of a train. Wiles cookers were used in many countries and both theatres of the war and updated versions stayed in use with the Australian Army until 1980.

German Rations of World War Two

The German foot soldier at the start of World War Two had a wide variety of foods available to him. Rations were developed to supply nutrients, calories, protein and other essentials. These rations were developed to be portable, filling and easy to use. Rations included a base tin of meat such as turkey, beef, pork and chicken. Also included were hard bread and crackers of various varieties including whole wheat. Like their Allied counterparts the Germans added varied items and packaging solutions for rations for different needs. Tins, wraps, water resistance packaging were all used.

One thing the German forces did not have was the amount of variety that Allied Forces enjoyed. German soldiers were often amazed at rations that were captured when they stormed across Europe. But there are numerous stories of Allied forces enjoying better tasting items from certain German offerings. German cooks relied heavily on the food available from the local area. Simply put, the lack of variety was not a problem when captured foods were available. This luxury was short lived as only a few troops were able to take advantage of this situation during the beginning of the conflict. As the war progressed, food and other goods were shipped from occupied areas back to the homeland to meet the needs of the German people. Shortages began to develop and the common foot soldier was relegated to weeks of the same ration meals or field cooked meals that often mimicked the rations they were already eating. Field cooking was used and the bread and other fresh items used at the outset of the war were becoming a thing of the past as the war progressed.

The Germans utilized a multi piece mess kit like many Allied and AXIS forces. The remains of a German Mess kit, complete with shrapnel hole and spoon, were recovered in Russia by Matt Fox of Quarter Ton & Military. Mr. Fox noted that these items were most likely from members of the Totenkopf SS Group Simon according to maps of known troop locations. Note the German S makings on the spoon which was not part of a standard issue kit.
Items pictured are from the collection of Matt Fox, as well as the Veterans of All Wars Museum, Chickamauga, Georgia and *The History Co. & Southeast Veterans Museum—photo by Kent Whitaker.*

Through out the war the German cooks tried to deliver as many hot meals to troops as possible but as with other armies during the conflict this was simply not a reality. A battalion kitchen was set up and meals were prepared and hand delivered to front line forces. The hot meals were packed with assorted candies, sides, breads and more. The problem was that often fighting simply did not for the hot food deliveries to make it through and the delivery and production of field rations was not to a point where German troops had enough to eat during many battles. Often German soldiers would go for days with little to eat.

During the closing stages of the Second World War German forces were strung out across the war zone and constantly moving. Setting up a large battalion size field kitchen to prepare food for front line troops was not possible. Not only were the food supplies of the military becoming limited the population of the major cities were feeling more than just mild shortages. The supply chain had almost completely shut down. Towards the end of the war and for extended periods of time after many citizens of AXIS countries and their military members lived near starvation until relief supply lines could be fully implemented. Food production as a whole in occupied Germany was in ruins.

WWII Canadian Rations at a Glance

The Royal Canadian Air Force had a peak strength of over 215,000 including 15,000 women. The RCAF provided a large amount of pilots and crews to the RAF and Allied efforts during World War Two including service during the Battle of Britian.

After World War One the Canadian military took a strong look at improving and developing their own rations separate from the British. The decision to move forward with a similar, but separate, ration program from the Royal armed forces was helped by the fact that Canada and the United States were neighbors. Canada, like the United States, was far removed from any ravages remaining from World War One and industrial capacity was beginning to come out of the depression. Despite the problems with the economy the Canadian military was able to improve their own rations to a point that when the next world war was beginning to rage in Europe Canadian forces heading to mother England had a growing variety of rations available for its troops. Canada entered the war in 1939 with a declaration of war against Germany.

The Canadian forces were a major influence in defending North Atlantic shipping lanes, the war in the Pacific, fighting at Normandy as well as across Europe and Africa. Canada provided Britain with forces including pilots that served in the Battle of Britain. One out of six bomber command units flying in the RAF were RCAF trained aircrews.

While serving in France in June of 1944 Canadian Highland Light Infantry Sergeant C. Orton takes a few minutes to enjoy a drink from a captured bottle of cider.

76

The Canadian rations followed much of the thinking of the British and the United States in the sense that certain rations were developed for certain needs and situations. They made full use of increased knowledge of production, safe packaging and even variety in menu items. First the Canadians focused on providing an improved menu for camp and kitchen cooking for mess and chow halls which fall under the blanket term of a Food Service Ration. These Food Service Rations were meals made from ingredients that were as fresh as possible much like the improving cooking methods found in the United States as far as food safety, training, delivery, shipping and production.

The next level feeding the troops came in the form of Field Service Rations. These rations were transportable foods with a longer shelf life, improved packaging, required no refrigeration and had a variety of items and were packed in bulk in order to feed larger numbers of men. These rations could feed a few troops or as many men as needed depending on how many rations were combined. Like the rations of the same type from other nations the Field Service Rations could be used by the group or broken down for smaller numbers and possibly individual use if needed. They contained a combination of canned and packaged foods including meats, stews, soups, crackers, juices, drinks, condiments and assorted personal items. The Field Service Rations could easily be adjusted to meet the needs of any situation as well as adjusted to use ingredients and items that were available if something were unavailable due to shortages.

This flexibility also was planned into the development of the Operational Rations which were a step away from the larger rations that could be used in the field or in a mess kitchen setting. The Canadian Field Operational Rations were to be used under situations when a soldier could not get to a mess hall. Simply put, if you were in the field for a few days chances are you were going to be issued a ration for a twenty four hour or forty eight hour use. These rations were designed to provide basic substance for only a few days and also include a wide variety of items in varied packaging ranging from canned and tinned goods to wrapped items packed in improved packaging designed to better survive combat conditions. These rations were similar to the British Compo rations and even the American 5 in 1 ration while also being geared towards individual use as needed.

Canada also developed specialty and supplemental rations for use in mountain regions, emergency situations, survival settings, tank, aircrew and water survival rations, general purpose rations and Individual Emergency Rations and several more. All of the Canadian rations tried to take advantage of newer and safer production and packaging and placed a high regard on shelf life and variety.

The majority of troops from the United States used outdated mess kits when the war began. Many from WWI stockpiles. Small changes by designers made for welcome improvements by GI's. The new kits were more versatile. They were light, had deeper compartments which could separate foods and store more items. They could also be made faster and more efficiently than the older kits with the modernization of US production facilities. Pictured are an original WWI design on the left, and a 1943 WWII version on the right.
From the collection of The History Co. & Southeast Veterans Museum
Photo by Kent Whitaker.

CHAPTER FOUR

Welcome to Cooks and Bakers School

To make things as real as possible for students these field ovens were placed on the lawn of the American Institute of Baking in Chicago. The classes were a mix of officers, non-commissioned officers and privates. As graduates from the U.S. Army Training School for Advanced Baking Instructors, they, in turn, will be able to supervise and instruct others.
Photo courtesy of the Harold M. Freund American Baking Museum, WWII Collection. Original photo by the United States Signal Corps.

According to the 1948 Quartermaster Messing Operations World War Two report the military had learned that the methods in which troops in the field were fed in World War Two had undergone some major changes from previous wars. Heading into World War two they knew that

79

the old "scorched earth" methods of sustaining troops on the move, at least in part, off the land were no longer viable. The food that was obtainable by purchase and commandeering while troops moved about was always an important part of providing daily provisions. This would hold true on many levels but the need to be able to better supply and feed soldiers with less reliance on local foods was something military planners decided to work on. An improved combined system of deployable pre packed rations combined with better cooking and messing operations. The age of "scorched earth" was at an end.

Photo Courtesy of the Veterans of All Wars Museum, Chickamauga, Georgia

Things had improved vastly over conditions in World War one by the time the Second World War was over. Efforts were made to make sure a decent meal could be had by soldiers, sailors and airmen anywhere in the world. Whenever possible the meal could be served hot. As the 1943 October Quartermaster Review states, "Americans like their food hot." Of course this was not always possible and many soldiers suffered eating the same canned rations day after day, week after week. In some situations food was not available or in short supply. This happened in situations such as when supplies were cut off, during prolonged battles, while being held as a POW and even when being shot down or stranded. Prison camps were not known for great food. In one case a group of American sailors were essentially stranded in Murmansk Russia waiting on repairs to their ship. For many months the crews normal meals were replaced by a diet of yak meat, soup and pressed caviar. But overall World War Two cooks and bakers did their best to perform the duties of what was actually a highly skilled job that required many weeks of training.

Improved education and training did not only apply only to cooks and bakers. The changes made over the course of time between the start of the First World War and the end of the Second World War in areas affecting food, rations and supplies was multi level. Besides cooks and bakers almost every aspect of providing subsistence to troops was looked at including the role of Mess Sergeants, Noncommissioned Subsistence officers and more. Procurement procedures were studied. Even the way dishes were washed and sanitized received attention.

Overall, leaders knew that "good food" would play a major part in keeping moral up. They also knew that the food should meet improved dietary and nutrition guidelines and it should be safe. Pre-packed rations were improving in variety and growing in number all of which served a purpose in feeding troops. But the smell of hot coffee and the aroma of fresh baked bread had an amazing affect on weary soldiers and sailors. This was not a new thought to World War Two military leaders. The effort to improve Army, and military cooking and food supplies in general actually started years prior to World War Two. The first Army cooking school was started at Fort Riley Kansas in 1903. The Army Quartermasters cooking school opened in Philadelphia in 1910. The Navy issued it's standardized *General Mess Manual and Cookbook* written by Paymaster F.T. Arms in 1902.

During the Spanish American war so many problems with tainted supplies, spoilage, food poisoning, and overall issues such as kitchen safety and sanitation were brought to light that it was understood that better methods and training were needed. In fact it was a national issue and scandal that raged in the government as well as the newspapers. Everyone knew that something had to be done to improve things. With the establishment of cooking schools, cooking manuals and the start of an emphasis on safety and sanitation the old style military cook was being replaced by a trained, professional, military cook. All of the various service branches from the early 1900's to the outset of World War Two had realized that the old adage of a military traveling on its stomach was not only a good saying, but it was also a very true statement.

Prior to the United States entering World War One Major General Henry G. Sharpe, considered by many to be the father of the modern Quartermaster corps, realized that improvements could be made in the way the American military men were supplied and served. Using his own funds Henry set out on a learning trip to Europe to take a look at how different militaries handled supply operations. He visited English, French and German forces taking note on things he saw that he thought should be incorporated into American supply efforts. One area that Henry focused on was how various cooks and bakers schools operated. Upon his return Henry was able to use his newly gained knowledge to help improve rolling kitchens and more. But not all of Henry's knowledge was put to use. Henry was made Quartermaster General a mere six months before America entered World War one.

Henry called for consolidating many of the efforts of the way troops were supplied and the way goods were procured. With consolidation would come better organization and the ability to better track, procure and deliver items and services in a timely and more efficient manner. Henry submitted his ideas for improvements and consolidation when he returned from his overseas tour in 1907. While his suggestions were not adopted at that time, they were revisited four years later. With the United States now entering World War One Henry was now Quartermaster General and had only six months to prepare. Six months was not enough.

During the First World War many shortages often were the result of a surge of materials being ordered by various eager supply bureaus. They ordered everything they could as quickly as possible in a rush to make sure the troops had what they needed. Procured items began arriving to supply depots at one time overwhelming the workers and the ability to properly ship them. They simply could not load enough trains fast enough with the materials most needed.

During the time between World War One and the Second World War the United States worked hard to better organize the procurement and supply process at the same time that an attentive eye was also turned towards the way cooks and bakers were trained. Cuts after the end of the first war slowed the process but progress was made. The Quartermaster

Subsistence Research and Development Laboratory was opened in 1936 in order to address many of the food and ration issues that still lingered from World War One. The opening of the facility ushered in a new era in the thinking of what military food for fighting troops in the field should be. It was a great start. Sadly for American forces during the outset of World War Two many types of older style rations were used in conjunction with only a few new rations that had been developed, tested and in production. Older stored items were utilized to feed the growing military because they had to be used. Newer rations on a large scale and with lots of variety were not available yet. But they were coming.

In World War One soldiers were fed an assortment of hot meals, cold meals and various rations. Many early rations lacked proper packaging and were prone to rust and rot and sometimes did not properly protect the food. Over the course of the war progress was made in packaging and durability of the rations as the technology of the day would permit. Many of the rations that were used in World War One were developed for Trench style warfare. The combination of pre-packed meals and field cooked meals were delivered by hand from kitchens to the front lines as conditions allowed. This combination of cooked hand delivered meals and under-performing rations and did not meet the nutrition needs of the troops. Plus, many of the soldiers used to deliver food in this manner, on both sides of the battlefield, were killed while doing so.

The entire system was not very efficient. The military started looking for some solutions. These early efforts to solve the problems included the introduction of nutritional survey parties. These units were sent out to the field to try and do a better job in informing cooks about nutrition and other food topics. They perceived that many problems with the quality of meals, and providing food to troops, could be improved in kitchens. Ration improvement and development was still an issue still had to be addressed.

During the years that the United States remained neutral steps had been taken by the service branches to improve the way military cooks were trained. By 1941 the work towards better daily food preparation had come a long way. Cooks and bakers were receiving better training and many service branch cookbooks and manuals were being updated and supplemented. Other measures were addressed as well. The way food was procured, shipped and stored saw advancements. Improvements were made in food safety along with overall nutritional content of daily meal plans were improved. However in a situation similar to ration development much of the military relied on older methods to cook and prepare meals. Progress on this end was coming but it was slow. The Navy was renowned for the quality of meals served on their ships. The larger ships had more storage and refrigeration capacity. For the foot soldier in the field refrigeration was limited as were storage facilities depending on where they were stationed or deployed.

This picture was taken at the mess table at MacArthur's HQ at Tacloban, Leyte, Christmas 1944.
Photo courtesy of the MacArthur Memorial Norfolk Virginia

A large number of soldiers learned their cooking trade by attending one of a growing number of cooking schools. These schools started popping up at bases across the country during the Second World War after the initial first Quartermasters Cooking School opened and continued to do so. As bases were built and the standard mess halls and kitchens were put into place many base commanders sought a cooks and bakers school for their facility. After all, it was to the advantage of the facility to have a cooking and baking school in order to serve better food on base and also in the field. On the Quartermaster side of the cooking equation there is one statistic that shows how many cooks were available in the QM ranks. On average fourteen trained quartermasters, in a variety of duties, were used to properly handle one soldier during World War Two. And one of those fourteen QM's was a cook.

The logistical side of cooking three meals a day for home based servicemen and those overseas was as big of a challenge as the work done to improve rations. Each facility with a mess and kitchen would rely on a combination of fresh, canned, powdered and ration style items. To supplement these stockpiles fresher local items were procured when possible. The variety of food served would vary depending on factors such as the purpose of the facility, location, service branch. It also helped if there was a good cook available.

Every kind of food stores imaginable were purchased and shipped to waiting kitchens by the tons on a daily and weekly basis across the globe. Regardless of the use of fresh or canned prepackaged ingredients the amount of food used was enormous. Baking bread for a large camp meant truck loads of flour and other ingredients were used daily.

During World War II, the required cooking and baking class lasted over six weeks. The cooking classes covered a vast amount of information in a relatively short period of time. The new cooks not only learned recipes and cooking in general, they also learned to cook for a crowd. The majority of approved recipes available were set for feeding 100 men. Because of the large quantities recipes required military cooks also learned methods for reducing recipes as well as increasing them. More importantly in many ways was the fact that the new cooks also learned about topics ranging from sanitation, food safety, nutrition and more.

The War Department Technical Manual 12-427 (TM-12-427) of 1944, Military Occupational Classification of Enlisted Personnel, defines the duties of trained cooks, bakers, Mess Sergeants and Subsistence Noncommissioned Officers in the following ways.

COOK (060)—Prepares food for the personnel of a military organization, using a daily menu as a guide. Seasons and cooks meats, soups, deserts, vegetables, sauces, and gravies in accordance with military methods of food preparation. Must be familiar with regulations governing kitchen sanitation. Must be capable of setting up and operating a field kitchen.

CHIEF BAKER (017)—Bakes bread and allied flour products, such as rolls, cakes, pies and pastries, in a fixed of mobile bakery. Requisitions supplies and maintains simple records. Weighs proper amounts of ingredients and mixes them, using an electrically powered mixing machine, or kneads by hand. Places dough in proofing room or rack to ferment. Cuts dough into uniform portions with dough knife. Shapes chunks into loaves, places them in greased pans, and inserts them in oven. Regulates oven temperature by manipulating drafts or thermostatic controls. Removes baked bread. Cleans all machinery and equipment. In a mobile kitchen, aids in loading and unloading equipment, digging oven pit and firing trench, and assembling field ovens.

MESS SERGEANT—(824)—Supervises and controls the activities of mess personnel in garrison or field kitchen installations. Prepares menus from a master menu. Supervises the preparation of food in accordance with established sanitary and dietetic principals. Makes authorized requisitions and purchases of supplies. Inspects delivered supplies for condition and proper quantity and inspects stored food for spoilage. Keeps record of supplies, equipment and mess account. Must have sufficient knowledge of dietetics to maintain a balanced diet. Must be able to direct and control the preparation of palatable meals under unfavorable field conditions. Must be familiar with Army methods of accounting and inventory as they apply to food.

SUBSISTENCE NONCOMMISSIONED OFFICER (820)—Directs a subsistence supply section in drawing field rations in bulk and in making equitable distribution to the various companies or similar units in his organization. Checks work of section leaders who handle meats and produce and the work of dry-issue clerks. Draws dry rations from commissary or supply dump and counts number of cases of each item. Supervises a detail in loading cases on trucks and in delivering them to units. May supervise delivery of rations to unit mess sergeants.

Just by reading the job descriptions one can tell that the skill level and training had increased for cooks and bakers and issues such as diet, nutrition, sanitation and supply were addressed on all levels. From cooks and bakers to Subsistence non-coms the variety of skills and knowledge learned from increased training raised the quality level of chow.

This increased education came in several ways during school including classroom, kitchen time and the use of various multimedia items such as training films. Basic cooking, safety and sanitation skills were all covered in classes. In addition the cooking students studied ways to adjust their abilities to adapt to different situations. They could be called to duty on a large installation, sent overseas to cook with a unit and of course work towards the front. Any situation was possible. The idea being that the basics of safety, nutrition and sanitation would remain a standard, the tools and equipment used to cook and prepare food could change depending on where the cook served. And if the equipment was not there… they could improvise.

This training gave many cooks the ability to adapt to their situations. A general field kitchen could be up and running in a relatively short period of time. It could be on located in a secured area, a forward position, a bombed out enemy hut or building. It could be driven to the soldiers in the form of a mobile field kitchen or simply a quickly assembled oven made from salvaged drums or even metal from a wrecked airplane. In one instance the remains of an outdated French Bomber and its expansive wing made for a perfect setting for a kitchen. Mess sergeants, non-coms and cooks became masters at tossing tarps over something securing a few lines and before long they were serving chow, passing out rations or at least had some coffee flowing. The 1944 January 21 edition of the *Quartermaster Review* summed it up this way.

"Fighting men eat their food where they find it. And Chow Time, is anytime there is a long enough lull in the fighting. When hot food is on tap, the surroundings, the menu, and the mess gear are of secondary importance. Main idea is to get it quick. Men eat ankle deep in mud, dipping the food from their helmets; or they stand in the blazing sun; or they flop in the jungle grass."

This ability to use their training in order to adapt cooking methods to just about any situation helped cooks and bakers provide hot meals to troops just about anywhere troops traveled. Additionally, on the smallest level, soldiers in the field often had the ability to heat and warm rationed items themselves. Training allowed cooks to determine temperatures simply by holding their hands close to a heat source and counting how long they could keep it there. Many cooks would use a "four count oven" as a temperature in recipes. The more numbers in the count, the cooler the temp. A count of one or two meant the heat source is very hot. Or, the oven was on high! A longer count meant the heat source was lower in temperature. It was not an exact science, but cooks were very good at knowing what temperatures were by this time honored cooking tip. Because of the improved training American World War Two cooks were better prepared than ever before. Even if supply chain issues and shortages came into play they could generally serve up chow, coffee and bread that was hot and very less likely to make anyone sick as in previous wars.

Another aspect of the training was that some emphasis was put on the ability to save food, reuse items and make use of leftovers with a policy of limited waste. A great example of this is the instructions for slicing fresh bread in a manner that eliminates the waste of end pieces since few people enjoy a sandwich made of only the end crust slices. Cooks and bakers were taught to try and pinch every cent out of the money spent on supplies. Not only was this an effective means of cost savings it also helped in keeping units supplied. If a cook could get the most out of the supplies he had then the wait for new supplies would not be as strenuous.

During World War Two cooks and bakers served everywhere fighting took place or where troops served. Make no mistake about it. Cooks were in the same war as everyone else wearing a uniform. In many cases kitchens and food stores would be a target. Convoys, supply lines and more were popular targets. Kitchens had to be mobile, and yet be versatile enough to dig in, camouflage and eventually be packed up and move as needed. This meant that the same effort that went into the proper development of rations to be able to be used in extreme, wide ranging, conditions also applied to cooks preparing daily meals.

In the tropics cooks had to adapt to the heat which could spoil a wide variety of food and make cooking over a hot heat source a very unpleasant activity. In remote areas of the frozen Arctic cooks also dealt with extreme conditions on the other end of the temperature spectrum. However, instead of the heat the issue was cold temperatures. Cooks would refer to frozen milk as a "brick of milk." Frozen meat could be sawed and even chopped with an ax. Any frozen meat "sawdust" could be saved and used.

One the other side of the coin the cooks were able to take advantage of cooler conditions that allowed for many items to last longer. Even the handling of greases and fats was easier due to the colder climate. In some cases cooks learned how to carve ice for use as a water source. They learned how the color of the ice, bluish to clear and even milky looking, would affect the quality and taste of the water.

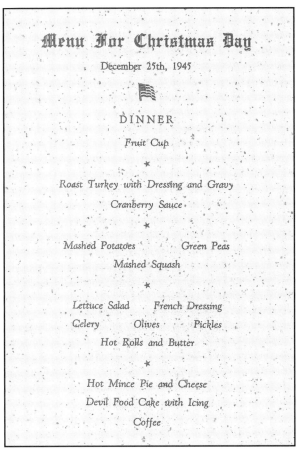

The Fort Olgethorpe Post Christmas Dinner Menu from 1945.
From the collection of the 6th Calvary Museum, Fort Olgethorpe, Georgia

The 1943 March 14th *New York Times Magazine* proclaims that the average soldier consumes on a daily basis: 1 pound of meat, poultry, fish or substitutes; 1 egg; 1 pint of milk, or equivalent; 3 ounces of butter and other fats; 12 ounces of grain products; 4 ounces of tomatoes and citrus fruits; 7 ounces of leafy green and yellow vegetables; 12 ounces of other fruits and vegetables; 3 ounces of sugar; and a standard serving of coffee, tea, cocoa, fruit juice, bread, pastry, ice cream, jam, jelly or salad. Obviously this article never took into consideration where the "average" soldier was serving and exactly what type of meat would be used.

The variety of items available locally to supplement stores and shipped in items varied for cooks serving in different theatres. One could well imagine the assortment of meats, poultry, fish; vegetables and breads cooks would have in Europe and even the Pacific. But for a cook serving in Arctic climates instead of shipped in standards such as beef; pork and poultry the locally procured items could be anything from caribou, seal and on occasion; a polar bear. Which in one case was referred to being "like pork, but it is stringy, gets between the teeth, and causes sore gums." Even though what could be ideal cooking situations rarely existed, United States and Allied, cooks were able to provide hot, nourishing food in a timely manner to troops in almost every setting imaginable. When this was not possible, a growing number of field tested rations were put into play by military planners. Overall, America's World War Two fighting forces were consistently the best feed troops in history.

This picture, from the 1944 January publication "Headquarters Bulletin" shows classic KP duty with onions instead of potatoes.
Courtesy of the Historical Reference Branch, Marine Corps History Division, Quantico VA.

CHAPTER FIVE

Chow on Trucks, Planes, Boats and Battleships

This picture shows a crew grabbing some chow in the galley of a PT boat near Bougainville Island Picture taken March 31, 1944.
From the collection of the National Archives.

The war time efforts to make improvements in the training of cooks, bakers, procurement, equipment and the entire supply was done in order to better feed the troops. It also served as a way to improve moral and to make sure troops were properly nourished. Sanitation and food safety was also part of the overall plan. The processes, recipes, equipment and training methods developed by the various military branches had to be put to use where ever troops were serving. Cooks and bakers served in everything from fully equipped galleys to field kitchens near the front lines. Some had

91

mobile units while some constructed homemade ovens in the ground or out of salvaged materials. There was an amazing amount of ways troops were fed by cooks.

For an infantry man the meal of the day was often packed rations, d-bars and whatever else could be had as they moved about fighting. In many cases the frontline Marines and Army units would eat the same rations day after day and possibly for a few weeks. The cooks did their best to provide as many hot meals with hot coffee as possible. Every once in a while a cup of hot coffee and a doughnut from the Red Cross could be acquired. Seabee cooks in the Pacific were known for their ability to adapt a kitchen and mess to just about any situation. For most men in the trenches a "real" meal would come when you were rotated back, hooked up with a field kitchen or if you were possibly injured and sent to a medical facility with a larger kitchen.

Even with the limitations the United States Military faced, the cooks and bakers did an amazing job getting hot meals to fighting forces on the ground. In the European campaign The Surgeon of the First Infantry stated that they never had a man suffering from malnutrition. In the article *Feeding the Infantryman in Combat* by Major General Robert M. Littlejohn—Chief QM, European Theater, Littlejohn states that more often than not a riffle company under combat could expect its kitchen to prepare two hot meals a day while operational rations were issued for a third, and possibly a forth. Any operational ration served should be heated and hot coffee, cocoa, bread and hot soup should be available.

Major General Littlejohn also noted in his article a very important factor that was relayed to him by one of Battalion Commanders.

"If a hot meal is prepared, the chances are ten to one that it will be served. The kitchens are operated on a 24-hour basis. There can be no strictly observed meal hours, because they depend entirely on the tactical situation. All kitchens must learn the art of feeding while the kitchen is on the move, because that is frequently necessary."

Another factor for commanders to consider when in the field would be where to locate a kitchen. Often a mess or field kitchen had to be placed close enough to men in the fighting to be able to access them. But they also had to be far enough away from the enemy as to not make them too much of a target. Factors that had to be considered, other than trying to be as available to the troops as possible, when making a decision to locate a kitchen included terrain, supply chain, the possible available use of existing buildings or structures and more. In one instance a battalion commander utilized an abandoned German pill box approximately 500 yards from German lines and had his men come back for meals. In many cases the artillery and service branches of an infantry unit would make great use of a built up mobile kitchen while an infantry company might not have found that tying up a truck as a mobile kitchen as always practicable.

African American soldiers take a break and a few grab some hot chow in this photo taken in Massacre Bay in the Aleutian Islands on May 20, 1943.
Photo by Vincent A. Wallace from the National Archives

Cooks were generally appreciated in any situation, especially the front. Cooks, bakers, Mess Sergeants and that were good were highly valued. Especially appreciated were personnel that could perform their duties in a combat situation and who never forget that they were on the same team as the men up front fighting. In many instances cooks and bakers fought well when called to. In any location, especially a forward position, a cook that could combine the normal canned rations heated up with some fresh bread and coffee would be revered as a master chef by weary ground troops.

General Eisenhower said "The tempo of battle has increased immeasurably during the span of this conflict... Never have soldiers been called upon to endure longer sustained periods with a vicious enemy nor greater punishment from weather and terrain." Troops were moving faster and further than in any previous war and with them the chow had to move just as fast.

The Mobile Mess Unit

Mobile Mess Kitchens have been around for a long time. Packing up all of the cooking supplies, equipment and food on a wagon, cart, trailer or truck only makes sense. Chances are that if you watch a western movie you will see the Chuck Wagon, which was a simple mobile mess kitchen, in use. Mobile mess kitchens in some form were used in just about every conflict leading to World War One and World War Two. The major difference would be that as technology progressed the newer modern versions of the old Chuck Wagon could travel further, faster and be more versatile.

A crew shows their enthusiasm at the arrival of the rations truck with Christmas turkey's. 5th Army, Bisomo Area, Italy 1944
Photo Courtesy of the Fort Lee United States Army Quartermaster Museum

A favorite tool of the Military during World War Two was the truck. Trucks could haul people, weapons, clothes, food, equipment and more. It could also serve as an ambulance, mobile office, storage unit, operating room or a host of other uses. The Quartermaster Corps decided to "cram" everything needed for a full sized kitchen onto a 2 1/2 ton 6x6 truck. The Quartermaster Board at Fort Lee Virginia, Camp Lee during the war, fine tuned the methods involved with packing, stocking and using a 2 1/2 ton truck mobile kitchen in order to utilize the space more efficiently. They defined and set standards for mobile kitchens that served in a wide variety of combat zones and which very adaptable for each situation.

Private First Class George E. Neidhardt, with 9th Army in Germany, opens a holiday package sent from his home, Dec '44.
U.S. Army Center of Military History

Corporal Charles H. Johnson of the 783rd Military Police Battalion, waves on a
`Red Ball Express' motor convoy near Alenon, France.
National Archives - Bowen, September 5, 1944.

Mobile kitchen trucks carried water, ice chests, cutting area, stoves, lights, storage, cooking utensils and more. It provided space for working, ventilation, mobility and a relatively safe working environment. And with the flow of information coming from the Quartermasters Corps units already in the field could adapt, or customize, their trucks for better use. Adaptations could include adding steps, additional serving tables, extra storage, tarps for extra coverage and work space. Many times if somebody thought of a better way to change or customize a mobile kitchen in the field to better suit a situation the work was done.

Some things were simple. The top of the ice box, fitted with a leak proof top, doubled as a cutting board. The leak proof top would keep any drippings or anything else from contaminating the items in the ice box. This is a good example of sanitation efforts being translated to the field. Crews added items such as bottle openers, meat grinders, hand bars to

96

hold onto when under way and extra lighting. In the field untold numbers of impromptu adaptations were made in order to get a job done. A popular customization was extending the height of the work area. The average truck cover was only about five feet above the bed of the truck. By adding extra height an additional couple of feet could be gained. This made cooking and simply moving about more comfortable.

Countries on both sides of the conflict used various types of mobile kitchens and cookers in order to feed their troops. A very successful piece of equipment made in Australian was the Wiles cooker which was so versatile that it could be trucked, towed, used on a jeep, mounted to trains and transported in just about any manner available. The American version of a field cooker was the M-1937 field range. The M-1937 combined a gas powered burner with a range top and oven complete with racks and rails to accommodate a wide variety of pots, pans and cooking sheets. The M-1937 could be used by itself as a standalone unit or combined with others to increase capacity. They were relatively lightweight, could be carried comfortably by two men, or pushed around by one man. They were used by cooks and bakers of the various service branches in just about every place that American and many Allied forces served. One unit could help feed around 50 men or more, three would fit on a truck side by side and depending on how the cook set up the movable heat source could be used as an oven, range and griddle. The M-1937 fed soldiers, sailors, marines, air corps members as well as countless allied troops. It was in officially in service from World War Two until during the Vietnam War.

Another great advantage of using a truck with several M-1937 field cooking units on board was the fact that it was still a truck. It could go just about anywhere that it was needed. Not to say a few didn't get bogged down in mud or stuck in deep snow or slush, but for the most part the truck mounted mobile kitchens were able to deploy to some of the most remote places. And, like any good truck, it could haul something such as a trailer. For mobile kitchens this was a trailer that was packed with more food, equipment and supplies.

By combining the cooking skills of the new breed of trained cooks with a better supply lines, skilled mess sergeants, proper tools and a wide variety of rations U.S. ground forces ate better than any American army before them, arguably better than any army in history.

Chow On a Bomber

A visiting YMCA Tea Car is surrounded by RAF crewmembers at one of RAF
Sleap Airfield's nearby dispersed sites in 1945. Today Sleap Field is fully
operational as Shropshire Aero Club.
*Picture from the collection of Gordon Taylor and Courtesy of Rob Truman UK, of
www.controltowers.co.uk .*

Limited time forced many aircrews to forgo hot meals at airfield mess halls.
That's if a mess hall were to be found. In flight meals were limited to smaller
rations, snacks and anything that could be wrapped in paper and stuffed in a
pocket. This picture, of an SAAF crew grabbing some chow on the dirt airstrip
in Libya, was taken in March of 1941. It was common for air crews to seek fresh
air and eat a meal as fast as possible while their planes were serviced and
reloaded by hurried ground crews.
Picture from the collection of Duncan Archer.

98

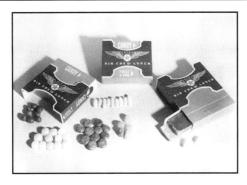

This picture shows an Air Crew Ration used during the war.
Photo Courtesy of the Fort Lee United States Army Quartermaster Museum

The Army Air Corps utilized many of the cooking operations, equipment and supply chains that the Army provided by way of the Quartermasters. According to the Air Force Historical Studies Office the majority of air crews, pilots and other personnel enjoyed the same dinning as other Allied military branches during World War Two. Aircrew members, except on some of the remoter Pacific Islands, usually ate the local fare in combination with food provided by the US Government which included powdered eggs, milk, tinned beef and the like. Of course these items included every combination of rations available. That worked great while crews were on the ground. But what about when they were on a mission, or if they were to be shot down over enemy territory or had to ditch a plane in water? You could not fit a large oven on a plane. And canned C rations would be hard to work with while trying to float. For the most part pilots and their crews were seemingly left to grab what they could for an in-flight meal or snack from kitchens.

If possible aircrews would pack a small meal prepared by a cook who understood what they could use and store. The meal, however large or small, could be as simple as a thermos of coffee or soup and a few slices of bread and with whatever was handy to make a sandwich. Other times the use of the growing variety of rations available to troops was utilized. Favored items were selected out of available rations. The items selected by the crews were, small easy to handle and prepare while in flight. If it was a long mission some type of nourishment was needed. In most cases due to altitude and weather factors something warm was needed as well.

Consideration also had to be given to weight and even the amount of space items would take up.

When efforts to develop a better air crew specific ration were started developers immediately took into consideration what pilots and crews already considered valued items. These were items that were easy, provided something quick, took little space and could be tossed aside in an instant if needed. This aspect of designing a ration was especially true with fighter pilots and crew members on smaller aircraft with little, or no, extra space. Smaller items for snacks such as fruit, candies and the always popular coffee seemed to fit the bill. Some development was given to a sandwich style pack that the crews already were making themselves but a true version was not in use until after the war ended.

Some larger craft did in fact have the ability to house a small warmer for heating items more than actually cooking them. The heated rations that were being designed proved to be a step forward in ration development in many ways. Due to the limitations of the planes, the time constraints, space, and other duties the crews had to perform it did not seem to make sense to pull crew members away from more important duties in order to warm up dinner. It could be done, but it was not a favored way the pilots and crews preferred to grab some chow. In addition rations that were designed bailout and other issues were addressed and were developed over the course of the war. Attention was given to size, amount of calories, durability and of course packaging.

Like any other unit in the field the airbases ability to cook and serve food differed from base to base. It depended on factors that affected all services such as size, location, supply chain, enemy location and more. Smaller kitchens served chow ranging from pre-packed and heated rations and more secure larger bases could possibly have a larger kitchen, bakery and more staffs. According to the Air Force Historical Studies Office WWII Air Corps crews ate the same daily meals and foods that were available to any other Army unit in any given situation. A combination of rations, dried goods and more supplemented with local items when possible.

Jackson Tanner Fahl remembers several things about military cooking while serving in WWII with the 9th Bomber Group, 5th Squadron, 313 Wing of the 20AF. First, food was ok on the ground when you could grab some chow hot or cold. Secondly long flights demanded mostly snacks as

"We filled up before we left. Sometimes we didn't eat too much at all, it just depended on the mood you were in." But one thing that Fahl will remember forever was the site that greeted him and the rest of the crew as they flew low passes over POW camps dropping supplies to feed and take care of prisoners.

"Even from that height we could see the ribs of these guys on the ground. They looked like they were half dead."

Feeding the Royal Air Force

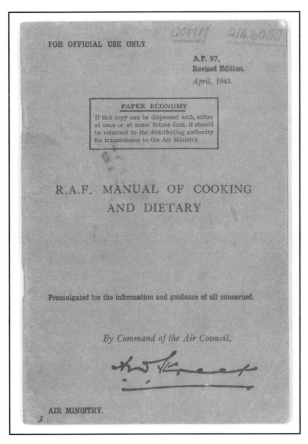

Cover of the RAF manual of cooking and dietary, 1942
Submitted by the Royal Air Force Museum, London. R.A.F. Manual of Cooking and Dietary, Air Command, April 1942. British Crown Copyright, RAF Museum.

Pages from the 1943 Royal Air Force Catering Bulletin
Submitted by the Royal Air Force Museum, London. R.A.F. Manual of Cooking and Dietary, Air Command, April 1942. British Crown Copyright, RAF Museum.

Pictured is Flight Sergeant James Hyde of San Juan, Trinidad. Hyde was a Spitfire pilot who arrived in Britain in 1942. The picture was taken in 1944 with his Squadron's mascot. Flyers from over thirteen countries, including the United States, served alongside of British pilots in the RAF starting with the Battle of Britain. *From the collection of the author. Original photo by Royal Air Force Museum, London. British Crown Copyright, RAF Museum.*

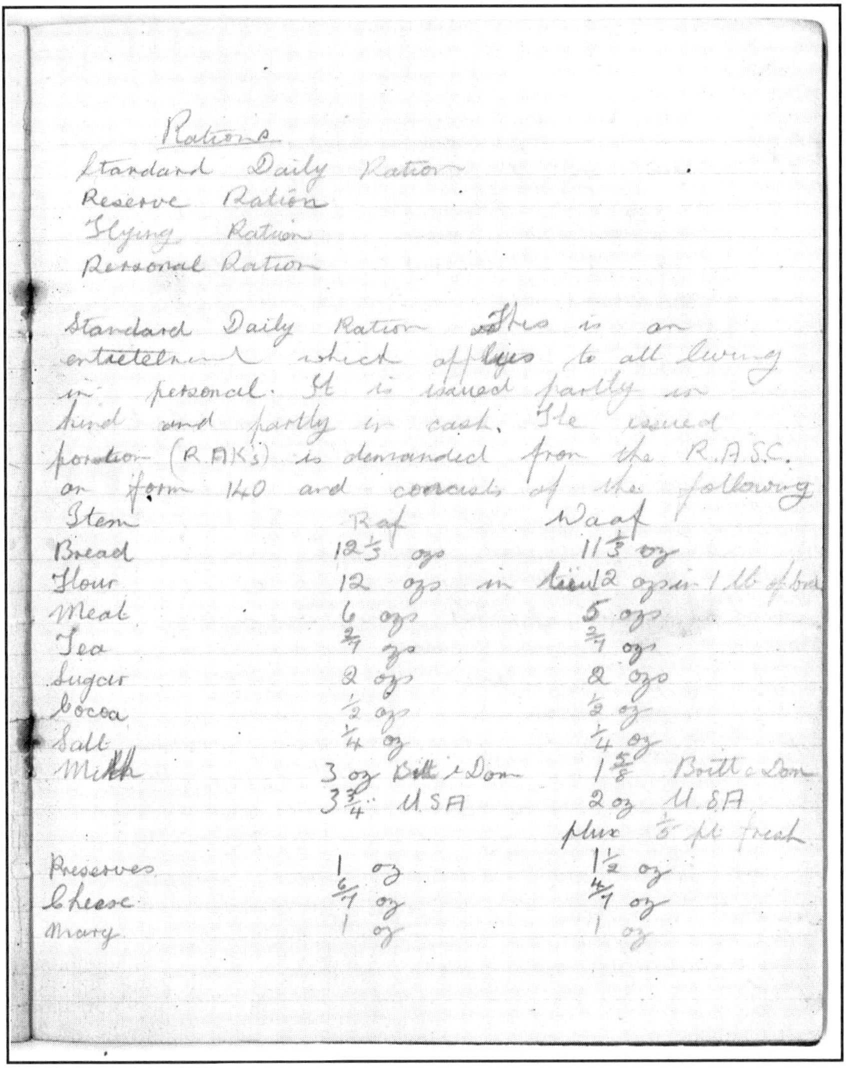

Rations
Standard Daily Ration
Reserve Ration
Flying Ration
Personal Ration

Standard Daily Ration This is an entitlement which applies to all living in personal. It is issued partly in kind and partly in cash. The issued portion (R.A.K's) is demanded from the R.A.S.C. on form 140 and consists of the following

Item	Raf	Waaf
Bread	12 1/3 ozs	11 1/3 oz
Flour	12 ozs in lieu	12 ozs in 1 lb of bre
Meat	6 ozs	5 ozs
Tea	2/7 ozs	2/7 ozs
Sugar	2 ozs	2 ozs
Cocoa	1/2 oz	1/2 oz
Salt	1/4 oz	1/4 oz
Milk	3 oz Bott & Dom 3 3/4 USA	1 5/8 Bott & Dom 2 oz USA plus 1/5 pt fresh
Preserves	1 oz	1 1/2 oz
Cheese	6/7 oz	4/7 oz
Marg	1 oz	1 oz

A Handwritten recipe from a Notebook belonging to LAC Marion Edith Gomm
RAF Cooking handwritten.jpg
Submitted by the Royal Air Force Museum, London. R.A.F. Manual of Cooking and Dietary, Air Command, April 1942. British Crown Copyright, RAF Museum.

The RAF, Royal Air Force, became legendary during World War II for its ability to defend the skies of Britain. The RAF also took the fight to the

Nazi forces early in the war on several fronts, often in obsolete planes when compared to the planes their opponents were flying. RAF bombers searched the North Sea for German ships to attack while also flying night missions over Germany in order to drop over thirteen tons of leaflets in hopes the propaganda would help avert a full scale war. Despite the lack of success of the leaflets being able to avert war, the missions did give the crews needed practice in flying over Germany in darkness. Night bombing and flying was a skill that would be needed for future sorties. With the war being limited during the early days the RAF crews were already mounting losses.

When Germany attacked Norway and Denmark the somewhat limited war turned into a full scale war, and would soon become a global one. The RAF tried to push back and bomb the advancing Germans but they were met with superior equipment and were outgunned. While an amazing number of troops were rescued from Dunkirk, in the now famous effort, the pilots and the flight crews of the RAF were not so lucky. Because of the attacks from German fighters only a small number of planes were able to make it safely back to their bases.

As the war progressed the RAF depended on its fighter crews to defend the skies over Britain and the English Channel. The RAF fighter pilots were so successful in their efforts that many credit their skills during the 1940 Battle of Britain with helping delay and cancel any invasion plans that Germany may have considered which is referred to as Operation Sea Lion. Any German invasion plan would most likely require complete air superiority over the channel as well as a significant presence over Britain itself. The few hundred fighter pilots of the RAF made this impossible. This was noted by Winston Churchill. "Never in the field of human conflict was so much owed by so many to so few." The RAF efforts combined with the Royal Navy's commanding presence made German invasion plans on the isle as being simply too risky. As the Invasion of France loomed planners realized Hitler's dilemma. Allied forces would also have to have complete control over the channel as well as the ability to strike over and over again deep into Germany.

Along with heroic efforts of the British RAF crews, help came from the commonwealth as well. Royal Canadian Air Force crews and squadrons were soon able to bolster the RAF with fresh crews and equipment. The

Royal Australian Air Force joined in the fight as did pilots and crews from many other nations. All were trained and ready to go. This wide variety of nationalities made the RAF a very diversified, but united, group of fighters.Nationalities ranged from the aforementioned British, Canadians and Australians but also included New Zealanders, Poles, Czechs, South Africans, French, Americans, Jamaicans and Rhodesians.

Even with the initial losses suffered during the beginning of the conflict the RAF, now bolstered by additional air crews and Allied bombers, was able to improve all of their aircraft and make great advancements in technology. With the improved aircraft came the ability to perform a non-stop strategic bombing campaign against the AXIS forces. Air crews could fly from Britain to targets deep into occupied territories as well as Germany itself. As fighter escorts improved, along with tactics, the RAF and Allied bomb crews flew an ever increasing number of sorties against targets almost twenty four hours a day. These missions originated from airfields dotted across the country and Europe as Allied forces pushed towards Germany.

Life for a RAF pilot, or aircrew from Britain or one of the commonwealth Air Forces, during the war was a stressful one. Down times were often hard to come by. Some bases were also more permanent that others as temporary bases had the ability to pack up and move to avoid bombing. Other bases were quickly put into action as close to the front lines as possible by engineers. But as German forces zeroed in on the location shells would begin to fall in hopes of shutting the runways down which caused every pilot and crew in action to get the planes in the air as quick as possible in order to beat the closing of a runway due to damage, or losing a plane from the shelling. An RAF pilot could expect to be called into service at any time. Missions could range from a few hours to long range, high altitude affairs or they could find themselves flying close to the ground to avoid detection.

When on the ground the RAF pilots and crews enjoyed a varied range of chow. Of course this all depended on supply, the size of the station or airfield and the skills of the members of the Catering Corps assigned to cook for the men. Each station had catering staff which used a combination of official manuals and recipe guides that went along with their training. But, due to the fact that many items were either rationed, short in supply or simply not available the catering staff became experts at working with what they had.

Just because a food or ingredient was listed as a rationed item did not mean it would actually be available. Each catering staff determined an amount of food for each person per day. The menus were developed from there, cooked and served in an organized mess. Because of the supply issues and rationing the various catering staffs developed their own notebooks that were like food diaries. They could keep notes on what recipes worked and which ones did not due to rationed or missing ingredients. These new menus were created with limited supplies in mind. The catering cooks used all of their training, including properly cutting meat to avoid waste, to the test in order to create and use recipes. All of the recipes had to feed the set number of men, avoid waste at all cost, use only available ingredients and of course provide a proper meal to the pilots and the crews.

As with many crews the RAF forces also made use of prepackaged rations ranging from full meals to emergency and flying rations. Some crews managed their own snacks for a flight. But every effort was made by the catering staff to provide a hot meal whenever possible. Upon return from a mission, which would often be quite cold due to altitude, the catering staff would do their best to have a hot breakfast waiting in order to help fill up and warm up the tired men. A sad end result of trying to prepare enough food for a returning set number of men is that quite often some of the crews did not make it back. The mess staff certainly found the empty places of missing crewmen upsetting.

Chow On a PT Boat

It is often said that during World War Two the best chow in the world could be found in the service of the United States Navy. While the argument can be made that this was the case in many situations, it was most likely applied for those serving on one of the larger ships, battleships or aircraft carriers, the rest of the men in the navy may take issue with the statement. One group of sailors that would argue with you about the best chow in the military would be the men who served on PT boats during world war two. To many PT boat crews, having to eat and prepare meals while underway on a patrol or extended mission seemed to be the last thing PT boat designers had on their minds when drawing up plans for the boats.

Jim Stanton found this photo of his grandfather, James J. Stanton,
RON 15 PT 209 and RON 23 PT 243, hauling some extra chow. Note the
bananas hanging from the railing. On the back of the photo is written
"243 underway off Romblon with bananas," in pencil.
From the collection of Jim Stanton, Stanton Family Collection

In fact, there could be some partial truth to the statement when you
look at the mission the boats were to perform. The boats were designed to
be lightweight compared to other crafts, inexpensive to build in comparison to larger craft, make use of more wood and utilize every inch of available space. The boats had to be prepared to run a patrol, provide security
and attack a target and return to base with the minimal amount of preparation and turn over as possible. In other words, PT boats always had to be
ready to go. And their crews, however small in number compared to larger vessels, had to be ready to go as well. Thankfully, planners managed to
squeeze in room for a small galley and dining area. The Galley was actually

107

a corner of the boat housing some storage, a compact range and what amounted to a small picnic sized table that served duty as a place to eat, work on parts, plan missions or whatever needed to be handled that required a flat surface.

PT boat crews often felt that the Navy actually forgot about them in the plans to feed and supply their small vessels. The boats and crews relied completely on getting supplies from their bases or from a supply system that utilized medium sized ships called "tenders." The tender boats would arrive and the smaller PT boats would pull alongside and load needed supplies ranging from munitions, paint and repair items to whatever food could be found. What food was passed over the side of the tender to the PT boat, or loaded from the dock at the base, was what they got. Most often the PT boat cook, who also served a variety of duties including manning a deck gun, was handed week after week of the same foods including an unrelenting number of cans of SPAM.

The arrival of fresh eggs, or items acquired locally, was considered a feast. PT boat cooks became masters of preparing meals with the bare minimum of supplies, ingredients and even cooking space. As one veteran PT boat said; "You can have whatever you want for chow. As long as it was SPAM or dehydrated meat. You could have it plain, peppered, covered in hot sauce, with eggs, with bread, with marmalade and even with beer." One place that the crews of PT boats were able to come across good food was from the supply stores of grateful merchant marine ships who appreciated any extra protection the PT boats could offer. A large amount of trading with bases on shore and Pacific native people also helped supplement supplies.

Being a PT boat cook was a tough job. Earl Richmond, cook on PT 108 during the war stated the situation in no uncertain terms when it came to preparing meals. "You had to use what you were able to scrounge up from the base or beg from another larger ship." Despite the fact that a NAVY training manual for new PT boat crewmembers described the "grumpiness" of some PT boats cooks Richmond says everyone understood what cooks had to deal with. "It seems that the PT boats and PT bases were the last ones on the island bases to get food. We only had one fresh egg the whole time I was on a PT base or ship. We hardly had any fresh meat. It was mostly dehydrated or powdered stuff. We did the best we could with what we had. It wasn't much but the crews were so hungry they ate almost anything I could cook up."

Chow On a Submarine

One of the most impressive weapons in the arsenal of the United States military during World War Two was the American submarine fleet. The fleet grew from a small force that was battling issues with problematic torpedoes and an overly cautious initial group of commanders, into a dominant multi-class fleet with some of the most aggressive and well trained crews in any submarine force in the world. The American sub fleet did have an initial rough start during the outset of the war. However; the submarine forces of the United States improved to a point where they were effective in sinking much of the Japanese merchant fleet. This effectively cut off Japan by severely limiting needed imported items. These items were needed not only for the massive war effort but also for a dwindling industrial base and for any consumer items.

A Balao Class submarine was powered by 4 diesel engines that also charged batteries. Under diesel power, while cruising on the surface, the submarine could average speeds of about 20 knots and had a range of about 22,000 miles. While submerged the craft relied on its battery fueled motors and ran close to 10 knots for less than 100 miles. Essentially the World War Two submarines were boats that had the ability to submerge and return to the surface. This made them deadly killers. As the war progressed the American submarine fleet grew in numbers and continued to improve its vessels and its crews training and tactics. At the outset of the war Japan had over 2,300 merchant marine ships. At the end of the war the number was less than 250. The American submariners also sunk one battleship, eighteen aircraft carriers, and eleven cruisers, over thirty destroyers. They also provided unlimited escorts and security patrols to Allied forces.

Life on a submarine was filled with the daily smell of oil and fellow sweaty crew. Cramped living areas and limited space for activities were not related to sinking enemy ships. Many of the crew wore shorts and sandals during extreme heat only donning their "official" uniforms when required or when pulling into a base if needed. Unlike surface ships there was only a small amount of room topside so any activity there was limited than taking a deep breath and catching a breath of fresh air while scanning the skies for enemy planes or the horizon for ships.

The life of a cook based on a submarine was nothing like a shore based cooks life. Everything on a submarine was crammed into as small of space as possible. There were no large kitchens like those that could be found on land bases. A submarine galley was not much bigger than a closet with a stove and storage was limited. This forced cooks and crews to stash items away in every nook and cranny available. It was not uncommon to open a hatch or turn a corner only to find a stack of canned goods or boxes of food crammed into a space. Crews became masters at spreading the food. Despite the limited space and prep room the submarines still had a good reputation for great food on board. The smaller crew size made this possible as well as the efforts of the Navy to make sure that the volunteer crews of the submarines had decent food. A large number of submarines during the war enjoyed the use of an onboard ice cream maker as part of their standard galley equipment.

This photo shows the Wardroom Galley on board the USS Pampanito. The Pampanito is now on display at the San Francisco Maritime National Park Association in San Fransisco California.
Photo courtesy of Dave Hall, Colonel USAF.

Howard McMahon is pictured on the USS Parche baking cinnamon rolls in the cramped galley. According to USS Parche's Bob Hall, who served as the subs cook, every extra space that could be found ended up being used for his galley's storage space. It was not uncommon for Bob, Howard and the crew to stuff cans of food under decks, pipes, crawl spaces and more. *Photo courtesy of Bob Hall, USS Parche.*

Shelton Doyle Blalock, or "Steve" to his submarine friends, served aboard the USS Tambor, and other subs, during WWII. He relayed several stories to his grandson Lance Dean about better pay and food for submariners. "If I was gonna get paid to die, I might as well make the most money I could while doing it!" In October of 1944 the USS Tambor was attacked with twenty plus depth charges. During the attack the sub became stuck on the ocean floor for over two hours before rising. Pictured is the crowded mess of the USS Tambor.
Photo Courtesy of Lance Dean, from the collection of his grandfather Shelton Doyle Blalock USN.

Storage space was limited on submarines so cooks and bakers were pretty
creative on finding space for storage. Baker 1st Class Bob Hall is shown
retrieving some hidden away items while underway on the USS Parche in 1944.
Photo courtesy of Bob Hall, USS Parche.

Cooking on a Battle Ship

The portside galley area on the USS Alabama, along with other galley's, served
meals three times a day, 24 hours a day, to over 2500 men during any given
deployment. The galley tables were removable so hammocks cold be hung from
hooks in case the ship had extra passengers. This was the case on many ships.
Photo by Bill Tunnell, USS Alabama, Battleship Memorial Park, Mobile Alabama

The Gedunk stand and soda fountain on the USS Alabama. Pictured in the foreground are assorted types of Hershey Chocolate bars produced during World War Two. The ice cream was stored in compact car size freezers while under way.
Photo by Bill Tunnell, USS Alabama, Battleship Memorial Park, Mobile Alabama

According to the museum staff of the USS Alabama, and staff of the USS North Carolina, if you want to know about feeding large numbers of sailors then you should look no further than the galleys on a massive World War Two battleship! According to both museum staffs the multiple galleys on board each ship, combined with butcher shops and bakeries set the tone for efficient military cooking at sea.

The Galley is not only a ship's kitchen it's also one of the most vibrant places on board. The galley is where food is prepared and cooked for the crew and as many veteran sailors will tell you the galleys on any ship are the busiest places on any ship. As with any military kitchen hours of prep work are logged in order to have meals ready for the men as they come in for chow. The problem with ships as large as a battle ships and a carriers is that multiple shifts are running and the crew will require meals at just about any time of day. Of course there were standard set meal times for the majority of the crew but kitchen prep and having smaller meals ready for

113

crewmembers on a late watch meant that seldom would any galley be completely void of activity.

The combined galleys on the USS Alabama served over eight million meals during the course of its service. More than 2,000 men were fed three times a day. On the USS North Carolina breakfast was served at 0630, lunch at 1130, and dinner at 1630. Early chow for watch reliefs was served a half an hour earlier. Sandwiches and coffee could be had if needed during other hours for crew on watch. Coffee is a mainstay on just about any ship around the clock. On average twenty-five cooks worked in the main galley along with one hundred plus messmen. The messmen helped serve food, assisted the cooks, and performed general mess duties such as serving tea and coffee, putting away condiment containers, and cleaning the mess area. All non-rated enlisted crewmembers had to serve a duty.

The battleships had huge refrigerators and freezers, called "reefers," that stored fresh meat, vegetables and fruit. The units were so big that buttons and alarms were installed in case someone was accidentally locked inside one of the cold rooms. These coolers were broken down into various rooms that stored frozen items and various walk in refrigerators for fruits one, vegetables in another, eggs, dairy, meats and more. There was even a cooling room that allowed frozen items to thaw without going bad. The items were gathered as needed and taken to the galley prep areas. The butchers worked with an assortment of knives, saws, bone cutters, fish cutters, meat slicers and grinders in order to cut down and prep pieces of meat. These pieces, when delivered to the shop, would often weigh up to one hundred pounds or more. The larger slabs of meat were hoisted from the refrigerators using a block and pulley system.

Once on the right level it was carried to the butcher. When the fresh meat and stores began to run low the massive storage areas then yielded a wide variety of canned and powdered substitutions along with just about every condiment your could think of. It was not uncommon to see a guard posted outside of a refrigerator or storage area and in general food was kept under lock and key. On average a battleship could carry fresh foods for thirty days and canned provisions for ninety days. They could be restocked in port or at sea from supply ships.

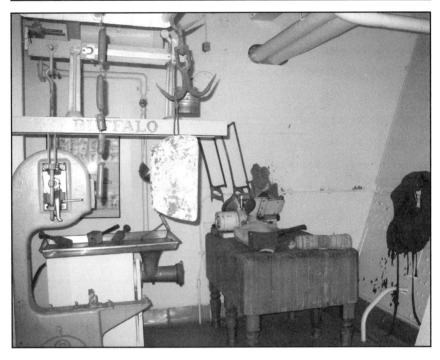

This picture shows the tools of the trade in the butcher shop on the USS Alabama. Traditional cutting blocks, grinders, knives and hand saws helped the butchers provide meat for the crew when available.
Photo by Bill Tunnell, USS Alabama, Battleship Memorial Park, Mobile Alabama

The galleys and assorted shops always seemed to be active. The bakery would turn out bread and rolls as the vegetables and fruit items were prepped in the galley. The butcher shop would gather its needed supplies and start hard at work cleaning and cutting thousands of pounds of meat poultry and fish. Mess areas were cleaned and trays and utensils washed. Hours later, once the food was prepped and cooked, it was placed in large steam tables to be served. The enlisted men stood in mess lines which led to the large steam serving tables. The mess men stood behind the serving tables and served the food cafeteria style on stainless steel trays with indentions to keep foods separated much like a lunch room tray. The mess men not only served food they also staffed the scullery, assisted the cooks and bakers, and performed many other duties associated with feeding the crew and keeping the mess areas clean.

115

Once a meal was served and complete everything was cleaned and the process seemingly started over again. Actually the process had started days before with prep work and menu planning. The the cooks and assigned help would make the daily trip to the refrigerators and storage areas to start gathering the needed ingredient items and collecting the additional fruits, vegetables, eggs and deserts in advance as needed. The butchers would follow suit and start cutting meat for the next day's meals.

Being on a battle ship, or other large ship in the U.S. Navy, did have its advantages as far as chow was concerned if you were a crew member. You were almost certain to get at least one or more hot meals served on a tray every day most likely more. Then if you missed a hot meal you usually had a pretty good selection of cold cuts or quick meals as you came off watch along with a hot cup of coffee. The USS Alabama had a rather well stocked gedunk or iceream and sweetshop as did some other larger ships. It was almost a certainty you would enjoy your meal seated at a table using real knives and forks unlike a foot soldier who once headed towards the front would survive on rations and the occasional meal hot meal served up from smaller cook stations.

The only complaint crewmembers would have was the same meal was often served on the same day every week of every month for the entire year. According to some Navy veterans you knew what day of the week it was by what was being served in the galley. As with other service branches extra care in providing a special meal was done during holidays or for special occasions. Christmas and Thanksgiving always received special attention.

Submarines, PT Boats and Battleships were not the only ships at sea. There was a seemingly endless variety and number of vessels manned by Navy, Army and Coast Guard crews. The Army and Coast Guard ships faced the same challenges that the Navy faced when feeding crews and keeping things fresh on smaller vessels as compared to much larger vessels. Space was always limited to the actual sides of the vessel; there is no room to expand. In many cases the galleys were not too much larger than those found on submarines.

Despite the limitations in facilities, refrigeration supplies and time, Cooks on Coast Guard Ships and Navy Vessels of all size made amazing attempts to bring the best meals possible when possible. For many service branches these opportunities to shine for troops and crews came during the serving of holiday meals.

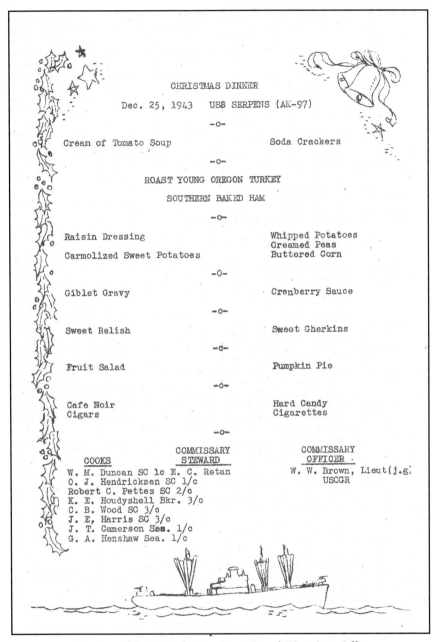

CHRISTMAS DINNER

Dec. 25, 1943   USS SERPENS (AK-97)

-o-

Cream of Tomato Soup   Soda Crackers

-o-

ROAST YOUNG OREGON TURKEY

SOUTHERN BAKED HAM

-o-

Raisin Dressing   Whipped Potatoes
                                        Creamed Peas
Carmolized Sweet Potatoes   Buttered Corn

-o-

Giblet Gravy   Crenberry Sauce

-o-

Sweet Relish   Sweet Gherkins

-o-

Fruit Salad   Pumpkin Pie

-o-

Cafe Noir   Hard Candy
Cigars   Cigarettes

-o-

	COMMISSARY	COMMISSARY
COOKS	STEWARD	OFFICER
W. M. Duncan SC 1c	E. C. Retan	W. W. Brown, Lieut(j.g)
O. J. Hendricksen SC 1/c		USCGR
Robert C. Pettes SC 2/c		
K. E. Houdyshell Bkr. 3/c		
C. B. Wood SC 3/c		
J. E. Harris SC 3/c		
J. T. Camerson Sea. 1/c		
G. A. Henshaw Sea. 1/c		

Courtesy of the United State Coast Guard Historians Office
The men of the Coast Guard Manned USS *Serpens* (AK-97) enjoyed a

117

full Christmas dinner according to this menu from 1943. The Auxiliary Cargo Ships, AK for short, was one of the most important links in the military supply chain during the war. The smaller AK's, like the larger Liberty Ships, were loaded down with as much supplies as possible. They were packed with gasoline, bombs, medical supplies, food and everything else. Once underway the AK's rarely returned to the same port but traveled from location to location in a constant effort to deliver cargo. In the book *U.S. Army ships and Watercraft of World War II* By David H. Grover states that much of the "cargo" fleet of US forces was an Army Fleet. Grover puts the total of Army vessels at 111,006 compared to the 74,708 vessels in the Navy. The Army's fleet was centered on transport or maintenance ships with the Navy's being mostly combatant. Many men heading off to War were surprised when they boarded an Army ship!

Tragedy struck the *Serpens* in 1945 when it was anchored of Lunga Beach, Guadalcanal, Solomon Islands undergoing a loading of depth charges. The ship exploded causing one of the largest loss of Coast Guardsmen life in history. The blast was so large that ships nearby were damaged and one soldier was killed onshore. The unidentified remains of 250 Coast Guardsmen, and additional personnel, killed in the immense explosion are now buried at Arlington National Cemetery.

This photo shows the Galley on board the USS Pampanito. The Pampanito is now on display at the San Francisco Maritime National Park Association in San Francisco California.
Photo courtesy of Dave Hall, Colonel USAF.

CHAPTER SIX

Hitting the Beaches—
Invasion Day Chow

This picture shows Herbert M. Sifford assistant field director of the American
Red Cross, grinding coffee at an ARC camp near Tebessa, Tunisia before heading
out to visit the soldiers on February 19, 1943.
Signal Corps Photo: NA ZEI-43-987 (Zeigler),
U.S. Army Center of Military History.

119

Sometimes the setting makes the meal. These three men enjoy a cold beverage
and a snack somewhere in the pacific during World War Two.
Courtesy of The National World War II Museum, New Orleans

Invasion days in the European theatre and the Pacific theatre shared
many similarities. Both involved an incredibly large amount of planning.
Both were backed by efforts to properly place the needed men, equipment,
rations and other supplies at the right place quickly and effectively. Along
with equipment such as guns and ammo needed supplies such as rations,
food and field kitchens in huge numbers were required. Cooks, bakers,
mess sergeants, supply officers, Quartermasters and mechanics and more
found themselves alongside frontline troops in many situations during
pre-landing training as well as supporting them as close to the moving
fronts as possible. In many ways the invasions in the two theatres were
similar while being completely different in many aspects.

In Europe the invasion forces massed in a relatively small area, the
English coast line, and traveled across the Smaller English Channel. The

fighting when they arrived was by all accounts a living hell. In the European theatre D-Day was essentially a massive, and bloody, invasion based on one landing date across several locations near each other on the same coastline. It was set to secure a beachhead in order to move troops forward for an extended period of time. The "D" in D-Day stands for the un-named day in which a military invasion is set to begin. In Europe D-Day was June 6th, 1944. The Allied troops fought and died in order to gain the foothold in Europe. The fighting continued every inch of the way until the end of the war.

The Pacific D-Days were different. There was no "single" coast such as France in which to attack. Japanese forces had to be forced off every island they occupied. D-Day happened over and over for many troops in the Pacific. Some were more deadly than others, but in every case the mental aspect of troops getting ready to storm an enemy occupied beach was faced by fighting forces over and over again. And in each case the efforts were planned for which included the gathering of needed supplies, equipment, troops, ships and air cover. According to historian and author Donald L. Miller's research there were 126 D-Day landings in the Pacific by American and Allied forces. The Pacific D-Days began with five large scale amphibious assaults on August 7, 1942. The five initial islands were Guadalcanal, Tulagi, Gavatu, Tanambogo and Florida. These assaults were followed shortly by the landings on Adak on August 30, 1942. The Pacific D-Days continued as American and Allied forces Island hopped across the Pacific fighting for every island one at a time until the war was over.

In all of these landings, in the Pacific to Normandy, every fighting man had to be equipped and fed. Everything a soldier needed had to be on hand to make sure front line troops had every advantage possible. According to the Fort Lee Quartermasters Museum for every one soldier an average of 14 QM's efforts helped supply and prepare him for duty.

Training on the Emerald Coast

According to Don MacLean, WWII veteran and volunteer for the Camp Gordon Johnston Museum in Carrabelle Florida, practice for amphibious training and beach invasions began up north near Massachusetts. "Then somebody said, Ya know…it don't snow in Guam…

or anywhere in the South Pacific!" So the search was on for a suitable location for amphibious assault training, with a more realistic feel.

Practice on the Gulf Coast. Camp Gordon Johnston is the beach pictured, not an Island in the South Pacific. Many amphibious troops trained for both European and Pacific landings at the Carrabelle Beach, Florida training facility. In the distance one of the Gulf Coast's area light house can be seen above the tree line. *From the collection of the Camp Gordon Johnston Museum, Carrabelle, Florida.*

World War Two veteran, and Camp Gordon Johnston tour guide, Don MacLean shows how items were stored on his Higgins boat during operations in Okinawa. The model, built by Maclean, is loaded with peaches, supplies and about "50 cases of beer. We re-appropriated the destination of that beer for our guys." *Photo by Kent Whitaker, Camp Gordon Johnston Museum, Carrabelle, Florida.*

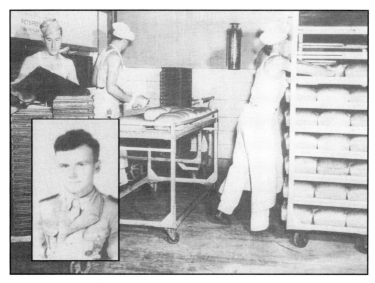

POW's often manned the bake shops at Camp Gordon Johnston in Florida. They were a vital part of daily life on many stateside camps working in a variety of positions. According to Herman Blumhardt, (inset), a German POW who returned to live Florida after the war, the people in the picture are Blumhardt fellow POW Franz Schollhamer. Also pictured is an American baker named Louis.
Picture from the collection of Camp Gordon Johnston.

Leonard Wieloch & Archie Anderberg, Company C of the 594th were stationed at Camp Gordon Johnston Florida when this picture was taken during the war. They are both enjoying a "cold one" at an area that was commonly referred to as "The Beer Garden."
From the collection of the Camp Gordon Johnston Museum

123

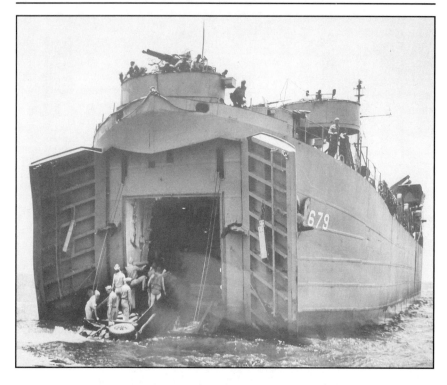

Training and testing was standard practice at Camp Gordon Johnston during WWII. Not only were men trained and tactics tested, the military had the opportunity to evaluate how equipment, supplies, vehicles and anything else involved in an amphibious assault would perform.
From the collection of the Camp Gordon Johnston Museum, Carrabelle, Florida
Original photo by Joseph A. Pulli, 1944

"They came to Carrabelle and opened the camp because the beaches were similar to what we would be fighting in real combat in the Pacific. Of course lots of Normandy guys came through here too. At the time Florida was real rural, real open, so the towns were small and you could really only get around by train. We had full scale invasion practice right here on the beaches right down from current tourist places. Back then, there was not really anyone around that would be in the way. There were hundreds of bases all over Florida. There was just plenty of room for 'em." Maclean said.

From 1942 to 1946 Camp Gordon Johnston's scenic location on the panhandle of the Gulf of Mexico was home to over a quarter of a million men who trained how to storm a beach. Not only did the men get to practice, but the equipment that they would be using was also tested and evaluated. "The guys trained with everything here. They tested and trained on transports, Higgins boats, used those big balloons to fly over an invasion force, guns... everything," MacLean said. Simply put, if it didn't work on the beaches in Florida, it would not work somewhere else. "And if it didn't work all too good, then these guys had to learn how to make it work better." According to MacLean the men even tested food. "There were mess halls and such. But they wanted it real so many times the guys ate what they would expect to get in action so they ate rations and at field kitchens just like during battle."

The idea behind the location and training methods was simple. If you could not unload men, gear, supplies and truckloads of food and rations on a beach on the quiet shores of the Gulf Coast then chances of doing so effectively on a beach in France or an Island in the Pacific, was slim. The answer was planning and creating as realistic of a battle ground as possible. This included men, equipment, supplies, explosions, noise and whatever could be thrown at the men. "During World War One they were trying to train guys with painted sticks and broom handles and stuff. They knew they had to make things as real as possible for the men to be able to react." MacLean said. Camp Gordon Johnston was a leap forward in realistic training methods.

The camp, like many doted across the country, was also a temporary home to a few thousand POW's mostly from Germany and Austria. Many POW's were utilized around the base in jobs such as cooking and baking. One such man was former POW Herman Blumhardt. According to MacLean, Herman fell in love with Florida. "Herman is a good guy. He was a POW who worked in the bakery. After the war the POWs were sent home and when he left and got to his home town it was pretty roughed up from the war. He found out he missed Florida and decided to move back when he could. He came back, still lives in Florida and comes to the Camp Gordon Johnston reunions when he can. He is just one of the guys."

Fine Dining On The Pillars of CGJ

Despite being a huge facility that helped with the advancements in beach landings, training methods and scenarios, Camp Gordon Johnston was built as a temporary base. Today only a few buildings remain. Most were built from temporary wood frames, tar paper and used the hard packed sand earth for floors. If two men sleeping on bunk beds weighted too much, or moved too much, their bunk beds would shift in the sand much like a beach chair. Many men joked that sleeping on base and camping in the woods during training were very similar.

When the base was to be closed the Army let locals know that they could come and salvage what they wanted or bid on items at a reduced price. One area resident came and bought truckloads of scrap wood from the base and built a restaurant nearby in Panacea Florida. That man was George Petrandis. He bought wood, nails and even large pilings from the camp.

He built some of his new restaurant, Angelo's Seafood Restaurant, with the scrap material from the camp. It was located out over the water in order to serve alcohol because the property on land was in a dry county but across the water was a wet county. Since there was no electricity he also bought generators from the closing of the camp," MacLean said.

After just about everything of value was sold and carted off the base and put to use in business and homes in the area. Any remaining material and buildings on the base were bulldozed into huge piles and burned.

Guam & The Pacific

Before World War II the Island of Guam was a quiet and yet vibrant island with a small, but growing, local tourist economy. In short, it had island charm. But it was also a key location for two sides of a coming global conflict. The island had strong ties with the United States and was a stop for U.S. Navy vessels and at the same time was often visited by people such as Ernest Hemingway. The local island people, Chamorro's, retained much of their island culture while still managing to adopted many things from the people of the United States, especially the Navy lifestyle. When World War II began the local Navy band on Guam was comprised completely from local Navy recruits. The main crops were locally grown fruit and vegetables along with a growing seafood trade.

On December 8th Japanese planes and bombers appeared in the skies over the island for an attack. The only large ship in port was the mine

Grateful marines thank the Coast Guard crews that landed them on the beaches of Guam. During assaults on the many islands of the Pacific both Coast Guard and Navy manned vessels landed with men and supplies. Then they loaded the injured for the return trip. Along the way the crews made countless impromptu rescues. Often all of this was done while trying to provided cover fire.
Courtesy of United States Coast Guard Historians office.

sweeper USS Penguin. It managed to slip out of the harbor and return fire. The crew of the Penguin did manage to drive attacking aircraft higher but eventually became the focus of several strafing and bombing runs. After suffering damage, several injuries and the death of a crewman the ship was scuttled in order to keep it from enemy hands. The surviving crew made it to shore on life rafts to join the under equipped personnel trying to defend the islands and its population from attackers. The assorted group of defenders did include some marines but was mostly made up of none combative Navy personnel and other troops with minimal combat training. To make matters was that many of the limited weapons on hand were outdated and some were stamped with a warning to only use for training . . . not to actually load and fire. Guam was under Japanese control from December of 1941 until July of 1944. During this time its economy was devastated, the local crops destroyed, abandoned or harvested for Japanese forces.

When the Allied invasion force started to mass for an assault on the occupied island, the men aboard the ships had no idea when they would be called upon to take back the island. Many of the troops waited at sea for weeks until everything was in place. When word was given to land on the island over 500 ships and support vessels were positioned for landing on the island's beaches. These were large troop transports with just about every type of fighting man and specialist fighting routine and boredom, and weary of the same type of meals served week after week. The ground troops waiting on board were not used to long periods at sea. The long wait increased anxiety and stress levels. Eventually the word would be given to "go." A sure sign of a Pacific invasion day for many of the troops waiting to go ashore was the standard boring and routine meal being switched from the regular chow to a breakfast or early lunch of steak and eggs or at least something better than normal. In Normandy the troops knew they were heading into battle in short order due to the relatively short trip across the English Channel. In the Pacific troops waiting on ships for days on end had a longer wait. When a plate of steak and eggs came your way you knew you were going ashore.

When invasion time came many of the forces that had waited for so long on the ships suffered from a bad case of sea legs. Having to wade or swim ashore and then cross reefs while being shot after being cramped up on a ship for an extended period of time was extremely difficult. Once on shore problems with supplying the initial invasion troops became evident. Despite heavy planning the ability to get needed food and supplies to troops involved in fighting seemed to be more difficult than first thought. Factors for delays ranged from being able to land enough supplies on the beaches because of enemy fire as well as bottlenecks at the outset of the invasion with incoming craft and craft returning with injured men and the problems of reefs and tides.

The overall conditions encountered by the fighting men on the beaches was horrific as were conditions for Coast Guard crews manning ships in harbors and on craft between the shore and supply ships. These crews didn't leave their smaller vessels for days at a time and their vital supplies were lowered to them in buckets from larger ships. At night the Coast Guard crews slept in the open at anchor while being awakened by shots from the shore. In some cases, such as in the battle of Peleliu, water hastily stored in un-cleaned containers with a fuel reside tainted drinking water. Many soldiers became ill and a few died. That problem was fixed as soon as possible. Allied forces often felt the issues with supply during the initial days of conflicts until safe beachheads were secure which allowed more and more supplies to be distributed even though items were hitting the beach almost at the exact same time troops did.

During the invasion of Guadalcanal the marines that landed on shore suffered through weeks and months of fragmented and shortened supply lines as the fleet of ships offshore that were there to protect and supply them were forced to flee after a sea battle. The Allied ships, mostly American ships were attacked and harassed many times as the Japanese made several efforts to retake the Island. During the initial confusing sea battle Japanese and American ships came so close to each other as to intermingle and cross paths. Eventually a near hour long nighttime sea battle erupted that was compared to a "bar room brawl with the lights out." While the U.S. ships suffered enormously, the Japanese ships sent to resupply and attack the Allied troops, evacuated leaving both forces on shore to fight with limited supplies and re-enforcements.

As the Japanese repeatedly tried to retake the Island and airfield over the course of several months they began to use faster and lighter ships that could carry men and light equipment more effectively through Allied patrolled waters. This fast delivery, via smaller vessels, became known as the Tokyo Express. While this succeeded on many levels the inability to land larger equipment and limited rations kept the Japanese at a disadvantage. Eventually the American and Allied supply lines to Guadalcanal, and the surrounding islands, improved. During battle on many of the islands in the Pacific both sides were hard pressed for rations and food in many cases. Allied troops would supplement their own supplies with captured Japanese goods. And the Japanese would make efforts to raid and steal American supplies often under the cover of night.

The Japanese were crippled by shortages and had limited rations and ammo, and in every case eventually had no hope for reinforcement or resupply. After many months of not being able to retake the airfield captured by the Americans, or the island, many knew they were going to be fighting to the death instead of surrendering. Towards the end of the fighting troops began to capture many Japanese soldiers that gave up because they were starving and dying of thirst. All Japanese central command on Guadalcanal was eventually lost and remaining forces were left to fend for themselves. Those Japanese troops that did not surrender either killed themselves or continued to fight while hiding in the jungles, caves, tunnels and swamps of the Island. They survived by stealing from the same people that had been used as forced labor during the occupation. A special patrol was formed from island volunteers to seek out these die-hard stragglers. This mop up mission was a hard one as only five remaining Japanese fighters surrendered and over one hundred were killed.

Across the Pacific supplies seemed in short supply for many Allied troops. The expansiveness of the theatre, number of places where fighting was taking place and where troops were located, was staggering. It was truly a logistical nightmare which actually was handled quite well although many troops suffered through the same menus day after day, week after week. Every effort was made to get as many hot meals to the men as possible but the expansive size of the Pacific theatre made it a difficult task. The cooks and bakers of the Pacific theatre made the most of short supplies and became masters at improvised kitchens and ways to feed troops using pre-packed field rations, baked bread, canned meat such as SPAM, coffee and an assortment of tropical foods including fruit and seafood when it could be procured or acquired. Sometimes the gathering of fish could include a grenade or some high explosive tossed into the water. The gathered dead fish would become food for the troops, but only after local island people pointed out the fish and sea life that could cause a soldier to get sick.

One group that gained a great reputation was the cooks and bakers of the Seabees. The Seabees were becoming known for hitting a target alongside attacking troops, holding it, working it, repairing it and improving it for use by the Allied troops. They were masters of improvisation and worked with just about everything available in order to get an airfield back online and in action or to build a road, bridge and more. Cooking and supplying troops was no different. Their ability to think outside of the box in order to get a job done allowed them to adapt to feeding fighting men as well as rebuilding a landing strip. They improvised kitchens of all sizes, mobile kitchens, grills, cookers and even delivery trucks made of small trailers which were utilized to get hot food fast to hungry troops.

A Tender Ship feeds needed supplies to waiting PT Boats. This picture is from the collection of Randall J. McConnell Jr., commander of the PT 361. *Submitted by Randall J. McConnell III. Photo was possibly taken by Jerry Nolan*

On Guadalcanal, and on other islands as fighting progressed, as Allied forces began to take control of the island the immediate concern of properly providing for ground troops was met head on with another food and supply concern. In many cases the Allies had to provide relief in the manner of food, supplies and medical care for a population that was not in much better shape than the men that stormed the beaches. This added an extra strain on a supply line that was already working at a maximum. The same was to be found after the D-Day invasion of France. As troops moved forward the number of injured enemy troops, prisoners of war and refugees grew. So did the efforts to feed them and provide proper medical care.

131

Getting Ready for The Normandy Invasion

On June 6th 1944 a massive Allied invasion force began to hit the beaches of France after departing from the shores of England. The liberation of Europe had begun. Before the Allied forces left the somewhat safe soil of their British base camps they spent several weeks massing for the attack. This build up was a massive undertaking. Allied military planners had to move an incredible amount of men, equipment, supplies, ships, planes and more into place.

Efforts to draw attention away from the growing mass of men and equipment to be used in the invasion included the use of an entire fake inflatable army. Allied planners hoped the Germans would believe the inflatable force, which was being led by General Patton, was the main thrust of any planned invasion. The fake force was built of inflatable rubber tanks, planes, temporary buildings and even landing craft. To complete the deception that a massive force would attack somewhere other than the beaches of Normandy fake radio transmissions were broadcast and false information given to known spies. Hopefully all of the false information provided would cause confusion among German forces, or at least force the Germans to stretch themselves too thin while trying to defend a wider area. The deceptions continued during the invasion and Allied planes even dropped massive amounts of radar- confusing foil strips in order to convince the Germans that Allied forces were attacking elsewhere.

Weeks before the actual Normandy assault men, weapons, planes, tanks, landing craft and a massive assortment of supplies were stockpiled. For many men this meant weeks of waiting, sitting, training, sleeping, eating, boredom, practical jokes and trying to sneak off base for an in- town drink. Games of pickup football were soon shut down because too many men were getting hurt. But according to one soldier at least the food was OK. Sgt John Robert Slaughter noted in his writings that besides fresh eggs and ice cream the men also enjoyed some great main dishes. "Steaks and pork chops with all the trimmings topped with lemon meringue pie." Slaughter noted that the good food did more than keep GI's happy. "They're fattening us up for the kill."

While the European invasion troops waited and suffered between bouts of boredom and periods of training planners were hard at work getting things ready. Heavy use of camouflage to conceal roads, camps, railheads and more were put in place. Huge field kitchens were brought on line to serve meals to the growing number of men. Some kitchens had a few portable M-1937 field ranges to work with. Other kitchens had too many M-1937 ranges lined up to count. Kitchens seemingly cranked out chow almost twenty four hours a day. Bakers also picked up the pace by supplying fresh bread, rolls and other baked goods to the troops. Thousands of loaves of bread were cooked everyday and distributed along the camps and bases that were growing along the English coastline.

The food, rations and equipment that was not being used to feed the amassing troops was packed and stockpiled into trucks, trailers, jeeps and more and being loaded onto LST's, and supply ships. The task was enormous. Everything that was determined to be needed and more" was procured was procured, stocked, distributed and packed into the appropriate craft. Everything had to be ready when the word was given to go.

Before the actual invasion began the fighting men were served up a huge variety of meals. What a soldier ate on a daily basis while waiting for the actual invasion largely depended on where he was, who was cooking the chow at that camp and simply what was available. Daily food ranged from simple warmed up rations to hot meals supplemented with as much fresh fruit and vegetables that could be procured. In all cases an effort was made to make sure the best food possible was available to each man before heading to the beachheads. Good food was considered part of plan to keep up morale.

Steak and Eggs

By many accounts it really didn't matter what was being served. Many of the soldiers either ate light due to nerves, or did not eat at all as rumors of the impending date of the invasion came and went. A quick reminder from officers that everyone would need as much energy as possible may have sparked some to force in as much nourishment as possible. Others ate as a way to forget what could happen next and try to keep up a feeling of normalcy. High energy rations and foods were planned for invasion day menus. When the word "go" was given all of the kitchens were putting out as much food as possible to ensure every man involved had a good meal.

To make sure everyone was served, several special emergency kitchens were readied at points of embarkation. These kitchens handed out what PT Boat veteran Earl Richmond termed as hot "grub" to any man who wanted it. After much training and waiting the troops actually did not fully know what their invasion day plans were.

Once the forces were loaded up and heading across the channel the men were given their orders and missions. The word went down the chain of command and finally troops were briefed on what their duties were. After going over the plans and making sure gear was in order many men took a moment to reflect on their inner thoughts, while others chose to keep busy by checking and rechecking their equipment. At dawn before the invasion many of the troops enjoyed, or tried to enjoy, a breakfast of steak and eggs.

Once on the landing craft which were heading to the beaches of France the rough waters, combined with the limited view inside the deep walls of the craft, and caused many troops to get sick. Nerves also were a factor. Once the door opened on a landing craft... food was the last thing on the men's mind.

While food was not on the minds of the men fighting a live and death battle across the landing beaches of France, it did occupy the thoughts of military planners. The months of hard work and planning hopefully would pay off. Even if the initial landings were successful any inability to properly supply the invasion forces could prove to be disastrous. The massive stockpiles of provisions, gas and other materials were now being moved across the English Channel. Once across the channel someone had to bring it ashore. Members of the quartermaster corps landed along with the invasion forces. When the first boots of fighting men hit the beach, equipment and supplies were starting to be unloaded in order to support and fuel the Allied efforts.

On invasion day some vehicles were so over packed with gear and equipment getting them ashore would have proved a problem during perfect conditions let alone during a pitched battle. Planners did not realize in some cases that some troops, in an effort to make sure they had everything possibly needed, packed as much gear as they could carry including extra rations, ammo and even cigarettes. The overloading, combined with rough seas and overall conditions, caused several problems with overloaded vehicles. Despite the rough conditions, overloading and being shot at—the quartermasters managed to bring supplies ashore in an amazingly short amount of time.

Special "integrated" roller bearing conveyors transported and built in interlocking sections were developed and brought in to help land supplies from vessels to the beaches. Specially designed temporary docks and loading zones were soon in place and more and more men and supplies were ferried back and forth between France and England. Patrol boats manned by Coast Guard crews dodged enemy fire, and returned fire, as they rescued injured men from the water. As new supplies came in, the empty landing craft and supply ships returned to England loaded with dead and wounded. Even with the use of specialty ramps, docks, LST's and more it was often pure manpower that proved to be the best tool in unloading until more permanent facilities were in place. In many instances the men unloading and moving equipment forward, and that were braving the German efforts to repulse the invasion, literally dragged equipment onto beaches by their bare hands and brute strength. If a large piece of equipment bogged down or was stuck in sand or surf then it slowed the whole process down. It either had to be brought ashore or moved out of the way as quickly as possible.

In a report printed the *Quartermaster Review*, July-August 1944, Quartermaster General—General Gregory listed the following facts about the supply effort that went into the invasion planning.

- "First of all the Quartermaster Corps furnished the assault troops with a high energy-content ration so that the invasion forces would be in tip-top shape on landing. This was the B ration, with high energy foods substituted for low energy foods. Such foods included grapefruit juice, tomato juice, canned milk, roast beef, corned beef hash, coffee, tea, coca, canned peas, canned tomatoes, jams, string beans, sliced pineapple, potatoes, canned peaches, fruit cocktail, sugar, and corn."
- "A special ration was furnished for issue to the wounded as they were returned to England."
- "For the assault troops, also, the Quartermaster Corps furnished 10-in-1 rations; C and D rations. The troops were likewise supplied with a condiment kit designed to vary the taste of the C

ration, packed in water-proof containers and issued to small units. This contained salt, pepper, mustard, ketchup, and lemon powder."

- "A special medical kit was procured and distributed by the Quartermaster Corps to be issued at forward field dressing stations for use by the wounded. The kit was packaged like a K ration and contained 100 bouillon cubes, 600 cigarettes, and 30 packages of matches."

The war effort helped produce huge strides in packaging, storage and longevity or shelf life. Better packaging was needed for rations falling into the waters of the English Channel, heating units, low light camp stoves, water proof and water resistant clothes and gear were all developed for invasion forces. Every day items were also brought ashore including mobile kitchens, hospital and medical equipment, clothes, toilet items, radio equipment, trucks, jeeps, tanks and more. A huge amount of pre-packed sacks of coal were carried ashore to help heat water for beach based hospitals and provide cooking heat for troops away from the front lines. Thin plastic "vinylite" weapon covers that were developed for the African invasion to prevent rusting not only provided protection from moisture for the Normandy landing forces weapons but they also provided a make shift float for many of those swimming and wading ashore.

The Normandy invasion, as well as invasion operations in the Pacific, saw some of the largest strides ever made in providing quality food and supplies to fighting troops. Many of the later problems of shortages simply became about as a matter of troops out pacing supply lines.

"The Quartermaster Corps was ready with these so called "unusual" items which it had developed, stored, and issued in preparation for the invasion. Officers and men of the Corps may well be proud of the job that was done in supplying the invasion forces."

General Gregory—Report to the Quartermaster—Quartermaster Review—1944

As Allied troops eventually worked their way across Europe and the Islands of the Pacific they came across similar situations. They entered ravaged lands with starving and shell shocked people. The enormous number of displaced people included starving Allied prisoners of war and captured

Axis troops that had to become part of the supply, and now relief, efforts. Eventually many of these people ended up surviving on the same rations Allied troops had become used to. Special care was needed for those in POW and forced labor camps who had not eaten a real meal in years. Their bodies could not handle the foods included in most field rations. If they ate too much food too fast they could get sick or possibly die. Many were placed on very restricted diets that very slowly increased in fat, calories, fiber and more as their bodies were able to handle it. For many refugees eating a C-Ration was their first introduction to American style food and flavors.

Bob Hope became a legend with military troops across the globe during World War Two and he continued his USO trips until failing health halted his efforts during the Persian Gulf War in 1990-1991. In all, Hope is credited with hosting or appearing in 199 USO shows.
From the collection of the 6th Calvary Museum, Fort Oglethorpe, Georgia.

Known for hard work and enjoying good food and good times in port Sinbad, the Coast Guard's most famous mascot, is shown manning his station ready to take aim at a German U-boat. Sinbad was adopted by the crew of the cutter Campbell prior to World War II. Sinbad served faithfully through thick and thin, surviving combat with the Germans and Japanese. He even had a book written about him.
Courtesy of the United State Coast Guard Historians Office.

Troops enjoy a serving of coffee and doughnuts near Cervaro, Italy.
From the collection of the National WWII Museum.

Sgt. Edward F. Good feeds his buddy, Pfc. Lloyd Deming, a leg of Christmas
turkey on December 24, 1944. Both are casualties at the 2nd Field Hospital.
U.S. Army Center of Military History.

138

The panzer "Santa," with well-filled sack of radios, books, cookies, and other gifts dear to soldiers hearts, glides up to the door of the barracks in Camp Lee's Quartermaster Corps and it isn't hampered by lack of snow in Virginia. Camp Lee, Virginia, Quartermaster Replacement Center. December 1941.
U.S. Army Center of Military History.

CHAPTER SEVEN

Victory Gardens & Rationing on the Home Front

The familiar home front ration card was part of everyday existence.
The Collection of the Hamilton Co. Bicentennial Library, Chattanooga, Tennessee

Citizens across the globe faced many hardships during World War Two. American's were not the only ones that had their daily lives disrupted. Americans possibly fared the best out of many of the Allied Countries and Axis nations. Countries in Europe were under the clouds of war for years. The land was bombed, factories, destroyed, infrastructure devastated and this does not even take into account the toll on human lives. All things considered, the United States and Canada were pretty good places to be during the war.

One of many Coca-Cola ads designed during the war years depicting
refreshed soldiers.
Courtesy the Coca-Cola Corporation.

Rumford Baking Powder was one of many companies that produced easy, and rationed related, cook books and pamphlets during World War II.
The Collection of the Hamilton Co. Bicentennial Library, Chattanooga, Tennessee

Hang this up in your kitchen!

Save your WASTE FATS to make explosives!

1. **The Need Is Urgent.** War in the Pacific has greatly reduced our supply of vegetable fats from the Far East. It is necessary to find substitutes for them. Moreover, fats make glycerine. And glycerine makes explosives for us and our allies—explosives to down Axis planes, stop their tanks, sink their ships. We need millions of pounds of glycerine and you housewives can help supply them.

2. **Don't** throw away a single drop of used cooking fat—bacon grease, meat drippings, frying fats—every kind you use. After you've got all the cooking good from them, pour them through a kitchen strainer into a clean, wide-mouthed can. Keep in a cool, dark place. Please don't use glass containers or paper bags.

3. **Take Them** to your meat dealer when you've saved a pound or more. He is cooperating patriotically. He will pay you for your waste fats and get them started on their way to the war industries. It will help him if you can deliver your fats early in the week.

SEE FURTHER INSTRUCTIONS ON THE REVERSE SIDE OF THIS SHEET

10—29835-1

Wartime reminders were common place in every newspaper and other publications.
The Collection of the Hamilton Co. Bicentennial Library, Chattanooga, Tennessee

This photo, by Alfred Palmer taken during 1943, shows the efforts taken at educating even the youngest of Americans about the realities of rationing.
From the collection of the National Archives.

While clowning for the camera's this Department of the Navy photo shows Betty Hutton during a stop at a chow hall for a visit with sailors and Marines somewhere in the Marshall Islands during December of 1944. Virginia Carrol, a dancer with the Hutton troupe, is the lady smiling over Hutton's shoulder.
From the collection of Charles Sturt University Australia.

The war effort included rationing as is shown by this group of people waiting in line for sugar.
From the collection of the National Archives.

Lena Horne shows how to conserves fuel during lean times on the home front in this picture by N.d. Randt Studios, Inc.
Photo from the National Archives.

145

(Booklet Cover, Blue Ribbon Creamery
From the collection of the National WWII Museum.

146

The Hormel Girls performed across the United States to raise spirits of both the military and war weary civilians.
Photo courtesy of the Hormel Corporation.

"We'll have lots to eat this winter, won't we Mother?"

Grow your own
Can your own

This 1943 World War Two poster by Al Parker promotes home canning and home gardens during the victory garden movement.
From the collection of the National Park Service from the US National Archives.

147

This does not mean that hardships were not felt. In the U.S. and Canada millions of families faced the uncertain future of loved ones serving in the military. There was a large amount of stress placed on the citizens due to the constant warnings and threats. Shipping was affected off the coasts as enemy submarines tried to stop the flow of aid and men overseas. And daily life was anything but normal with the introduction of rationing. The United States was not the only country to limit the availability of certain items. Britain, Canada, France, Russia, Japan, Canada, Germany and more all implemented some form of rationing.

Rationing was a way to keep certain items available to the public and to make sure needed items were available for the war effort. There was a very real concern that mass buying and stockpiling, called hording, would lead to shortages. This could strain a system already burdened with supplying the war effort. The American public used ration books to regulate when they could buy certain items ranging from sugar to gasoline. War and rationing came after the country, and the world, had suffered through the great depression. People were already used to hardship and the call for rationing and conservation was a tough sell.

In order to get the message across about issues such as rationing the government utilized a very effective propaganda effort that hoped to show how it would help the war effort and give troops the tools needed to win the war. Citizens had to appear before a local rationing board in order to be classified for a ration book. This included everyone in a household including children and babies. Ration books had a limited lifespan and limited the amounts of any rationed item that could be purchased at any given time or over a period of time. Americans in huge numbers paid attention to the patriotic message. Citizens accepted the rationing and they bought war bonds, recycled materials such as metals, rubber and oil all in an effort to help the war effort.

People may often think of things such as beef and sugar when talking about rations however the first thing rationed in January of 1942 was actually tires. This was due to a wartime shortage of rubber. The rationing of tires was aided by the efforts of the government to educate the public on conservation and recycling. A combination of printed pamphlets covering a staggering amount of issues, motivational posters, celebrity appearances, and news reel reports worked very effectively in getting the message out.

Rationed Items included tires, cars, bicycles, gasoline, fuel oil and kerosene, solid fuels, stoves, rubber footwear, shoes, sugar, coffee, processed foods, meats, canned fish, cheese, canned milks, fat and even typewriters. When the war ended the need for rationing was slowly lifted. Most items rationed returned to normal purchasing for the consumer by the end of 1945. But the limits on sugar remained until 1947.

The call for conversation and rationing from the government was met with an outpouring of supporting materials from corporate America as well. Companies across the country printed material filled with tips about cooking and energy conservation, cost saving recipes, tips on how to extend recipes, make home repairs and more. The PR campaigns echoed the message from official offices. Everything that could be done should be done for the war effort. The only difference was that the information produced for commercial use naturally highlighted the company's products as a great addition or solution. People learned about mock food dishes such as Ritz Cracker Apple Pie, cost saving recipes featuring Heinz products and more.

PR companies and marketing departments looked for any way to connect their products with helping the war effort. After all, many of these companies were consumer driven corporations. The commercial success of their products was as important as helping the war effort. Companies had to keep their names and product in the public eye. World War Two public relations ad campaigns constantly reminded consumers that their product and company were working hard to provide the best for servicemen. A great example of this is the marketing for products such as SPAM, M&M's, Tabasco brand hot sauce, Heinz products and Coke. In the case of M&M's the product was actually a relatively new one. After being introduced in 1941 the use of the candy in rations because of its durability and resistance to higher temperatures made it a GI favorite. The candy coated bite sized chocolate pieces had a devoted following after the war.

Coke became a product known around the world during the war. According to the Coke Cola company 64 bottling plants were set up around the world to supply troops during the war. This followed an urgent request for bottling equipment and materials from General Eisenhower's base in North Africa. Many of these war-time plants were later converted to civilian use.

A cablegram from General Dwight Eisenhower's Allied Headquarters in North Africa. Dated June 29, 1943, requested a shipment of materials and equipment for building 10 bottling plants overseas as well as 3 million filled bottles of Coca-Cola. Within six months, a Company engineer had flown to Algiers and opened the first plant, the forerunner of 64 bottling plants shipped abroad during World War II. The plants were set up as close as possible to combat areas in Europe and the Pacific. More than 5 billion bottles of Coke were consumed by military service personnel during World War Two, in addition to countless servings through dispensers and mobile, self-contained units in battle areas. While working hard to supply fighting men with a Coke, the company also took the opportunity to put out its share of marketing material letting the public know that its product was at the front lines with them.

Marketing and public relation efforts were not limited to food items, recipes and cost saving tips. Ads appeared in papers and magazines daily from producers of clothes, cars, trains and just about any product available. If a plant was converted from making something for the consumer and now manufactured tents or even planes the word had to get out. After all, when the war ended the name of the company had to be remembered. These ads usually highlighted advancements and usefulness in items used by soldiers, new airplanes, trucks and more. On the food side of the marketing campaigns the ads generally fell into touting how the product was being used in the war effort or offered recipes or tips on how to extend a meal or save money. Others tied their products in with efforts such as Victory Gardens.

Victory Gardens worked in World War One and they returned with a vengeance in World War Two. During the depression similar efforts were known as relief gardens. The depression era garden was geared towards food relief for the poor. It was more of an individual or family type activity. Whatever the title, the World War Two version was backed by both a commercial and governmental marketing and public relations campaign that tied the gardens to victory in the minds of the public. The ability for many "city" dwellers to successfully plant Victory Gardens to supplement their own pantries helped relieve pressures on food supplies. Victory Gardens were planted everywhere. The call for Americans to plant a Victory Garden in order to help the war effort was answered by nearly 20 million Americans. The gardens were no longer for the poor or limited to a single family or person. It seemed everyone was involved. Eleanor Roosevelt's even had a Victory Garden on the White House grounds.

Official pamphlets, newspapers and magazines ran informative pieces about how to make a Victory Garden work. Topics included seed selection, planting, keeping insects and animals out of a garden, harvesting, how to involve children and how to combine your efforts with your neighbors. Families were also encouraged to can their own vegetables and to combine efforts with family, friends and neighbors to produce food for everyone. The sale of pressure cookers used in home canning skyrocketed. Combined Victory Garden Cooperatives were started. Victory Gardens appeared in empty lots, backyards, on rooftops, in planters and just about anywhere something could be grown. The US Department of Agriculture estimated that the 20 million victory gardens that were planted produced 9-10 million tons of food. This was food that would have come from commercial sources which was now needed for the war effort. This was about 44% of the total amount grown.

There were several goals that the use of Victory Gardens in the United States hoped to achieve. The goals were similar in other countries that utilized garden programs. The main public relations message was that the gardens would take some of the demand off of commercial supplies. This of course would make more produce available to the Armed Forces and the lend-lease programs. Keeping the troops fed! This message was tied in with planning for the future in case of shortages down the road. Increased home grown food could be canned and saved. Another aspect was to tie the message of a Victory Garden in with the moral aspect of the war. It was simply the right thing to do as a citizen.

On the industrial side, the gardens helped reduce extra demand on materials that were used in food processing and canning but which were also strategic and used in supplying the military such a packaging supplies, metals, chemicals for processing and more. All of these items were needed in packaging and canning food for the troops but also in the making of weapons, shells, jeeps, food, packaging, medical supplies and more. Less material for commercial consumer canning meant more for the war effort and more industrial capacity could be focused there.

Another goal was to reduce the amount of transportation needed for consumer produce needs. By growing as much food locally the need to ship large amounts of commercial based produce was reduced. This meant that the capacity of railroads used in transporting munitions and soldiers was increased simply by reducing the amount of produce shipped. Trains were vital in moving men and supplies around the nation.

Not only was the use of Victory Gardens a great way to help keep the food supplies plentiful for the war effort it gave people a feeling that they were actually doing something to help. When buying a bond the transaction is easy and over. Ration books were so integrated into the daily lives of people that it became common place. Gathering items for a recycling drive only lasted a while and much of the recycling message was built into rationing and conservation. When people planted a Victory Garden they got dirty, used tools, worked the gardens over a long period of time and in many cases on a daily basis. People living in many metropolitan areas across the country were not used to planting and farming as their rural neighbors were. The gardens helped bridge a gap and bring communities together. Victory Gardens were hands on and this gave people a sense of being part of the effort to win the war. It also relieved stress as people worked towards a goal which they deemed vital.

In Germany the use of gardens was also common place. The message was not as strong as those in the United States and other Allied countries but there is no doubt that the use of homegrown gardens helped supplement the dinner tables of German citizens. The use of gardens in many areas of Europe during and after the war was an absolute necessity in many cases as production and agriculture capabilities were often destroyed during the war.

In Canada the message on Victory Gardens was very similar to the message in the United States and England. Citizens used available space to plant a variety of produce. The use of commercial messages and government pamphlets was very effective as it was to the South. In England the message of Victory Gardens was also well received. An abundance of crops such as carrots were available and quickly carrots became an ingredient in all kinds of recipes. Special pamphlets geared towards using carrots in every possible manner were distributed in order to make sure nothing went to waste from spoilage. Everything needed to be used.

While the wartime efforts in raising awareness about homegrown food sources was incredibly successful in Allied Countries the message was lost when the war ended. As the war ended so did the majority of government promotions of the gardens. As a result many people in the United States, Canada and England did not replant Victory Gardens in the spring of 1946. The message to do so was not there, the war had been won and the extra capacity was not needed to send food overseas for the troops which were now returning home in massive numbers. The problem was that production had not yet fully switched from supplying the war effort back to production for grocery stores and consumer foods. Several food shortages occurred at the market place on many items. Thankfully part of the overall message about Victory Gardens included saving and canning. So many people turned to their war time stocks of canned food. Eventually the production was able to catch back up with demands as more and more industries switched back to peace time production.

Another factor in the lack of Victory Gardens planted in 1946 was the fact that many were built on loaned property, vacant lots and donated space in parks or on private property. As the war ended most control of private and civic property used for public victory gardens returned to the property owner. This left the majority of any remaining gardens relegated to those found in residential back yards.

One aspect of the war on the United States Agriculture business was the incredible amount of improvements the overall system saw. As America entered the war the majority of produce farming was very regional in nature and relied on many smaller farms. Over the course of the war advancements in production, equipment, transportation, markets, storage, packaging and even seed and crop selection had dramatically increased. The way farmers selected crops, planted, treated, harvested them and shipped to market had improved in a few short years. These wartime advancements in agriculture on a commercial basis were not lost. Agriculture had quickly changed, and continued to change, from smaller operations to larger corporate style farms.

The modernization that took place on many commercial farms across the United State was also seen in other areas. The overall transportation system had improved. There were better roads, shipping and railways. All of this had been improved as part of the war effort. Communication across the country had improved as national networks, and local radio stations, gained massive new audiences. People were used to listening to the radio and reading newspapers. Suddenly the world seemed a lot smaller as people now knew about distant lands and people. On the industrial side factories had been retooled and improved in more ways than can be named. The amount of new production methods, packaging, products and technology now available to corporations was staggering.

Simple things, including neighbors picking up a shovel to plant seeds for a victory garden, allowed businesses the room to improve so much that by the time the war had ended the country had gone through a wartime industrial and technical revolution.

CHAPTER EIGHT

Memories from the Chow Line

Cpl. John A. Maceri of Bristol, Pennsylvania, stirring food which he and his helpers have prepared for the 2000-odd released prisoners at the Los Banos Prison in Manila, Luzon, Philippine Islands.
Huge batteries of GI cans were used as cooking pots.
Photo and original caption from the collection of the National Archives.

Chow Time for the 19th Engineers and SeaBees.
War In The Pacific National Park Collection.

A frozen World War Two chow line serves men of the 347th Infantry Regiment
on their way to La Roche, Belgium.
Photo from the Collection of the National Archives, January 13, 1945, Newhouse.

Shortly after being liberated from prison camps these internees are heading for
their first real meal in a long time as well as medical attention. The group
consists of civilians, clergy and military personnel. The original photo from the
National Archives notes that the Priest pictured was held at Lost Banos Prisoner
of War Camp and was taken in March of 1945.
Photo from the collection of the National Archives.

Liberty Phone Call From Scotland. U.S. Coast Guardsmen make use of a telephone booth in Scotland while on liberty from their ship. From left to right: Officers' Cook Second Class Joseph Andy, Officers' Steward First Class Casiano Aquino, Gunner's Mate Second Class Vincent G. Igoe, Electrician's Mate Second Class George Trigony, Radioman Third Class Carlton Lee, and Officers' Steward Second Class Daniel Riley.
Photo courtesy of the United States Coast Guard Historians office.

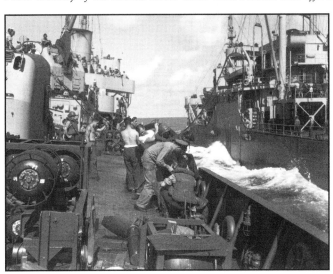

The USS Taney takes on fuel from the USS COSSATOT. Being able to transfer supplies and fuel while underway was an Allied time saver as well as a way to keep ships moving instead of becoming sitting targets for attack. The Coast Guard Cutter Taney served at Pearl Harbor and was in service until the late 1980's.
Photo Courtesy of United States Coast Guard Historians office.

Overture

Celery Soup and Crackers . Sung by the entire Audience
without Silencers

Prologue

Mr. Pickles, and his Sweetheart Celery . Relished by All

Cast of Characters

The various members of the cast are listed in the order
that they appear. The management hopes that the audience
will appreciate the strain under which our Star, Mr. Turkey,
is acting.

ACT I

A California Gentleman . . . . Mr. Tom Turkey

A One Nighter . . . . Oyster Dressing

Greasy, his pal . . . . Giblet Gravy

Berry Joe . . . . Cranberry Sauce

Rolly Polly . . . . Stuffed Celery

Virginia Ladies . . . . Candied Sweets

A Flirt . . . . French Peas

ACT II

Mr. Big Ears . . . . Mr. Corn

A Leafy Lady . . . . Miss Lettuce

Her Boy Friend . . . . Red Tomatoes

Their Mutual Friend . . . . Miss Mayonnaise

Intermission

COLD FOAMING DRINKS

This 1944 Thanksgiving day menu from the Third Marine Division at Camp
Elliot, California shows the creativity of the staff as the menu was presented as if
it were a program from a theatre presenting a three act play. Of course the star
of the play was Mr. Tom Turkey. Guest stars included his pal "Greasy"—the
Giblet Gravy, and "Mr. Big Ears"—corn on the cob.
Source, Courtesy of the Marine Corps History Division.

Marine Corporal Fenwick H. Dunn gives the candy from his K-rations to an aged woman on Okinawa. The Japanese fled as the Americans landed on Easter morning, abandoning the aged, infirm, and small children.
From the War in The Pacific National Park Collection.

A makeshift bar setting provide some resemblance of home to servicemen in the Pacific.
From the War in The Pacific National Park Collection.

159

The men enjoy homemade ice cream from their ice cream maker that was assembled from salvaged parts. The photo was taken on Bougainville Island in April of 1944.
Photo Courtesy of the Fort Lee United States Army Quartermaster Museum.

Two French soldiers give handfuls of candy to advancing American soldiers in Rouffach, France, after the closing of the Colmar pocket on February 5, 1945
Photo from the collection of the National Archives.

This entire book stems from one conversation, one brief story that a veteran told me about military food. The story was about cooking barbecue over a drum filled with scrap material set on fire with the aid of helicopter fuel.

This book is centered on the best and worst chow of World War II. The memories recounted are from veterans of the various service branches, some allowed me to use their names; others preferred to remain anonymous. The stories are often humor based. Many of the veterans corresponded by letter or email, and when interviewed used safe topics like food or "chow," as a means to communicate about the events they witnessed and the battles they fought. It's much easier to talk about an amusing event involving a hastily constructed raft and a hand grenade fishing trip in a lagoon, than horrific events many of us can only imagine. To capture the personality of the storytellers, the following stories are unedited

Corby's Baked Beans and Hangover Cure

Looking back on it, I still wonder how it was we had so many excellent cooks. We submariners were members of an elite corps and as such I know we were spoiled. There was never any stinting on the supplies of quality food we had. We even had fresh sweet cream. We had 3 cooks: a head cook, an assistant, and a baker. One of our head cooks, a man named Corbesierre, was a genius. He came from New Haven and said after the war he was going to go back there and open a restaurant. We called him Corby and he served delicious meals 4 times a day, every day, even when our supplies ran low towards the end of the patrol. We carried 25 pound metal cans of flour in the engine room between the outboard sides of the engines and the pressure hull. Once our initial supply of bread from the tender ran out, our baker began baking fresh bread early every morning.

You could smell it throughout the hull and it was a wonderful smell. I considered myself the gourmet of the ship, and I once persuaded Corby to serve a curry dinner. He did so against his better judgment. It was delicious but not popular with most of the crew and Corby was heart-broken and it was all my fault. Corby also made the best baked beans in the world. He soaked the beans overnight then placed them in deep pans and covered them with brown sugar and thick slices of bacon. I have never tasted baked beans like his since. There was a submarine custom when in port called "10 o'clock soup." It was just that. A large tureen of freshly made soup was served every day in port at 10:00 am. It was delicious and was especially good if you had been ashore the night before and had a hangover.

From the papers of Dick Hawn USS Trout and the collection of Dave Hall.

Dinner on Downing Street

My dear fellow:

I was in the Army during the WW2 Blitz in London. That was in my opinion the worst part of the battle by far. We women generally worked in ammunition factories but some like me joined the effort as student nurses and medics. Princess Elizabeth was an ambulance driver then. Sometimes we worked during the day and became female soldiers only at night or during an emergency situation. The very best meals are usually simple meals one can remember because they were eaten when you were very hungry, sort of starving and suddenly you are presented with something to eat without warning. This is my story;

I was dispatched to Downing Street right after a bomb hit and arrived there with the ambulance only to find debris all over the road that made it impassable. My driver and I ran a part of the way with my medical bag slung over my shoulder. As we got closer my heart started pumping real fast because I realized that our destination was Number 10. What if I should find a broken and very injured Mr. Churchill inside there? I scrambled over the debris to find the big man, Mr. Churchill attending to his cook, a woman of about forty who had sustained minor abrasions and his butler was faffing about throwing bits of kitchen appliance out of the way.

The bomb had hit just outside the kitchen window and had taken with it a large part of the outer kitchen wall. Fortunately no one was in the kitchen at the time. The cook was in the pantry, closing up for the night when the bomb struck. Mr. Churchill was so happy to see me, and after I had attended to the cook, she gave me some of what was apparently left of Mr. Churchill and his visitor's supper. It was cold ham, home-made bread and a salad of some kind, and Mustard. I will never forget the mustard. It must have been home made. It was a lovely combination.

It was probably the best meal I have ever had in the Army. Simple, but who else on this forum can say that they had been invited to Number 10 Downing Street for supper?

Submitted by anonymous—England

Enjoy the Company

During WWII I was in Germany and it was months after fighting. Lots of guys were gone or heading home and there was only a small group of us stationed at a small village. We made friends with an elderly local who was a pastry chef or something before the war. He stopped by all of the time to say hello and talk. He spoke great English and was a very nice man. That's all there was to do around there for a long time, talk. Before I shipped out later he brought all of us two big baskets of some of the best food I had ever eaten. He had landed a job as a cook was cooking for big wigs and such. But he wanted us to have some decent food before we left. That was ok by all of us. All we could offer him was some coffee. He seemed very pleased just enjoy the company.

Submitted by anonymous

Beans, Beans good for Your Heart

I was reminded of a story my father used to tell me about being in the Army during WWII. I don't remember where he said this took place but it was one of his favorite stories. He often told a story about clearing out houses, door to door, checking for enemy, wounded, injured, fallen soldiers and locals who were scared to come out. They were often told not to touch too much due to traps or hand grenades or such that had not gone off. Dad said he walked into a kitchen area and after days of not touching anything he walked over to a counter top and found a can of food.

The can had no label so poked it with his gun. The next thing he knew there was a loud bang. My father said he knew that he had set off a grenade and expected to look down and see his hand missing and to be covered in blood. Instead he as covered in some sort of canned bean stew that had gone bad and fermented. The pressure had finally made it explode. He said one of his buddies came running from the other room and dropped to the floor laughing at him covered in goo. For the rest of his time in the service, and for years after that, everyone called father "Beans."

Submitted by Allison Carter

The Day of the Big Fish Explosion!
Mr. Whitaker:

My husband, Robert A. Ptacek, was on Guadalcanal during the worst fighting there. In putting info about his experiences together, I got this story from him.

On Guadalcanal in early November 1943, I and four of my buddies were discussing how tired we were of eating the same rations day after day. Having found some dynamite in a tent that had apparently been used to house sick Japanese (there were dead Japs on the straw mats), we decided to try and get some fresh fish. My thought was this story might be useful to you.

—Maxine Ptacek

We then built a raft out of coconut logs and, with the dynamite, took it down to the beach and went out to where the water was about 90 feet deep. One of the guys, who claimed he had civilian experience with dynamite, lit it, but held it too long in the wind. Seeing the short fuse and to keep from being blown up, he threw the dynamite overboard and we all dived off the raft. As it exploded, the raft was torn into splinters and blown about 30 ft. up along with us five men and a lot of fish that, as they came down, were hitting us in the head. We had more fish than we could handle and, after swimming to shore, gathered a lot of it in large bags that had been used for rations. We were told to eat only the ones with scales, not those with skin. The fish were very good.

The above was written from my oral discussion with him about what happened. He remembered the names of the other four, one of whom went back to Illinois with him and married his sister. He called it "The Day of the Big Fish Explosion with Jap Dynamite" and said they got "hundreds" of fish.

Submitted by Maxine Ptacek

Green Eggs
Mr. Whitaker:

I served in the Navy during WWII. I really don't have much to say about the food I ate in the service other than everyone always did their best to get things right. The only time I had a problem was during a St. Patrick's Day breakfast some cook decided to put green dye or something in the eggs.

But they didn't have enough food coloring so nobody really knew what was going on. The eggs had a faint tint of teal in them and around the edges which scared most of us off! We thought it was mold or something.

Word got around about the real cause of the discoloration and the guys finally started eating them. I had to cover mine with Ketchup. That made the color even worse. That story always makes me smile. Thank you. B.T.

Submitted by B.T. United States Navy Retired

The Best Breakfast Ever

I was in World War Two in the Pacific. I met lots of good guys. Food was not always the best - but we did alright. But this one time we came into this camp and it was just in time for breakfast. I was amazed; the cooks were serving up fresh eggs, bacon, toast and everything. I thought to myself that this place was not all that bad. This was the best food ever.

But the cooks kept coming over and giving us more, piling it on and all of the guys were eating like crazy and they were saying eat faster, eat faster and giving us more. I was stuffed and thought that I would really like this place if the food was always that good and we had so much of it. But I didn't think I could eat any more. Why were they feeding us so much and what was the rush?

Well, we finished up eating and they cleaned everything, all scraps of the food were gone in an instant and any evidence was buried. I thought, boy these cooks are fast.

Just as soon as they got done some MP's drove up searching for some… re-appropriated chow and supplies. It seemed that somebody had "liberated" a whole bunch of fresh eggs, bacon and such from some higher up. Everyone just shrugged their shoulders and the cooks and Mess Sergeants acted like nothing happened. The MP's looked around looking for the food and didn't find anything so they left. Best breakfast I ever had in the war!

Submitted by Jim "J.W." Watson, Uncle of the author.

Sugar Beets and Tulip Bulbs

Like myself many Dutch child must have heard it in the Fities and Sixties from his parents, when Mum had cooked meal that was not very much to the child's taste:

165

"During the "hongerwinter" (winter of starvation) we would have committed a murder for this. We were glad if we had some sugar beets or tulips bulbs we could cook. It tasted horrible, but you had something to eat." There are stories of people that ate porridge made of sawdust!!

A little bit of history: After the Battle of Arnhem the German occupiers of the Netherlands cut off almost all the food supplies to the not liberated northern and western part of The Netherlands. The winter of 1944-1945 was extreme cold. Many women, the men had a good chance of being arrested and taken to Germany for forced labor, went from the cities to the countryside to exchange with farmers whatever was valuable (table silver, cloth, etc) to whatever was eatable. Who was not capable of doing this had to rely on central kitchens which served most strange stews and soups.

Cooking for your self was troublesome. There was no or haphazard energy (gas, electricity) or water supply. People cooked on a small stove that was also meant to heat the house or rather one room a little. The stove burned anything, but there was hardly any fuel. People used wood from their own house or unoccupied houses or removed trees from parks and streets. Of course this was illegal. You can imagine the euphoric reaction of the Dutch on the Allied bombers that dropped from low level food supplies in and around the big cities in April 1945. Unfortunately for many thousands this help came too late.

Submitted by Levien

No Comparison

There is no comparison between training at the Naval Cooks and Bakers School and on the PT boats. At the school you had all the equipment and help you needed… but on the boat you did not have much in the way of equipment, help or supplies. The menus at school were pretty much laid out for you. On the boat you alone had to make it up and then scrounge for supplies. The school was spotlessly clean. The boat was as clean… as you could make it. We had daily inspections at school and none on the boat. It was up to us individual cooks on the boats to do the best we could. At school we only had to do cooking and baking.

On the boat we had to do all that plus cleaning and stand watches and, when necessary, man a gun at GQ. At school we had 150 gallon "kettles."

Pictured are PT 108 cooks Frank Akonowicz on left and Earl Richmond on right. While stationed with PT squadron 5 at Emirau Island, Solomon's in 1944. "I was the replacement for Frank. Frank had just replaced another man, Bell, who was killed in action in a daylight raid."
Picture and caption courtesy of Earl Richmond.

On the boat, we had little pots. On the boat we had an overhead rail to hold on to while we cooked underway. At base everything at meals times was stationery. At meal times while underway on the boat everything was all sliding around. Use your imagination and that is what is was like in comparison. There was a LOT of differences. It was not what we were pre-pared for in school. On our pt bases it was also different. On the bases we had to improvise also. We used field ranges mostly. We had supplies but not all we needed. We only had food that was doled out after all the other service bases got theirs. We on boats and bases had to contend with insects and rodents 24/7. It was rough. But we managed. We went from 3000 men to cook for at school down to maybe 500 at base and 12-14 men on a boat.

Two Dozen Eggs and A Bag Full of Potatoes

You ask for a WW2 best/worst chow experience. I take this to mean "memorable". The following excerpt from the reminiscences I wrote for my great-grandchildren, as a contribution to their WW2 school project, may serve the purpose. I find that the most memorable culinary delights are often quite simple.

I should explain that with the fourteen other Radar/Radio Engineers, one Cook, one Despatch Rider, Medical Orderly and MT Driver, under the command of a Signals Officer (Captain), we formed the advance detach-ment of a Mobile Signals Servicing Unit to provide technical backup to mobile Radar and Communications units that were intended to go ashore on Omaha Beach, since the US invasion forces had no such facility for interception of enemy aircraft. But, to set the scene, my enjoyable chow memory followed several weeks in a UK pre-embarkation secret concentration area, followed by several weeks in Normandy, post D-day, during all of which time we lived off K-rations.

Our Cook had accompanied a 'foraging' party, armed with two tins of corned beef, to visit a Normandy farmer, one of whose cider-apple orchards we had commandeered to set up our camp before moving on.

To our great joy the Corporal Cook returned an hour later bearing two dozen eggs and a bagful of potatoes. He issued us each with an egg, and two potatoes that he suggested we peel and hand back for him to boil the next evening. When the time came I decided to use one half of my mess-tin to mash and season the two boiled potatoes I'd collected from the cook and to spread this with the egg that I'd already soft-boiled in the other half of my mess tin, over a Tommy Cooker. After being denied both for many weeks the flavour was delicious. He had also 'requisitioned' the virtually inedible compressed fruit bar and the four hard tack biscuits, from our individual K-ration packs. After soaking these overnight he added boiling water laced with sweetened condensed milk to form a very acceptable dessert.

My worst meal followed the cessation of hostilities and was served in the RAF Military Hospital, in Hamburg, where my liver infection dictated a total fat-free diet. The menu that day was fried meat balls, with French fries. I was rather dismayed to receive three BOILED meat balls, with two slices of dry bread. The only saving grace was that a kind benefactor had decreed that any RAF personnel who were confined to hospital were to receive a pint bottle of Guinness each day. I benefited from the fact that some other inmates were tee-total!

Submitted by a British D-day Veteran and dedicated to his Royal Air Force comrades who died on Omaha Beach. —Dr Leslie G Dobinson

A Reminder of Daily Rations

My Royal British Legion Branch produced a small book last year in aid of our Poppy Appeal. It's called Ration Book Recipes with a collection derived from the memories of our WW2 Veterans and their wives. It reminded me that in 1941 the One Week Ration per person was; 4 ounces Bacon or Ham, 8 ounces Sugar, 2 ounces Butter, 10 cents—worth of Fresh

Meat, 2 ounces Tea, 1ounces Cheese, 2 ounces Jam (Jello?), and the equivalent of 1 small tin of Spam (or similar tinned item, as available).

Submitted by a British D-day Veteran and dedicated to his Royal Air Force comrades who died on Omaha Beach. —Dr Leslie G Dobinson

Thankful

My husband was in the war and his most memorable food was the pasta dishes, not always bad but not always great either. He said you could just about count on having some sort of pasta or potatoes no matter where you ate. His favorite though was the peanut butter and jam sandwich. He used to get those coming off watch late. He always said it was hard to make a bad peanut butter sandwich. But he loved cooks. He said they were the hardest working men in the military. They never seemed to sleep. There was always something going on in a kitchen or galley. He also said that the food on the carriers was wonderful and they got spoiled while on ship.

My uncle who was also a Marine always told me that any meal you got to eat while in the service was one to remember wither it was good or bad. If you got to eat while in combat it was a meal to be thankful for. He said some cooks, the thinks Seabees, rolled up next to him in a repaired Willy with a trailer attached loaded down with chow. They fed him and some other guys in a minute or less and sped off through the jungle with the trailer bouncing along.

Submitted by anonymous

Cooks used to make all the difference

I used to think that meat and vegetable was the best of the bunch until we changed coasts to join the Yanks. Our rations then changed dramatically for the better and we were to learn the delights of Spam, tasty Meat and Vegetable, Rice Pudding and even tinned Fruit Cocktail.

Porridge, a staple breakfast meal, was by tradition always made by the last man on guard, the one doing the 6am to 8am shift and so its quality used to vary from solid salty cement to ambrosia of the gods (that was when I made it)

Cooks used to make all the difference, of course, and I soon tumbled that the Battery cooks were never in the same league as the RHQ cooks and it would appear that COs guarded the chefs with their lives and never allowed them to be subjected to the risks that we other mortal faced.

Finally, when I switched Regiments from Light Attack to the Armored Corps I found myself acting as cook for two tanks (in addition to my normal duties). Here I had a chance to cook right from scratch even to meat issued in bulk. I used to carve the meat into manageable chunks, quick fry the chunks and then hang the meat in a bucket of salt water from the back of the tank. Later, when we had stopped moving for at least a day I would slice the meat and re-fry it until edible. I don't remember anyone ever dying of food poisoning.

Courtesy of Ron Goldstein —British Army veteran.

Re-appropriate the Destination

We trained on the Higgins boats. By the time we headed to Okinawa we mastered what we called Re-appropriation the destination, 'cause it sounded better than stealing. We re-appropriated the destination on about fifty cases of beer. And we had cases of peaches as well. At the time nobody was counting anything. We figured out you could open the cases and slide the beers one at a time down into the bilge. And I was standing on a case. When we needed a beer and would give a few out to guys they would wipe the green water off at first. But as we went on the guys did not care. They just wanted a beer and they appreciated it.

Submitted by Don MacLean USN, Camp Gordon Johnston Museum Carrabelle Florida.

Military Intelligence

I can't really say that I ever had a best food in the army… that's like saying Military Intelligence. The two just don't go together. Ha, boy I bet I get a rise out of some old Mess Guys - Cookies! But I can honestly say that most of it was pretty good. I remember being in boot and I got so tired of the normal food it was the same all the time. But breakfast was always good. Once we had a General visiting my post and some of us got steak as well some steamed shrimp. When he left the next day we had the same old stuff.

Then I headed overseas. I learned to eat lots of hot sauce on everything, while overseas and towards the front. I ate a lot of C's and other rations. I think they were much better than what I saw of our foes.

170

Almost all of the Nazis I saw looked hungry. Saw one Russian group and they looked starved. So I guess we had it good. We all just didn't realize it at the time.

Submitted by anonymous.

Stuck on S.O.S.

My Uncle was in the Army during World War II, and he said the best he thought was- SOS. He cooked some up for all us kids. It smelled pretty good. So we tried it and we thought it was good. It's creamed chip beef gravy over toast. Now I make it for my family at least once a month. My uncle said that he added hot sauce to his because he said he never ate a meal during the war that didn't have some hot sauce, or that he wished he had some hot sauce to pour over it.

Submitted by Karen B.

My First S.O.S.

I remember one of my first meals was S.O.S. The cook piled a big glob on it on my plate and I stood there looking at it. He asked me what I was waiting on and I asked what it was. He just said to move on down the line. It was not till I sat down that I realized there was some beef or something in the mix. Besides the weird looks that stuff was plenty filling and after a while I got too really like it. I sat there eating when I finally got somebody to tell me I was eating Shit on a Shingle or creamed beef. Bad news was, I had that stuff for about a week straight. I walked in one day and they were serving some baked chicken and I was so happy.

Submitted by David Walker.

Your Sister

I served as a cook during World War Two. Talk about hard work. We cooked, cleaned, fought just like every other guy. My worst memory is trying to get some food to guys in the front. Sometimes it felt like a last meal mission for them boys. Only one real funny thing happened. I was eating at the time and my buddy Rodney sat down but slightly missed the box he was aiming to sit on. He went off balance and fell straight back and lifted a small table up with one of his boots. That table had our mess sergeants food on it and the sergeant and I just watched that stuff shoot straight up into the air. Now we were all good friends by now and Dean, the sergeant, said, "DAMN IT RODNEY! You are so clumsy that I'm not ever going to introduce you to my sister when we get home!" Rodney was setting stuff back up and said, "That's OK, I've seen a picture of your sister!" Sarge hit him with a slice of bread or something and we all had a laugh.

Submitted by A. Harris —WWII Veteran.

High On The Hog

When I entered the Air force back in the day I came from a very rural and poor family in Southern Kentucky. The thing was I didn't know we were poor! We did alright, worked hard and did fine. But when I got in the service and sat down for my first real meal I was stunned by the amount of food there was. It was overwhelming in a way. I had the opportunity to try a lot of foods and such that I had never eaten before. Some of them I had never heard of before! As a country boy I figured I was living high on the hog during WWII.

Submitted by Bob B., United States Air Force.

They Looked Half Dead

Pictures and memorabilia from Jackson Tanner Fahl.
Photo by Kent Whitaker

172

Jackson Tanner Fahl describes pictures and memories from his days with the Air Force during World War Two to visitors of the 2010 Remembrance Day event at the Tennessee Valley Railroad Museum in Chattanooga, Tennessee.
Photo by Kent Whitaker.

I was with the 9th Bomber Group, 5th Squadron, 313 Wing of the 20AF. I think food was OK on the ground when you could grab some chow hot or cold. On longer flights, mostly snack and such, we filled up before we left. Sometimes we didn't eat too much at all, it just depended on the mood you were in. But right after the war we flew low passes over POW camps dropping supplies to feed and take care of prisoners.

We would fly in real low, real slow . . . and have food and such packed tight on pallets. Right there at the end we would shove them off. Try to get as close as possible.

I looked down and we were all silent. Even from that height we could see the ribs of these guys on the ground. They looked like they were half dead.

Submitted by Jackson Tanner Fahl, United States Air Force.

Begging Your Pardon

I served for several years abroad during the tail end of WWII and then in Korea. Most chow lines were set up pretty good under the circumstances. I walked up to a chow line about a week before I shipped back to the states and the chow line had a HUGE variety of food for some reason. I guess a truck had come in or something along those lines. I blurted out that if I had known the food was going to get better then I would come back for another tour. A voice from behind me said, "Heck, we can arrange that with no problem!" I turned around while saying something along the lines of "F#&@#$ There is no #$%^&** way I would ever come back to this @#!$hole!" I mean I let some curse words fly because we were all pretty raw nerved by that time.

I turned around to be eyeball to eyeball with a full bird! I was so stunned that I did not move, or salute, or even take a breath. A couple of my buddies were standing there with mouths wide open and I could tell everyone was stunned. Finally I eased the words... "begging your pardon sir." I guess the look on my face was so funny looking that he just started laughing. I was still standing there when he finally said not to worry about it because that is almost the exact words he would have used! He patted me on the shoulder and moved on while everyone began to laugh.

Submitted by M. Walker—United States Army Retired

The Chicken Song

My deceased father, a WWII vet always sang us a song . . . at the dinner table when we didn't want to eat our chicken. I thought it would be a fun inclusion.

"Oh the chicken in the army is mighty, mighty fine,"

"One jumped off the table and started marching in time,"

"Oh I don't the Army any more..."

"Hey ma I wanna go,"

"Gee ma, I wanna go,"

"Hey ma, I wanna come home!"

Submitted by Patricia A. Haubner.

Knee Deep In Mud

I was an Army Cook in World War Two. I was overseas in France and Germany. Some days we could make a spread like a Sunday dinner back home and other times we just did our best to get coffee and bread served while standing knee deep in mud.

Submitted by C. Tucker—United States Army.

Cooking For All

My grandfather, Lionel Kahn fought in World War II. He did a lot of cooking, and he was known to make really quality meals. The higher-ups, generals and such, found out about him and wanted him to cook exclusively for them. He refused. He said (and I paraphrase because I don't remember exactly!) "I cook for everyone or I cook for no one."

Best Wishes,

Submitted by Tammy Kahn Fennell.

Death From Within

My dad was an Army cook when he served during WWII. When I was growing up he was always the guy that church leaders came to in order to get some barbecues or something going. He could feed a crowd of people without even thinking about it. He always had a great sense of humor about things. He would tell me that of you gave him a dozen eggs, coffee, a potato, a can of beans and some hot sauce he could feed 50 guys! He had an old shirt that one of his buddies gave him that said. "Army Cook - DEATH FROM WITHIN!" He loved fun things like that. Of course it was all in jest. He was very proud of the things he did while serving in the Army. He took his service very seriously. He passed away a few years ago.

Submitted by Glenda P., Daughter of an Army Cook, deceased.

Thinking of Dad

Hello: I never served in the military, but my late father did at the end of WWII and beginning of the Korean War. He was a Seabee, and he always told stories about "shit on a shingle" -- otherwise known as creamed dried beef on toast. I actually liked it when I was a kid, haven't had it in decades but it wasn't bad back then. You probably have heard about this from others, but I think of my dad often and your inquiry reminded me of him, so I thought I would honor his memory by sharing. Thanks, Lisa.

Submitted by Lisa Hildebrand, Green Bay, Wisconsin.

Pretend Pickles

I served in France. Things were still crazy but our supplies were finally catching up with us. A supply truck met our unit near a small town and started handing out boxes of this and that. I yelled across the group of men gathered and asked if they had anything pickled. "Pickled" answered the GI on the back of the supply truck. I said yep, anything pickled! I love pickles, relish, vegetables, eggs anything pickled and I was having a craving. The GI scratched his head, reached into a box and tossed me a package of rations. "Sorry buddy, I guess you will have to pretend this time!" Later when I was coming home I was eating real food for the first time in a long time and low and behold at the end of the line was a huge pan of pickles. I bet I ate about twenty of those things. The next day I was on a boat steaming stateside and sick as a dog throwing up pickles. I hate pickles still.

Submitted by L. Wilson.

PT Boat Memories

My recollections of military chow and sharing leave much to be desired. Our first assignment in the Pacific was as relief of 4 boats Ron 3 by 4 boats of Ron 11, designated as 11-2. We drew our rations from the Marines, and as you might imagine, anything edible they took firsts on, ergo we didn't fare too well and G.I. Rations were our staple of the day. After the Marine subjugation and elimination of Tarawa we went back SE and started up thru the Solomon's, where we drew our supplies from Naval stores and fared very well, considering. A rare luxury was making contact with a Merchant Marine ship, them boys really would give us their best, thanks in part or because of the "Armed Guard" . . . us.

Submitted by Beaty Lay —US. Navy retired.

Best Meal-Worst Meal

More than sixty-five years have passed since my best/worst Service-connected food experience took place. At the time, I was stationed at the Marine Corps Air Station, Cherry Point, N.C. One Sunday we were favored with a particularly tasty dinner of fried ham, sweet potatoes, and all the fixings. So good, in fact, I could not pass up a generous second helping, which, as it turned out, was a big mistake. During the night, I was awakened with severe stomach cramps and nausea and could not find anyone in my area of the barracks to help me. Somehow I dragged myself downstairs and out to the street, where I lay in the gutter until an ambulance (some passerby called) arrived to pick me up.

When I arrived at the hospital, I found a lot of other guys there who had all eaten in the same mess hall earlier in the day. Aside from the pain, we all were suffering from insatiable thirst and pleading for water, which the corpsmen would not give us, explaining that this would make us even sicker. Anyhow, there was a lot of moaning and groaning going on, with some guys pleading to be "put out of their misery." Fortunately, within a few days we all recovered and later found out the "tasty" ham had been stored without proper refrigeration before cooking, which caused us never-to-be-forgotten ptomaine poisoning.

Submitted by Walter J Irving, U.S. M. C. 1944.

A Big Steak Dinner

There were three great pleasures in being a submarine man. The first was arriving back in home port at the conclusion of a war patrol. War patrols could last as long as 8 weeks, so we carried plenty of food and 114,012 gallons of diesel fuel. We made our own fresh water from sea water. At the beginning of the patrol we lived off the fresh food we had in storage but towards the end of the patrol we ran out of fresh food and lived on canned, dried, and frozen food. When we arrived in port there was always a navy band playing to greet us. The first thing to come aboard was the on-site admiral, the second thing was our mail, and the third thing was case after case of fresh fruit and containers of fresh milk. I remember once sitting on deck and eating 4 fresh cantaloupes one right after the other washing then down with fresh milk. You can't sit on the deck of modern submarines because they have no decks. Before WWII submarine decks were quite spacious even though they had a very low freeboard. In calm weather underway we would sit on deck and smoke cigarettes and drink coffee and "shoot the shit" which is a favorite navy pastime and means carrying on a conversation. Following the fresh fruit and mail call we were generally taken to the submarine tender and served a big steak dinner.

From the papers of Dick Hawn USS Trout and the collection of Dave Hall.

PT Boat Meatballs By George

Welcome aboard! Cooking on a PT boat was almost non-existent, although we had a very small galley, electric hot plate and a shoe-box refrigerator. Electricity was available only when the generators were up, not often. So we ate rations, bummed food from some other units or ate at the base if we happened to be in port at mealtime. Each boat had a cook, but usually he was reprogrammed to be a gunner's mate or something useful. Our cook was a potato peeler from a large ship, court marshaled and sentenced to hazardous duty. Not much funny happened in the war theater, but when nerves are strung tight, a small diversion seemed funny.

We had a big Motor Mac with huge hands, my friend George. Once when we were scrounging for a meal, our PT tender allowed us to join them but wanted us to supply a man to assist in the galley. We volunteered George. The cook assigned him to make meatballs and instructed him to grab a handful of hamburger, force it into a ball and drop it into the grease. They came out about the size of tennis balls. The ship's cook thought George was trying to be funny and our Skipper finally had to apologize to the cook and explain the situation.

Submitted by Robert, USN, WW2 PTI 67.

No Smoke Roast Lamb

When I was in Scotland & England I trained with some Gurkha guys an exercise on not being found… evasion. Once them Gurkha boys caught a lamb, killed & cooked it in a ground oven so there was no smoke. I thought that was pretty nifty, could be useful. We were out three weeks; then walked into base.

Later I was in France with two Brit fellows after our truck was blown up. No one was hurt but we heard them Germans coming and we didn't want to meet them. We hid everywhere trying to get back. Used evasion . . . but that trick for cooking with no smoke, no good. We didn't see a damn lamb walk by anywhere. We made it about a week on the ground before meeting up with some GI's. Ate the heck out of a few cans of stew. Best damn stew ever.

Submitted by anonymous

Three Down, Three Up

Squadron 22 was in the Mediterranean. We enjoyed Navy base Mess Halls and only had snacks on the boat and of course plenty of hot coffee. After VE Day, the Navy gave our food rations to the local French restaurants at Cape de Antibes and we had all our meals served to us from May t through June after which time we were on our way home to the USA via Oran, Africa.

Fresh French bread and Spam was my favorite snack. The rest of the crew thought I was nuts. To this poor kid from the slums of Cambridge, Spam on fresh French bread with plenty of butter was a treat. It is to this day.

I got sea sick all the time. Therefore I had six meals a day, three down and three up. Don't knock it. You never saw a fat sailor. Wish I could say the same thing for me right now. Bring on the Spain and rough seas.

Sincerely, Arthur John Frongello QM31C PT 302, Ron 22

You Get What You Ask For

I asked a cook in the mess to make me some eggs like he liked them. He said he hated eggs and handed my plate back with some toast only.

Submitted by anonymous

Earl's PT Boat Cooking Memories

I was the cook on PT Boat 108. There was no worse meal, or best meal, to cook on a pt boat. You had to use what you were able to scrounge up from the base or beg from another larger ship. Once we traded all our cigarettes with an Australian Korvette for fresh lamb, liver and chicken. Needless to say we had to start cooking right away until it was all cooked up. It would have gone bad on us quickly as we had not enough refrigeration space to keep it. The whole crew took turns cooking, eating and cleaning up. Another cook and I "borrowed" some crates from a guarded barge that had loaded from a ship in the harbor.

When we got back to our boats we found we had "borrowed" chocolate malts/candy and cookies. We split the proceeds. If we fished while at the buoy we cleaned and cooked them up. We also asked some natives who had speared large sea turtles thru the neck for a few. We dragged them to the beach where we cut the meat out and cooked it up. It seems that the pt boats and pt bases were the last ones on the island bases to get food. We only had one fresh egg the whole time I was on a pt base or ship. We hardly had any fresh meat. It was mostly dehydrated or powdered stuff. We did the best we could with what we had. It wasn't much but the crews were so hungry they ate almost anything I could cook up.

We stored our canned goods where ever we could find space. We stored stuff in the galley bilge or even under officer's bunks and in cabinets etc. We made ice cream in the ice trays. We always had coffee on even though it was hot out because it seemed that it helped us cool off some. We made our own maple syrup. We took jelly and diluted it a little with water and a little sugar and made popsicles in freezer. I always had sandwiches made up for the men to eat while going to or returning from patrols. I also stood watches topside/was loader on stem 20 nun/gunner on twin fifties.

For the spam I fried up the spam and then put it in a pot with my home made sauce made up of tomatoes/peas/catsup/salt/pepper/pimientos/onions/and chopped green peppers if i had them. We had a little problem with some pilots strafing the boats at night as they could not make out if we were a pt boat or Jap barges. The pilots were told to take rides on the boats so they could become familiar with them. I had to serve my evening meals, when going on patrols just after we left base as the further out we got the rougher it would become. It was rough to see that cup of coffee, knife or utensil that was intended to put food in your mouth all of a sudden go up past your mouth and then being brought back down. So I tried to feed the men when it was as soon as possible after getting underway.

I had to find out if and who our passengers were going to be and make up food supply list to draw from the base every day in order to make meals for patrols or at buoys. I had to draw extra food for this just in case I had to prepare the meals, clean up afterwards and then stand watch. There was always something to do.

Submitted by Earl Richmond PT I08 US Navy Retired.

New Guinea, New Ice

We had befriended a local couple of brothers, about nine years and six years old. We had trouble communicating with them. New Guinea natives were forbidden to enter our harbor for what that's worth. These kids had never seen ice or even felt anything that cold. We had a rare treat of ice from somewhere and gave the kids some. They giggled and screamed, put it in their mouth and stepped on it. The older one wanted to take some home to his mother. He wrapped up a couple of cubes in his shirt and headed home in 95 degree heat, he indicated he lived about an hour away. We saw him a couple times after that and he said he got home with nothing but a wet shirt. Simple things we took for granted were miracles to those poor kids. I wish we had had ice cream!

Submitted by Robert (Bob) Pickett, PTBoat 167 US Navy retired, www.rpickett.com

Great Glove Coffee

Lou Shirey took a cook's tour of Europe. But it was no picnic. Shirey, born Llewellyn E. Shirey in June 1921 in Robesonia, was a cook in Patton's 3rd Army. "We landed in France two months after D-Day and we moved east," Lou said. "Patton was right: The 80th never went backwards."

He was assigned to B Battery, 313th Field Artillery Battalion, 80th

Infantry Division. Lou was plagued by sergeants who wanted coffee at all hours of the day and night and then complained about how it tasted. "One morning the 1st sergeant was praising my coffee," Lou recalled. "I didn't tell him I later found one of my leather work gloves at the bottom of the pot."

Courtesy of Dan Kelly, a reporter for the Reading Eagle, Lou's local newspaper in Reading, PA.

No More Parrot Stew

The Mess Tent on Green Island in March of 1944.
From the collection of the National Archives.

This is a tale from an island far, far away at a time long, long ago. Specifically, Stirling Island in what is now the nation of the Solomon Islands. Food was very, very scarce and monotonous as our little, green "plywood" warships, actually just overgrown speedboats, tied up to the trees in one of several inlet arms. We could rest there, rearm and refuel before going out to beard the Imperial Japanese Navy and Army in their own lairs. The trees provided cover from the constant air raids with Jap planes hoping to smash our puny onslaught against them.

We were all in danger of contracting scurvy with the shortage of nourishing, fresh food, so the cooks on our boat, a guy named Larson, a Ship's Cook First Class, decided to build us a stew. France, Ship's Cook Third

Class, who was his helper, were really not doing much as "belly-robbers" or "stew burners" otherwise. They were included in the crew mostly to man the guns. The PT Base, was it 9 (?), was supposed to feed us after we had trekked through the jungle and after we had dipped our mess kits in a boiling, 55-gallon drum of disinfectant.

Now, the PT-103 for some odd Bureau of Ships reason had in its equipage a couple of .22 rifles down in the armory just behind the wardroom. And flocks of white parrots or perhaps cockatoos lived in the trees we were hiding under. "Parrot stew" it would be, so a couple of us began "harvesting" the birds. They would land and they would die.

Finally, we had collected enough so that with some withered vegetables begged from a nearby seaplane tender, we kids could feast right there on the boat. We had to be very careful to avoid the tiny bones. The beautiful birds filled our empty bellies and we enjoyed a respite from "corned willy," "meat and vegetable stew ration" and whatever that was in cans labeled as "Vienna sausage."

Later, our diet became largely coconut as those three entrees became unbearable. Ripe coconut like you can buy in a supermarket. Green coconut with a Jello-like substance and overripe coconuts containing a palm tree bud that became our "salad."

Little did we know that shark was delicious and even octopus tastes great. The "word" was out that most of the tropical ocean's denizens were poisonous! For some still-unfathomable reason the Navy always provided canned grapefruit juice for us to be forced to drink, also to prevent scurvy. A canteen cup of that was used to wash down the daily Atabrine tablet that was supposed to prevent malaria. If the Supply "wienies" managed to get that vile stuff to us, we called it battery acid, why didn't we get better or at least a larger variety of food?

The point? To this day, no grapefruit and no coconut. Now, I haven't tried parrot stew of late . . .

Submitted by Jack H. Duncan, Master Chief retired.

Now That's Fishing

The PT boats of our Motor Torpedo Boat Squadron 5 sneaked into the lagoon via the north passage in the reef at Green Island. I was one of several of the crew standing lookout on the bow as we very slowly inched our

182

way in with the coral heads clearly visible just below our hull. It was touchy inasmuch as our Nineteenth Century British Admiralty navigational charts were often wrong. It was February of 1944.

Green is a large atoll some forty to forty-five miles north of the large island of Bougainville, the top of the Solomon Island chain. Currently Bougainville is the dividing line between the nations of the Solomon Islands and Papua New Guinea with gold-rich Bougainville and the islands north of it part of Papua New Guinea. Green's lagoon seemed huge and idyllic in comparison with the more rugged, volcanic Solomon's.

I believe we were the very first boat into the lagoon while landing craft were still invading the islands from the outside everything seemed secure, so we proceeded a short distance to the east inside the lagoon where a nice beach seemed inviting. Dropping our anchor off the stern, the fragile plywood bow was eased up onto the sand. Jumping off the boat to the beach, we started to explore our surroundings when . . . WHOOSH, BLAM!

Some Allied artillery units began shooting over our heads at concealed Jap positions just yards beyond us. Someone was able to contact the gunners that we were there and also to arrange for a landing craft to bring us gasoline in drums so we could refuel and get on with the business at hand of eradicating Japanese military personnel.

From Green Island, our boats were able to run patrols up to Rabaul on New Britain, Namatanai on New Ireland and some surrounding islands where the Japanese had established small bases. As the island was secured, we began to set up housekeeping there on the beach. We moved empty gasoline drums to use as steps to get on and off the boat. Some of us purloined those excellent Japanese Army tropical shirts from those who no longer needed them. Lowell, a Motor Machinist's Mate First Class, even got a pair of Jap climbing boots . . . the kind that had the big toe separate from the rest of the boot.

Back on the boat, I spotted some fish off the stern of the PT-103; little pan-sized fish by the thousands. Food! Grabbing two hand grenades (we were forbidden to carry them—ha!) from the cockpit, I pulled the pins and threw the grenades into that huge school. Stunned fish floated to the surface by the score. The crew grabbed pans, helmets, buckets, whatever and over the side we went, gathering the harvest. Those two grenades fed most of the squadron with delicious little fried fish of some kind, augmenting the so-called rations of "corned willy" which everyone agreed with canned horse from Australia.

We also had sugar-sweet "meat and vegetable stew ration" in blue lacquered cans plus Vienna sausages. Those were our three entrees week after week along with every kind of coconut. Ripe coconut; the kind with meat you can grate. Green coconut; with its jelly-like meat. Over-ripe coconut; you ate the new nut growing inside, staying away from the meat which caused diarrhea.

Was it sporting to get fish that way? Of course not! It was an effective, though, to feed a bunch of hungry, half-wild, teen-aged kids with not enough palatable victuals to eat and far, far from home.

Isn't it strange how much of the privation and stress of combat fades as time goes on, but interludes such as this fish-fry linger on in the memory? This is military service . . . good times, bad times and boring times, camaraderie with people with whom you are close, but may never see again.

Submitted by Jack H. Duncan, Master Chief retired.

What The . . .

Here's one of my favorite memories of my year and half on a Higgins PT. We had a cook who was the calmest individual I've ever known a cook to be, but there was one notable exception. The guys were fishing from the bow of the boat and when they landed a nice one it flopped off the deck and got away. They decided to drop the next one through the hatch into the crew's quarters which is also the galley. Tate, the cook, was down there fixing chow, but they didn't think about that. They dropped the next fish on the table and it flopped off and all over the deck with Tate yelling at 'em, "What the f--- Y'all doin up theah."

Regards, Ken Nissen.

Some of Dad's Stories

These are some things my dad, Randall J. McConnell Jr., commander of the PT 36, told me about his food memories. I know he will not eat anything with beans in it; chili, three-bean salad, etc. after being in the Navy. He will occasionally eat baked beans, but that's it. He has also commented on how bad the food was. His squadron (27) often operated from open water rather than being at a shore base.

The PTs would 'nest' alongside the USS Varuna, a PT tender. The attached picture is of the Varuna and PTs in Subic Bay; photo credited to my father. He said that the food was prepared on the tender and passed down to the first boat in large pots, and then passed down the line to succeeding boats. He commented that they would pass every pot to the last boat where the contents would be dumped overboard. I'm sure there's some exaggeration to the story.

Grabbing some chow. To the best of my knowledge the picture was taken by Jerry Nolan, commander of PT 359. It's from the collection of my father Randall J. McConnell Jr., commander of the PT 361.
From the private collection of Randall J. McConnell III.

When I asked what they ate if they dumped the Navy food, he said they would barter with the local population for food. I doubt they did that for every meal. They would trade bed sheets that were provided by the tender but rarely used.

They also did hand grenade fishing. They'd take natives on the boat to good fishing sites, and lob in a grenade. The concussion would stun the fish and they'd float to the surface, but they would sink right away because their air sacs were ruptured. The natives would dive in and collect the fish before they sank.

They would show the sailors which ones were safe to eat, and divvied up the catch with the sailors. The rule of thumb was; the more colorful the fish the more likely to be poisonous. They did have an incident where a native dove in before the grenade went off. He floated up with the fish but didn't suffer any permanent injury.

From the collection of Randall J. McConnell Jr., commander of the PT 361. Submitted by, Randall J. McConnell III.

The Tuaca Italian Liquer Story
Mr. Whitaker:

Tuaca's inspiration may be traced back to the 15th century Renaissance, a period of cultural enlightenment throughout Italy. It is said that a brandy-based liqueur was created for Lorenzo the Magnificent, a ruler of Florence, Italy, and member of the Medici family. Lorenzo was considered by many as one of the greatest leaders of Renaissance times due to his patronage to the arts supporting such luminaries as Michelangelo, Leonardo da Vinci, and Botticelli. Lorenzo passed away just before the beginning of the "Age of Exploration" six months before Christopher Columbus set sail for the New World.

In 1938 Gaetano Tuoni and Giorgio Canepa, brothers-in-law, took inspiration from their Renaissance predecessors and re-created this legendary spirit. They crafted the liqueur based on their knowledge of a Renaissance recipe that had become popular so many years earlier. Gaetano and Giorgio derived the brand name from their own surnames and called it "Tuoca", which evolved to "Tuaca" over time.

The scene depicted on the Tuaca label is taken from a set of breath taking bronze doors that were created by Lorenzo Ghiberti in 1425 and are located on the eastern side of the ancient Baptistery next to the historic Duomo Cathedral in Florence. Michelangelo was so moved by the work decades later that he dubbed the doors "The Gates of Paradise".

Gaetano Tuoni had been a pilot and instructor in the Italian Air Force in the early 1930's but had resigned before the start of World War II. An anti-fascist, he became a leader of the Resistance movement in nearby Lucca. His group captured Tassignano Airport, near Lucca, from the Germans and held that strategically important position several days until the advancing American and British forces arrived. After the war, the Italian government honored him with the title of Comandante. Interestingly, the expansion of Tuaca is rooted in military beginnings.

Tuaca was first exported to America in the 1950's after American servicemen were introduced to the brand in the Livorno area and demand grew in the states. Since, the brand has become a favorite among bartenders who appreciate Tuaca's unique taste and versatility. It has subsequently spread to the U.K and Australia as a result of the interest taken by bartenders that have discovered the brand.

Submitted by Tuaca Italian Liqueur and the Baddish Group.

Sub Hangover Corned Beef

After a particularly exuberant night on the beach, while serving on the USS Bashaw (AGSS 241), we returned to the boat considerably hung over. One of our Filipino stewards told us he had a recipe that would get rid of our hangovers. Being ready to try anything we told him to bring it on! After a while he brought us each a plate with a helping of what turned out to be a Corned beef with lots of onions and tomatoes. After forcing it down and a cup of strong coffee we were amazed that not long after our headaches were gone and in general we felt much better! You figure it out!!!!!

The recipe is as follows:

1 can of corned beef

1 large onion

1 large tomato

Cut up the onion so that you have fairly large crescent shaped pieces. Place in frying pan with some butter and simmer until onion is tender. Add corned beef to frying pan and heat mixture until corned beef is warmed completely. While this is proceeding cut tomato into pieces similar to onion, after above mixture is heated add tomato pieces, gently mix so have a good mixture, continue heating until tomato is just warmed. Remove from heat and serve. Tastes great but can't promise it will cure hangovers!!!!!!

Submitted by Richard Hughes (Lt. SS).

Third Call Surprise

As a new kid, fresh out of "A" school and Sub School aboard, CROAKER it was a bit of a shock to me the day we ran out of ham at the noon meal and those of us in "Third Call" were stuck with steak. Never saw that happen in a shore duty mess hall.

Submitted by Dave Buchholz USS Croaker SS 246, USS Trigger SS 564.

Doc Parrish Remembers the Cook On "Scabby"

And then there was the Golden Greek 'Nicholas Constantine Christodoulou, the ship's cook who had expected to be a Navy Musician. He could play just about any wind instrument, but he couldn't read music and wanted the Navy to teach him how, and during wartime at that. But anyhow, his old man ran a restaurant back in Welch, McDowell County, Wes By Gawd Virginia in the coalfields where coalminers will just about eat anything put in front of them, they don't care you know! Dad told his little boy NEVER TO BE A COOK! (Guess his old Daddy knew more about his son than the Navy Classification yeoman, because the desk jockey saw that hellacious name, yelled with glee-Greek! Cooks & Bakers School for YOU!)

As the Ship's Medic, I can honestly say that 'Christy' hated that job. First, he almost chopped off his left hand with a meat cleaver, accidental of course, it was a mechanical device he didn't know how to operate, it got infected and I had to treat him with Sulfa drugs, sew him Up with cat-gut', and with plenty of hot soaks, I managed to pull him through. My beautiful stitching scars still show today!

The Skipper, Admiral Now, Lt. Cmdr. Then, Gunn, directed me to inspect the Galley DAILY. In the due course of this performance of duty, I went back and asked Nick what we were having for lunch. "Roast Chicken" he said, pulling a black pan from the oven. Now, you understand, I'd been in the Navy a long, long time, Regular Navy at that, and I quickly observed that the chickens were trussed with a familiar looking string. I said, "Nick, where did you get that string?" "Back in the Boatswain's Locker," says he, "in the after room." My favorite cook, Nicholas Constantine Christodoulou, had tied up the chickens with coal-tar impregnated MARLIN.

I pulled a chicken leg off and tasted it, YUK AND MORE YUK ... the phenolic taste was so strong, we fed the fish Roast thicken that day, and we had cold cuts something we ate most of the time when 'Christodoulou had the watch. It is of some interest, and maybe scientific study in case the Navy needs something to do, to find out why the fish wouldn't even eat Nick's roast chicken. We watched in amazement as the fish spat it back out.

From the writings "Ships Cook Christodoulou to The Captain!"
Submitted by the author Nick Christodoulou, Navy.

"Ships Cook CHRISTODOULOU to the Captain!"

I remember little things like sunny-side eggs stretched out three feet long when the ship rolls from starboard to port and the eggs follow gravity. The vision sickens me to this day. Or how about over-filled stew-pots either boiling over down onto the deck plates, or sliding off the range because I forgot to install the sea-mils at the end and sides of the range? There was another time when I was mixing a cake in the electric mixer in the galley, and playing 'poker, and winning' in the crew's mess waiting for the temperature in the oven to get just tight, when a 5 lb. can of baking powder was added to the cake mix a tablespoon at a time by several crew members seeking their revenge. Looking at the ship's clock, and noticing that it was time to get the cake in the oven ... I rushed into the galley, shut off the mixer, poured the cake mix into a greased pan, shoved same into the hot oven, wiped my hands on a dirty dishrag, and hurried back to my winnings.

I had been set up cause I couldn't play poker any better than I could cook, not

knowing What hand beat what hand, if you know what I mean. I should have noticed the excessive bubbles in the cake mix, for about five minutes later there was a muffled sound from the galley, followed by billowing, chocking black smoke! The cake had exploded inside

the oven, what with 5 lbs of baking powder lacing it ... the boat filled with smoke, the crew coughing and gagging, 'Pop' ordered emergency surface to air out the boat, followed by what was to become very familiar words to me, "SHIP'S COOK CHRISTODOULOU TO THE CAPTAIN."

I staggered my way to the Captain's Office, and he looks me straight in his eye, says he, "WHAT THE HELL AREYOU TRYING TO DO, SINK MYSHIP?" I tried to explain what happened, and being a reasonable man and a good skipper, he didn't hear a damn word I said ... Oh, well, that's naval officers for you!

From the writings "Ships Cook Christodoulou to The Captain!"
Submitted by the author Nick Christodoulou, Navy

Earl Richmond—PT Boat Galley Cook

I was a cook on pt 108. I would like to try and "clear up" our somewhat bad reputation for the cooking. We cooks did try our best to make the meals as palatable as possible but since we were on the move so much we could only cook what we got rationed to us. It seems like we only got what was left after the other services got theirs. We did not get much. It was either dehydrated or dried, etc. Yes, we got a LOT of spam and canned corned beef, canned pork sausage, canned Vienna sausage. That was about the limit of the meats. We tried every way we could to kill the taste of the spam. It still turned out like spam.

My best recipe was to make a tomato sauce, with onions and drained canned peas. I fried the spam part way and put it in a pan and poured the sauce over it. They men sort of liked that. They even used bread to sop up the sauce. On behalf of all the cooks that tried to do the best we could for our shipmates. After all, we had to eat the same meals too. a lot more to being am cook than cooking."

Submitted by Earl Richmond, Cook, PT 108—United States Navy.

Keeping it Safe!

I was the cook on PT boat 108. It seems like our biggest problem was keeping the food safe to eat because of the extreme heat in the galley. For some reason we all wanted something sweet to eat at breakfast and we all had orange marmalade, I still don't like marmalade. I guess it was to kill the taste of the other stuff.

We had plenty of Vienna sausage, we had a lot of hard cheese too. Besides eating it we also used it for fish bait!

Sometimes we were at treasury which I mostly stayed up at the base all the time in a tent with a foxhole outside it. I did stand watch at the upper part of the trail leading down to the boat area at night. Some times at the base galley we would store supplies next to the boat on skids that were covered with tarp. I usually was the first cook to go on duty at the galley. I started cooking breakfast at 4 am. One morning, in the dark, we heard a loud noise coming from the storage area next to the galled. The duty guard ran over to check it out with me. We found the tarp uncovered from the canned goods with some cans knock over. We never did see who was there. The noise of the cans falling must have scared them off. We assumed that somehow a Jap had tried to steal some food. They were still around the area during this time.

Submitted by Earl Richmond, Cook, T 108—United States Navy.

Noodles & Beer

One guy told me that he and a buddy stashed a whole bunch of pasta noodles away for a meal only to have it rain and an officer noticed the crate of oozing noodles and maggots. When he opened the crate lid the officer started heaving and was sick for an hour or so. Another told me he was saving a big bar of chocolate for a late in the day snack. He traded it for something better and by the end of the day had a few six packs of beer and a meal. He learned the art of bartering!

Submitted by G.R.

The Best Than Can Be Said about C Rations

Every solider can tell tales of Army chow, pick any era from any army the world over and you will soon understand that stories abound. My subject is C Rations of the Vietnam War time period which in military jargon were known as "Meal, Combat, Individual." About the best that can be said about C Rations (C Rats) is that, as food, they kept you alive, even healthy, and were vastly better fare than, say, your common Civil War ration and steady diet of hard tack and bacon. Well, except for the hard tack which was present in C Rations and issued at that time as simply "Crackers," which came in a little tin can containing seven of them and they were not a jot different than civil war era hard tack.

Each cracker was a quarter inch thick soda cracker about three inches across and, believe me, you could very easily break a tooth on one, in fact you didn't dare eat them right out of the can but soaked them in something before biting down. Soaking them immediately turned them into a sort of whitish-gray flavorless mush—so, the best thing to do with a C Rat cracker was Frisbee it at your buddies head and forget about it. C Rations came twelve meals to a case, each case contained three "Units" made up of various entrées and accessory items, B-1, B-2, B-3.

An example of at B-1 unit is the following:
- Meat: Ham and Eggs, Chopped (this was a greenish looking mushy mess)
- Fruit: Fruit Cocktail (just like you can purchase at any grocery store today)
- Crackers (7) (we know about these already)
- Peanut Butter (darned good actually—and organic!)

191

- Candy Disc, Chocolate (very hard, semi-sweet, pretty good)
- Accessory Pack: Spoon (plastic, Salt, Pepper, Coffee, Instant, Sugar, Creamer—non-dairy,
- Gum—two Chicklets,
- Cigarettes—four to a small pac
- Matches—moisture resistant
- Toilet Paper (small roll of a few sheets).

Submitted by Dave Parks.

Six Meals A Day

Squadron 22 was in the Med. We enjoyed Navy base Mess Halls and only had snacks on the boat and of course plenty of hot coffee. After VE Day, the Navy gave our food rations to the local French restaurants at Cape de Antibes and we had all our meals served to us from May t through June after which time we were on our way home to the USA via Oran, Africa.

Fresh French bread and Spam was my favorite snack. The rest of the crew thought I was nuts. To this poor kid from the slums of Cambridge, Spam on fresh French bread with plenty of butter was a treat. It is to this day.

Don't forget, I got sea sick all the time. Therefore I had six meals a day, three down and three up. Don't knock it. You never saw a fat sailor. Wish I could say the same thing for me right now. Bring on the Spam and rough seas.

Sincerely, Arhtur John Frongello QM3/C PT 302, Ron 22.

Basic Eats

In basic, when I went, They always said, "Take all you want, but, eat all you take!" You only have a few minutes to gulp down your food and the DS are posted at the door to make sure that your trays are cleaned off, well, I had two pats of butter left, guess what I had to do before I can leave the chow hall?! The trainee behind me put his sunny side up eggs in his field jacket pocket and got caught!

Submitted by anonymous.

General Foods

We had a General visiting my post(very small post in Germany) and we got steak cooked to order as well a steamed shrimp. . . Surf and turf.

And the best thing is that I did not have to coat it in Tabasco sauce! Thanks— Joe

Submitted by Joe.

Them Boys Tried Hard

I don't talk much about this but I do have a good food story for you. One thing I remember was how hungry we were most of the time. I was in France and lots of the rations were just enough to get you through when you had them. But lots of times during the first few months things were very slow getting to us. Sometimes we moved around so much our supplies could not keep up. Them boys tried hard though. After a while things started flowing in good. I remember us coming into a pretty big spread before I left and I had a real hot meal. I almost couldn't eat much because I was so used to not having nothing in my stomach worth talking about. That hot food felt like the best tasting lump in my belly. I was so full it hurt. But it was good. The next best meal I had was at home. Thank you for asking and remembering.

Submitted by anonymous.

Fighting the Same

Lots of people think that military food is not good. But I had some of the best meals I had ever had when I was in during World War Two. I cooked a bunch of it. Sure we had the rations as well. It is amazing how many mouths we could feed in a short time. Pots, pans, stoves, men, serve, wash done and do it again. All of the recipes for everything were for one hundred plus guys and hard to make better or mess up. We did take care not to do too bad of a job because we all were fighting the same.

Submitted by B.R., Army Retired, WWII veteran.

"Getter" Joe

You made me think about this story and it has been a while. I was in pacific towards the end and was stationed there several months after the war ended. We ate pretty good most of the time. During the war I had one really funny thing happen. We had a guy we called the "getter" this Joe could GET anything it seemed like. One day about four real mad looking MP's came by moaning about somebody lifting some supplies that were supposed to be for some bigs flying in. We all just shrugged and did not give it a thought. They moved on and old Getter just sat there until they were gone, didn't say a word. Next thing you know we all had a beer. Getter tossed all of us a beer, a cold beer. Somebody said "dag gum Getter your gonna get us in trouble with those MP's if they see us drinking this beer." He just said, "Well ya stupid idiot. Don't let them see ya drinking it!" He told me years later that he traded some other items from our unit with the MP's that came by that day and they were doing their job acting like they were searching for it.

Submitted by Randal S.—United States Army.

Quartermaster Cook Under Fire

When the 30th Infantry Regiment hit the beach at Anzio in January 1944, one of those to go ashore as a Quartermaster-turned-Infantryman, was the First Cook assigned to India Company—Tech 5 Eric G. Gibson. In the months before, Specialist Gibson worked out a deal with his CO that whenever the company went into battle, he could serve as a rifleman in one of the Infantry squads and go out on patrol. But as soon as B-rations were available, he had to return to his regular duties in the kitchen. Under this arrangement, First Cook Gibson wound up leading a pack train across several miles of rugged mountainous terrain in Sicily. Later he served as the Company's number one scout, locating several enemy positions, and managed to kill one German soldier and wounded another in succeeding firefights. He continued with his dual missions—as Company Cook and Number One Scout—and repeatedly distinguished himself in combat along the Italian coastline, after the battle of Anzio.

Then on 28 January 1944, Tech 5 Gibson joined the ranks of the immortal. Around 1200 hours, near the village of Isola Bella, Italy, India Company came under withering enemy attack. Gibson, with a tiny squad of replacements rushed out to secure the unit's right flank—and in so doing, destroyed four enemy positions, killing 5 and capturing 2 Germans. He then went out a full 50 meters in front of the squad, and running, leaping, dodging automatic weapons fire, he single-handedly knocked out another position with his machine-pistol.

He continued moving toward other bunkers, firing a submachine gun with almost every step forward, as enemy artillery began to zero in on his

194

position. Nonstop automatic weapons rounds passed within inches of his body, yet he never paused in his forward movement. He crawled much of the last 125 meters right through a concentrated artillery and small arms barrage, and dropped two hand grenades into a German machinegun emplacement—killing two more and wounding another. And was in one final face-to-face engagement when an enemy round finally cut him down.

For his conspicuous gallantry and PERSONAL COURAGE under fire, Tech 5 Gibson was awarded the Medal of Honor—one of 33 Quartermasters to receive that high honor.

Compiled by the U.S. Army Quartermaster Corps Historian Fort Lee, Virginia

Mutton Stew?

I remember some pretty bad mutton stew they served us on my first day in basic training. It was mutton stew with Navy beans. . . for breakfast. We had mutton stew a few times a week it seemed like somebody there really liked making it or they just had a bunch left over. It was horrible. I started in Ft. Belvoir in Maryland then headed to Mississippi, Alabama then to Louisiana in the Army Air Corps.

I think Keesler had about 26 mess halls that served thousands of men each a day, three times a day. Some of the food was pretty good over the years at different places. When I got paid I would eat as many meals at the PX as I could.

The worst thing for me was KP duty because we had to clean the grease traps and kettles. But they made a wonderful pancake on Saturdays and on Sundays we had pineapple fritters with some type of syrup. That was the best. That was at Keesler in Mississippi. But, the worst food I ever had in the military was the mutton stew and navy beans I had that first day. I still remember how bad that was.

Bob Williams—Army Corps of Engineers, retired

Real Meal

I flew bombers during World War Two. I flew lots of times with some great guys that didn't come back. I remember sometimes we had some rations in cans and stuff that were ok and other times we could actually have some good food packed up for us. The best was never the ration food.

The best was when "real" meal. Maybe some sandwiches and stuff. It all depended on what the whole unit had and what we could bargain for. Once it was so cold we had hot food loaded up for the flight and by the time we got up and had a chance to snack on anything it was already cold. It was almost frozen. Those long flights were rough. Some-times we got real hungry because they could take so long and other times I just didn't feel like eating anything.

Submitted by J. May—United States Army Air Corps.

They Forgot We Needed Food!!

On my PT boat It seemed like the Navy forgot we needed food, so we improvised, scavenged and begged. Only, we did have a small stock of C and K rations, mostly because patrols could be more than 12 hours long. Also, some PT tenders would not feed us unless we were there at regular chow time. I doubt that rations ever saved our lives, but they were sure appreciated when we needed them.

Submitted by Robert (Bob) Pickett, PT Boat 167—US Navy retired, www.rpickett.com.

Quarter Master Letter

No one seems ever to think a soldier in QM ever gets to smell any gun-powder, dig any foxholes, get into any fighting, go without food, mail and the like. Our QM outfit hit the beach on D-day right when the heat was on, and more outfits are hitting the beaches every day—to unload and load rations, ammunition, and all other equipment and supplies. Opening and running dumps under combat conditions is a tough job. We sleep in foxholes, wash and shave in helmets, dig slit trenches, eat in the open as do other Army outfits. We also have bazooka men, machine-gun men and operate twenty-four hours a day—about fifty percent of that time in the rain and mud.

Private First Class, James P. Hatchell,
(in a letter to the Stars and Stripes Newspaper, August 10, 1944)
Quarter Master Museum Fort Lee Virginia.

Thanks To The Cooks

I can honestly say that much of the time during the war I did not think of food at all. I was hungry some times, but I can't really say food was it. I wanted to do my job and go home to my girl. I knew every minute that I was going home. Even when I was shot I knew I was going home in one piece. But, when I heard you were looking for stories one came to me in seconds. I was in the pacific and things were tough supply wise. But the cooks never let us down. They worked their job and the manned guns and positions. Once after complaining about food one afternoon to one of the cooks we had a few Jap planes come over and take a swipe at us. The cook I complained to stood right next to me and loaded and shot like crazy. His name was Marty and after that fight he told me this. "I take ya'lls shit all day long about food (meaning us guys), I don't have to take anything from those sons of bitches!" I never complained about food again.

Submitted by K.S. Jr.

Spam & Pineapple

I remember the way our cook made Spam. I still have a craving for Spam these days because he would make it taste just about like anything. Granted, I didn't know much about good food growing up and I ate pretty good in the war for the most part. I lost a lot of weight over the couple of years I was in the pacific area but not as bad as lots of other poor men that were prisoners and starved. I remember one time all we had was about a box of Spam and some salt and pepper. We were all pretty tired of Spam and powdered eggs. Our cook came back from a run and had about five pineapples with him. He sliced them up and fried them with the spam and we ate that on some toast. It was pretty good. I still eat a Spam and Pineapple sandwich every once in a while. It tasted like a Christmas ham.

Submitted by C.T.

Kissing the Red Cross

I was coming back from Europe and had not really eaten or slept good in about six months. Seemed like we walked across Europe on our bellies behind tanks for years!! I remember looking over at one of my buddies, Thomas was his name, and telling him when I got home I was going to kiss the ground when I got off the boat. He said matter of factly. "Bob, I'm gonna kiss ANYTHING when I get anywhere close to home!" That became a joke between us and some other guys about Kissing this and that. What we would kiss first. About two months later we were rotated back to ship over and we were standing in line waiting to get some new clothes since our uniforms were so torn up and this Red Cross group walked up and gave us some things to eat and even offered us some coffee.

I didn't know what to think. For months we had almost nothing then I was standing there with some hot coffee and doughnuts. Years later I got a letter from Thomas saying that when he got home he saw a poster for the Red Cross at the bus station and he walked over and kissed it!

Submitted by Bob. C—US Army Retired.

Mess Hammocks

When the war was over, we took on about 1,000 passengers. We were transporting them from Okinawa to Pearl. Some stayed on until Boston. They all had to sleep in the Mess Decks in hammocks.

Paul Wieser, Boatswain's Mate 1/c, Courtesy of Battleship North Carolina.

Roach Bombs

Many of the memories in this book about PT boat cooking, and life on a PT are courtesy of Earl Richmond. During World War Two Earl served on PT 108 as a cook and baker and during General Quarters he jumped in as loader for the stern 20mm's. He also manned the twin 50mm's while standing watch on PT 108. While on shore during the war Earl also served as a cook and baker at various bases. Earl (pictured on right) takes a break with some of his buddies in 1945 while serving in the Philippines.
Photo courtesy of Earl Richmond.

On the PT boat we had to keep watch for roaches and rats. We had de-contamination detail one time. We threw "bombs" into the compartments and closed all the hatches for about 20 minutes/we all stood topside with brooms and whatever we could use and opened the hatches. The bugs and rats swarmed out of the hatches and we swept, kicked and pushed as many as we could over the side of the boat. The fish gathered all around the boat and really had a feast. Anybody watching and didn't know what we were doing must have thought we were a bunch of nuts gone wacky.

Submitted by Earl Richmond, Cook, PT 108—United States Navy.

First One Served

The first one served is the Officer of the Deck. He had to come down and look at the chow and eat it. If it is suitable to him, then the chow line starts. If there were any grievance he has about the looks of it or the taste of it, then the chow line would be secured until all this would be taken care of. There was seldom any time the chow line wasn't palatable. We ate very well on here. We had fresh baked goods all the time. They'd be baking pies and cakes and jelly doughnuts. We had ice cream all the time.

Chief Herbert L. Sisco, Courtesy of Battleship North Carolina.

Spam Burgers

I ate more Spam than you can imagine. We had Spam for every meal and for snacks it seems like. But I love the stuff. I still eat a good Spam Burger now and then. Just slice it thick and heat it up in a pan with some toast. Sometimes I add cheese and hot sauce. That's another thing we had a lot of with every meal . . . hot sauce.

Submitted by Johnny T.

Saving a Stuck Turkey

One Thanksgiving a huge turkey caught one of its legs in the dumbwaiter shaft and the turkey was stuck between decks. I volunteered to hang down the shaft and liberate the turkey. The other officers lowered me into the dumbwaiter shaft while holding my feet. Of course, I liberated the turkey by eating the drumstick, which caused the jamming. At 19 I had a rather prodigious appetite.

Ensign Richard Comen, Courtesy of Battleship North Carolina.

Famous Chefs

We had wonderful food while I was on the Ship. The Officer's Galley was fortunate in having an ex-chef from the Boston Lobster House. We also had an ex-dessert chef from an equally famous Boston restaurant.

Lieutenant (jg) Tracy H. Wilder, Courtesy of Battleship North Carolina.

Leftover Pies

I knew one guy on the ship that I grew up with. He was in the same high school I was. He was in the bake shop. Now, I was fortunate to know him because if anything was left over, he would call up the engine room, 'Neumann, send up a messenger. I have some leftover pies.' I would send up the messenger and he would come down with the pies. I always had something to eat. He would make a pie or a cake. He would actually make a flat pizza pie and he would send some down to us. He always took care of me like that.

Leo Neumann, Courtesy of Battleship North Carolina.

A Change of Menu

In 1942, everything was Spam, Spam, Spam for breakfast, dinner and supper with eggs. Back then they had powdered eggs and dehydrated spuds. They got a little bit better and a little bit better after a while. Now that I'm old and think about it, they had the finest food, but we were young and criticized the cook and everybody else. There was a Chief Steward, his name was Jackson. For a while, he started giving nothing but bologna. Somebody told the captain that 'they are going to throw him overboard.' If I recall correctly, they had a Marine orderly with him for a while who followed him around for a few weeks. They finally changed the menu.

Jerry S. Gonzales, Courtesy of Battleship North Carolina.

White Bakers

The flour was white and so were the bakers. They were covered head to toe. All you could see were two beady eyes peering out from behind flour covered faces. They looked like ghosts most of the time!

Lloyd Reedstrom, Radioman 3/c, Courtesy of Battleship North Carolina.

Battleship North Carolina Memories

The crew's "chow lines" formed on the port and starboard quarters of the Main Deck. The lines extended from the float planes aft and led forward on the deck to the opening of a large hatch and down the ladder to the mess halls below. The mess cooks, who were un-rated men drafted from the various divisions for a three-month tour in the Galley, were lined up behind steam tables to ladle out various items on the menu. The meals were served on aluminum trays indented to separate the different food types, and you would pick up one before getting into the food line. Sometimes they were just out of the Scullery and were very hot to hold, as were the blistering coffee cups that were made without handles for easier stowage. The mess cooks often delighted in serving pats of butter that they picked up out of a bowl of ice water with a fork. Two of those tines were bent like a pick and then with a flick of the fork against a knife they held in the other hand, they would shoot it into your coffee or milk. You also had to watch to make sure they didn't put gravy on your ice cream.

Bill Faulkner, Seaman 1/c, Courtesy of Battleship North Carolina.

Hefty Portions

When I had mess duty and served meat, I would get dirty looks if I did not serve a hefty portion.

Logan Owen, Seaman 1/c, Courtesy of Battleship North Carolina.

Fantastic Chow and Black Spots?

I always thought the chow was fantastic, I enjoyed every bit of it. Some of my favorites were beans for breakfast, beef on toast, eggs (out at sea they were usually powdered but sometimes we got fresh ones). Our bakery was exceptional; we had pies, cake, homemade bread and rolls. Seconds were sometimes available and sometimes refused, but usually if there was some leftover we were allowed. One thing we always were sure we did when we had biscuits or bread or anything like that was before we ate it we held them up to the light to make sure there weren't any black spots in them as we did have a lot of cockroaches! Quite often we would find them in the bread, sometimes so many of them we thought there were raisins in them!

Robert L. Palomaris, Courtesy of Battleship North Carolina.

USS North Carolina Mess Cook

I served twice on the Ship as a mess cook. My duties were to help set the tables and benches for each meal. The mess cooks were assigned either to work behind the steam tables [serving line] or to service the tables. This involved keeping the pitcher on each table filled with coffee for breakfast, tea for dinner, and tea or lemonade for supper.

Leo Bostwick, Machinist Mate 2/c, Courtesy of Battleship North Carolina

Old Tradition

The crew ate in the Mess Halls located in the aft part of the Ship. Six of them were for seaman rates and two for firemen. I think the separation was a holdover from the old sailing navy when the sailors greatly resented the "black gang" probably for their use of coal that dirtied the "holy" decks. Actually, I seem to remember that greasy soot came down on the freshly holystoned decks one day when the snipes were blowing the stacks to the outrage of the deck force. Maybe that old tradition was a good one.

Bill Faulkner, Seaman 1/c, Courtesy of Battleship North Carolina.

Potato Marbles

They had a big machine you put the potatoes in there with water. You turned the machine on. It had abrasive stuff on the inside, like heavy sandpaper. It would clean the outside tissue of the potato off, then you dumped that out and all you had left to do was to take the eyes out of the potato. The thing you had to watch and make sure the chief wasn't around because a lot of guys would let it run too much and instead of potatoes, you had marbles.

William A. Schack, Courtesy of Battleship North Carolina.

Bogie Hunts

"Bogie Hunts" was the term used for picking bugs from bread. The proper way to do this was to hold the slice of bread to the light-It would look like raisin bread but a lot smaller raisins. After a week or two of this you forgot about the raisins and ate it anyway.

Jerry Lape, Watertender 1/c, Courtesy of Battleship North Carolina.

Lost Track of Time

If you lost track of the days, you could always tell by what food was served. Beans were Saturday, chicken or ham on Sunday.

Henry Okuszki, Boiler Maker 2/c, Courtesy of Battleship North Carolina.

Wallpaper Paste

Food aboard Ship was generally good. We called the dehydrated potatoes wallpaper paste and probably wallpaper paste tasted about the same.

William Fleishman, Watertender 2/c, Courtesy of Battleship North Carolina.

Holiday Chow

Holiday chow was unbelievable. There is nothing nearer and dearer to a sailor's heart than plenty to eat. Good food, pumpkin pie, roast turkey, ham, steaks, mashed potatoes, gravy . . .

Donald Wickham, Musician 2/c, Courtesy of Battleship North Carolina.

German Death March

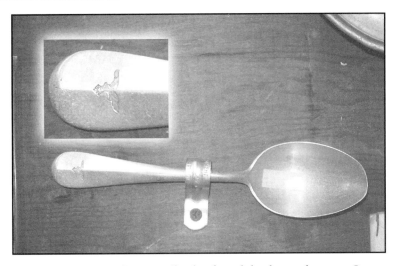

Bob Honeycutt survived a 800 mile plus forced death march across Germany. Now as owner and curator of the Veterans of All Wars Museum his collection includes this piece of silverware embossed with Nazi logos. See photo insert.
From the collection of the Veterans of All Wars Museum, Chickamauga, Georgia
Photo by Kent Whitaker

First off, this was in Europe—Germany. Not in the Pacific like most people think about death marches. I was shot down over Austria and ended up in a stalag camp. It was a nightmare to stay alive. They had no man zones and if you went close, the guards would shoot you. We had next to nothing to eat and we slept on beds made of wood and bags stuffed with something and bugs. That was about it. When forces got close, the Germans marched us over 800 miles. We were walking skeletons. If you laid down they would shoot you.

203

The big thing was what we called steak. We would talk about getting home and eating a steak about the size of our hand. By the time we were done talking we had a steak the size of a car. It passed the time of the forced march. When we were liberated I weighed close to 90 pounds. Me and a buddy decided to help some of our men that were still out there. We passed a farm house wearing our torn uniforms and hardly walking and I saw a big old flat bed truck. I said "If we can steal that truck we can go get the men." We jumped in and there was this big tank in it, right in the floor between us.

My buddy said he thought it was a bomb. I figured we had one shot to find out, so I started it up. It did not explode so we were ok. We later found out it was some sort of alternative fuel tank. When the truck started the owner came running out screaming. When he saw us he stopped. I handed him three or four American cigarettes and we drove off. We made several trips picking up men, some with guards from a British unit until they finally stopped us and told us we had done enough. They said we looked too rough to do any more.

They started feeding us doughnuts and coffee but since we had not eaten anything lots of people got sick. One guy ate so much he died. I guess his stomach busted. When they figured out that we could not handle it they put us on a diet of un-seasoned boiled chicken and water until we got our strength back and could handle food. I still remember talking about those steaks.

Bob Honeycutt Army Air Corps, Curator Veterans of All Wars Museum Chickamauga, GA.

Red Lantern Cooking

We had many nighttime air raids on a couple of the islands. The skies were lit up with tracers and searchlights. On one base we were close to the airfield and the bombs came mighty close to us. The boats were always a prime target for the Japanese pilots. When we heard the condition red sirens we dove into the foxholes next to the tent. Some it only lasted for a few minutes and many times much longer. We were very careful using lanterns at night. We had red globes on some that made it harder to be seen in the dark and only gave a little light for the path. In the galley, at night, I cooked also by a large lantern under the roof of the galley. I had to shut it down when the sirens went off though. I also had to shut down the stoves and restart them after the all clear.

Submitted by Earl Richmond, Cook, PT 108—United States Navy.

French PT Rations

Squadron 22 was in the Med. We enjoyed Navy base Mess Halls and only had snacks on the boat and of course plenty of hot coffee. After VE Day, the Navy gave our food rations to the local French restaurants at Cape de Antibes and we had all our meals served to us from May t through June after which time we were on our way home to the USA via Oran, Africa. Fresh French bread and Spam was my favorite snack. The rest of the crew thought I was nuts. To this poor kid from the slums of Cambridge, Spam on fresh French bread with plenty of butter was a treat. It is to this day.

Don't forget, I got sea sick all the time. Therefore I had six meals a day, three down and three up. Don't knock it. You never saw a fat sailor. Wish I could say the same thing for me right now. Bring on the Spam and rough seas.

Sincerely, Arthur John Frongello QM3/C PT 302, Ron 22.

The Chow

The food. I loved SOS beef on toast. I went in the Navy weighing 135 or 140 pounds. I came out weighing 225.

Jackson Belford, Signalman 3/c, Courtesy of Battleship North Carolina.

Flying Fish ad Boar Hunting

Sometimes we tried to shoot flying fish with our guns. It was good target practice and we figured we could eat them if we hit them. I don't think we ever hit one of those darned things. I used everything including my carbine and M1. They moved too fast. Sometimes we would tie up at and fish with cheese squares as bait. Sometimes we would pull the string up out of the water and the fish would jump out and hook themselves.

We once went on a special mission to pick up a Japanese water nipple mine so the demo men could check it out They removed all of the nipples and we netted the mine and towed it to an island beach so demo could find out more about it. While we were there we were bored and we asked the Aussi office to check with the natives to take some of us on a "safari" trek.

205

We started out loaded with ammo, guns and ponchos. It wasn't long before we got so hot and sweaty that we started shedding the ponchos and gear we did not need. We were able to shoot two wild boars before we got back to the boats. But they had so much lead in them they were no good. We kept the ears and told the natives they could use whatever meat they could salvage.

Submitted by Earl Richmond, Cook, PT 108—United States Navy.

Walton Alexander White, AM2 who was stationed at Naval Air Station Pearl
Harbor is pictured here with his Mess Pass.
Picture submitted by Chuck White.

Remembering Dad

Kent, my father never spoke of Pearl Harbor after the attack only about Pearl before the war. All information I have, came from his belongings. He was transferred to Midway Island in April of 1942, injured October 1942 (steel beam dropped on his leg and shattered it) and sat out the rest of the war convalescing at Oak Knoll Hospital. I was in Viet Nam when he passed away at age 48. I have so many questions now. But I found these pictures of him in his belongings as well as his Mess Pass.

Submitted by Chuck White.

Fruit Cake

I grew up in a military family and am now married to a Soldier. I remember being 6 or 7 years old and my dad bringing home boxes of MRE's. I was puzzled about what he expected us to do with them and in his drill sergeant voice he said, "Well, you like to picnic don't you?" as he huffed off. Wide eyed, I opened a can that had fruitcake in it. It was black with dark red spots. I couldn't imagine eating even a taste. It makes me laugh now, but being a WWII and Korean war veteran, I bet my dad ate lots of black fruitcake!

Sincerely, Kathy Partak.

Journal Thoughts

July 18, 1942. Chow is being rationed to maintain enough for us to stay out for two months—one egg or two pancakes for breakfast—baked beans for dinner. I might lose some weight on this kind of rations."

Edward J. Gillespie, officer, journal entry. Courtesy of Battleship North Carolina.

Galley.—Here is where the "cook" heats up the cans. A PT galley is much more than that. It can and has turned out American, Italian, French, Chinese, and even Japanese cuisine. Pies, cookies, and cakes flow from this modernistic kitchen if you've got a happy cook. Your refrigerator can make ice cream, ice cubes, and frozen delights (especially good is frozen fruit cup). Once a Jap bullet punctured a refrigerator unit and drained it of all its Freon. Several of the boats then decided to put armor plate about the refrigerator. So you see it's really very important, for it contributes to the living comforts which are all too few in the Area. Your refrigerator pump and motor need servicing.

This cartoon is from the WWII Know Your PT Boat handbook. The book notes the "grumpiness" of some cooks!
Courtesy the collection of Lou Gardner.

Don't let them wear down or overheat. To keep meat, your refrigerator must be in top shape. It is rare to have fresh meat and when issued it comes in 100-pound quantities. Hence the necessity for a good freeze or reefer. Have a drip pan properly placed or the meat juices will leak into the bilges and in a week you'll be accused of carrying a dead Jap around in your bilges.

A bit of advice about the cook. He's likely to be temperamental and have his moods. He needs help at meal time. So keep him in good humor by mess cooking without griping and helping him get supplies. He may serve you breakfast in bed some morning. Generally, he's a good gunner, too. You'll learn to count on "cookie."

From the Naval Department WWII booklet, Know Your PT Boat 1945.

Coast Guard Spar High Heel Chow

We weren't equipped, having come from California (to New York) in high heels, no hats and summer clothes, We got up with the bugle and started right out in a military way, high heels and all, marching to chow.

Seaman Second Class Patricia M. Raddock USCG, Spars, USCG Historian office.

The North Carolina Galley

Over eight million meals have been prepared in the Galley of the Battleship North Carolina. More than 2,000 men were fed three times a day. Meals started with breakfast which was served starting at 0630, lunch at 1130, and dinner at 1630. Early chow for watch reliefs was served a half an hour earlier.

Twenty-five cooks worked in the Galley and there were also one hundred men who served as "messmen" who helped serve food, assisted the cooks, and performed general mess duties such as serving tea and coffee, putting away condiment containers, and cleaning the mess area. All non-rated enlisted crewmembers had to serve a three-month mess duty.

Once the food was ready, it was taken to the steam serving tables to be served to the crew. The enlisted men stood in one of three "mess lines" which led to one of three "serving tables." Messmen stood behind the serving tables and served the food cafeteria style on stainless steel trays.

Being battleship sailors did have its advantages. You were going to get a decent hot meal served on a tray and sit at a table. For the Army or Marines, dinner would often be cold rations eaten out of a helmet. The only complaint crewmembers had was the same meal was served every week of every month for the entire year. Holidays or special occasions were the exception.

Coffee was always available.

Submitted by the staff of the Battleship North Carolina.

The Secret Door

(This memory from Joseph A. "Buck Craton takes place while stationed in Europe. Shortly before shipping home and a few weeks after General Patten told his group of men they would either be heroes or be annihilated.)

We are in Wels Austria now, set up in an old sugar-beet refinery when we get the news, "War is over!" We went to the small town of Linz near Vienna and took over a hotel (later I learned Uncle Sam paid for it). We were living like people again. We paired off two to a room and even hired local girls to be maids.

The hotel had two kitchens, one large and then a small one for the bar and coffee shop. The officers took over the coffee shop. That left the big one for us. The officers lost no time in stocking theirs with French four-star cognac. They stored it in their walk-in refrigerator. One morning when we went into our refrigerator we found this secret door that opened into the officer's mess. We would get two or three bottles of their cognac each day. Only Corporal Reid and I knew about this door, and for the next several weeks the officers questioned everyone but never did find out what happened.

We left Austria by truck, making our journey back to Le Havre, France. It took quite a while to get things organized, and as time drew near we would work on the way home. We decided all the workers and guards would board ship a day early so we could get everything set up. Now here is how the army thought in those days: cooks would take quarters on main deck and guards would quarter below deck (right next to the kitchen). The guards had to come topside each shift, and we had to go below each shift!

Courtesy of John Craton from the memoirs of his father Joseph A. "Buck" Craton. A Cook's Experiences in World War II.

Hammock on The Mess Deck

When the war was over, we took on about 1,000 passengers. We were transporting them from Okinawa to Pearl. Some stayed on until Boston. They all had to sleep in the Mess Decks in hammocks.

Paul Wieser, Boatswain's Mate 1/c, Courtesy of Battleship North Carolina.

Ketchup Wounded

Once when under general quarters, the boat took a sharp turn at high speed. I miss- stepped when going down the ladder from the cock pit to the crew's quarters below and found my-self on my ass on the deck in the crew's quarters. I thought the boat caught one. In the pitch dark I fumbled around and thought I was bleeding to death as I could feel a slimy substance all over me. I turned on a small flash light and was happy to learn that a shipmate had opened a gallon can of ketchup with a beer opener, the old church key, and placed the can on the deck. The can fell over and rolled around the crew quarters and with each roll painted the complete deck with ketchup.

I had mixed emotions. First, I was happy that I was not bleeding to death and second, I wanted to kill the person that caused the mess. When I went top side, the crew thought that I had been sea- sick again and as usual they had a great laugh. No I don't like ketchup to this day.

Sincerely, Arthur John Frongello QM31C PT 302, Ron 22

Mechanical Cow

Across from the Gedunk stand was the Daisy Mae. The Daisy Mae was a milk machine that converted powdered milk and butter into "fresh milk." The product was first class and made a lot of "Tin Cans," destroyers, and other lesser craft sailors happy when we refueled them and sent over ice cream and fresh milk. It took up a lot of time---at least one cook and one ship fitter to keep it running.

Don Grasby, Storekeeper 3/c—Courtesy of Battleship North Carolina.

Submarine Bread Baking

Bob Hall is shown cooking in his small galley on board the USS Parche.
Photo Courtesy of Robert Hall.

211

As a baker, I would do seventeen loaves of bread, a desert, and often cinnamon rolls for breakfast... I had a pie rack which stacked pies 14 or 17 high . . . It would take 14 pies to feed the crew and usually I made 17 or so for snacking. I'd start my baking around 8 pm and finish around 5 a.m. in order to be out of the breakfast cooks way.

Submitted by Bob Hall, Baker 1st Class USS Parche.

The Butcher Shop at Sea

On the Battleship North Carolina butchers processed all meat for the crew's meals in the Butcher Shop. Large slabs of meat weighing 100 to 150 pounds each were stored in the Ship's refrigerators ("reefers"). Butchers made a daily trip to the reefers to bring up the next day's meat. A chain and tackle lifted the meat out of the reefers. Workers carried the meat to the Butcher Shop for processing.

The Butcher Shop's equipment included a meat, bone, and fish cutting machine, an electric meat slicer, and a meat chopper for making ground beef. Meat was hung from the hooks overhead. Four to five men worked in the Butcher Shop. Their work day started at noon and ended when the work was completed. Supply ships delivered the meat when the Ship was at sea. The Ship would also resupply with food and other items when she was in port.

Submitted by the staff of the Battleship North Carolina.

Submarine Mushroom Explosion!

Why I chose a submarine, I don't know. Why becoming a cook and baker, again—I don't have a good answer for that. I love to eat!— grew up a little overweight because my mother was such an excellent cook. I took some of her recipes with me and used some of them on board the ship. We had about 85 men aboard, that's 75 men and 8 or 10 officers. The officers ate the same food that we did. The galley floor space was probably 7 feet long by 3 feet wide. If you worked with somebody else in the kitchen there just wasn't any room in a submarine kitchen and my wife wonders why I don't want anyone else in my kitchen now.

Cooking was done on electric heat, electric ovens and electric ranges. Those happened to be square, and if you used a big pot, those were square. And you had two oblong square pots that could be wedged into place so

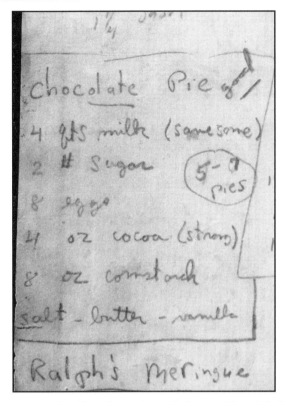

A hand written recipe for Chocolate cake by Baker 1st Class Bob Hall from the inside cover of the cookbook he used on the USS Parche during World War Two.
Photo courtesy of Bob Hall, USS Parche.

that they wouldn't slide around. But you had rough seas, and onetime I thought I would be smart and brace the pots so they wouldn't slide around so I used a can of unopened mushrooms.

Well, promptly… the can exploded. No harm, no damage. But I learned the hard way for that.

Submitted by Bob Hall, Baker 1st Class USS Parche.

The Cattle Boat

Along about February in 1942 we left Ft. Eustace and went to Ft. Slocum, New York. It was a small island close to New Rochelle. Boy, was it cold there! We only stayed there a few weeks then boarded a troop train.

The next day we were sidetracked for a while and found we were in Buffalo, New York. We were beginning to think we were going anywhere but Puerto Rico. We stayed one week on that train zig-zagging across the eastern U.S. before we finally pulled into the docks of New Orleans. We got off, had roll call, then boarded an old ship which looked like an old cattle boat.

This was my first experience traveling by ship. I must admit it was a very thrilling trip. We had problems eating. We all had queasy stomachs, and we would go through chow line and into the dining room. The tables were long counters about waist high. We had to stand while eating and when some guy at the table would get sick and vomit into his tray, that, of course, would set off a chain reaction as you probably guessed. The fish got most of the food!

Courtesy of John Craton from the memoirs of his father Joseph A. "Buck" Craton, A Cook's Experiences in World War II.

Seafood to Eat

(This memory from Joseph A. "Buck Craton takes place while stationed in Puerto Rico before being shipped to Germany.)

Things got so boring I signed up for detached service on another part of the island. This was done to train young Puerto Ricans. We lived in tents while there only about 100 yards from the beach. We had time more or less to become beachcombers. I bought a rod & reel and went fishing nearly every day. One Sunday morning I was fishing from a cliff jutting out over the ocean and was reeling in my line when I had a strike. I thought I had a fish that weighed at least fifty pounds. It took me about thirty minutes to finally bring it in, and I was disappointed because it only weighed 14 1/2 pounds. I found out later that was a good size for red snapper. I carried it back to camp and put it in the refrigerator, and that night our first sergeant caught one that weighed 54 pounds. It took two men to bring it in. Now we had nearly 70 pounds of fresh fish. We decided to have a large fish fry on the beach. Several of the men brought cases of beer and we all (including officers) had a great time that night.

Another of our sports was gigging for lobster. We used a gig similar to a frog gig and strong flashlight. We would wait till the tide went out, then we would wade out holding the light above water's edge. The lobster eyes would glow just like two glowing cigarettes. Then as we got near they would go under the water in the potholes. We would then gig them. We always had seafood to eat.

Courtesy of John Craton from the memoirs of his father Joseph A. "Buck" Craton, A Cook's Experiences in World War II.

Submarine Tale

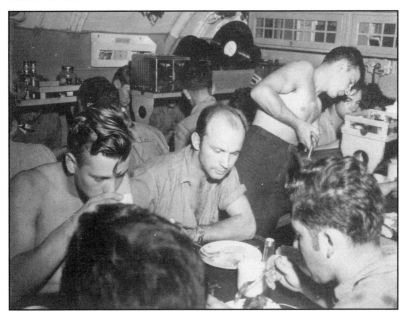

Sub crews made use of every tight space on a submarine. The crew of the USS Parche enjoys a meal in the mess, which also served several other purposes since it was one of the larger spaces on board. Note the record albums and other assorted items in the background.
Photo courtesy of Bob Hall, USS Parche.

When I graduated from submarine school and from diesel school, I and another man, Clabe Legget, had the highest grades and as a result we were given first choice of several assignments. We wanted to stay together as shipmates so we chose a new construction assignment to the USS TROLJT, SS 202 which was being constructed in Portsmouth, NH. Thus began my career as a submariner, all due to my first falling in love with the old "P" class. It was a wonderful career even during the war. Fortunately despite 11 war patrols and many attacks by the Japanese anti submarine forces, the submarines I served in survived, and I was no worse for wear except for occasionally having the daylights scared out of me by Japanese depth charges. However, after a few days ashore with girls and booze following a war patrol, I was ready again to go to sea.

From the papers of Dick Hawn USS Trout and the collection of Dave Hall, USAF

The 50 Cal. Mess Truck

(This memory from Joseph A. "Buck" Craton takes place while stationed in Austria.)

This is about me shooting down a plane. Our mess truck was equipped with a revolving 50 cal. machine gun mounted in the roof of the cab. If enemy planes attacked, no one would fire until they were in the circle of fire. One particular day I was alone with the mess truck and was serving coffee to our sergeant major. No one else was around. Suddenly there was a squadron of M.E. 109s overhead. Well, when all our batteries opened up they were so busy trying to get out of the circle of fire, I don't remember their firing a shot. It was at this point the sergeant major told me to use our gun. I always liked to fire those things, so I jumped in the truck and picked out a target. When you fired a large machine gun you could see the tracers and know exactly how you were doing. No one else was firing at my plane. The sergeant yelled to me, "Lead it a little more." You could see the tracers going into the tail of the plane. I took his advice and, lo, I got him! Smoke started streaming from the plane, and suddenly I got this feeling in the pit of my stomach. I thought, "God! I have just killed a man!" But suddenly I saw the canopy fly off and I saw a parachute open and I felt good again.

The sergeant major reported to my commanding officer and recommended that I get a medal, but our commander wouldn't believe his story and gave the credit and the pilot's side arm to the anti-aircraft officer. (Any soldier shooting down or capturing a German officer received his side arm).

Courtesy of John Craton from the memoirs of his father Joseph A. "Buck" Craton, A Cook's Experiences in World War II.

Hot Smokes and Gum

I didn't smoke when I joined the army. I did on occasion have a drink. But one thing that will make you smoke and drink is a war. Sometimes that was all we had to do to keep straight. I remember just about everyone chewed gum too. I never was much for gum 'cause people seemed to always chew with their mouths open and my mom hated us kids eating at the table eating away with our mouths wide open. But after awhile I didn't really notice. Didn't seem like something to worry about.

When we were in France after the main fighting was done we were rotated towards the back. We were bored so some particle jokes took place. I remember one time we dipped some gum in some Tabasco sauce and let it dry and wrapped it back up. A boy named Paul from New York was always bumming gum but never had any when you needed some. So he popped that in his mouth and started chewing. His eyes about turned red. He told me he would get me back. About a week later I lit a cigarette and after a few puffs I realized my lips and throat were burning like crazy. He had taken one of my cigarettes and took the tobacco out and dripped Tabasco sauce all in it. Then he repacked the paper. I had to give him credit—that took some effort.

I was running around looking for some water when a Chaplain asked me what was wrong. All I could say was "cigarette" and point at my mouth. That Chaplain said, "Never touch them. I suggest you start to chew gum son." The Chaplain walked off and Paul was just about dead from laughing so hard. I told Paul that I would get him back but before I could he was shipped back and soon I was and I never saw him again.

Submitted by P. Davis—United States Army.

Great Coffee

I seemed to get my fair share of C rations. We ate those things like crazy. They did the trick. The best thing we had for us was coffee. Seemed like somehow we could be short on just about everything but we could get some coffee.

Submitted by Terry H.—USMC

Fresh Eggs

When I got my first fresh egg cooked by a United States Army Cook after eating rations for about three months I thought I was in heaven. Never tasted something so good. Those guys could cook just about anything, just about anywhere. Never met a cook that didn't take his job real serious while I was in the service.

Submitted by T.H.—USMC

Red Cross Parcels Book Preserved by Son

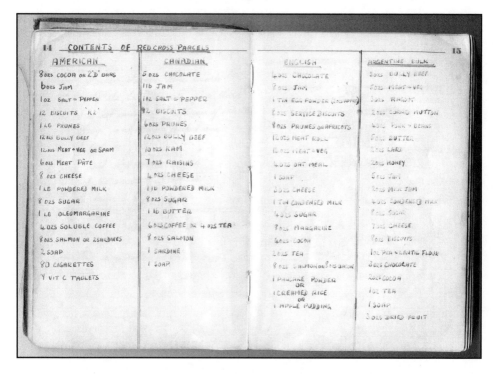

Two pages are shown from the prison camp journal of RAF Lancaster Wireless Operator Walter Henry Layne who was shot down over Mannheim Germany in 1943 and spent the next two years in several prison camps.
From the collection of David Layne.

This illustration, from the prison camp journal of RAF Lancaster Wireless Operator Walter Henry Layne, injects a bit of humor into the life of a POW as the prisoners decide how to equally divide a loaf of bread. Layne was shot down over Mannheim Germany in 1943 and spent the next two years in several prison camps.
From the collection of David Layne.

Hello,

My father was in the Royal Air Force (R.A.F.) and was shot down in September of 1943 when flying as a crew member of a Lancaster bomber. He was imprisoned in many different camps and during the early days of his captivity when times were "good" they were provided with Red Cross Parcels to supplement the meager rations given to them by the Germans. As the war turned against Germany the supply of Red Cross Parcels was greatly diminished. At the time that the parcels were more plentiful the prisoners managed to stash away raisins and other things that they kept hidden away from the Germans and were able to make an alcoholic brew with which they celebrated Christmas 1943.

This brew was so potent that it is my understanding that prisoners were known to have over indulged and died of alcohol poisoning! The practice of making their own brew was eventually banned by the Senior British Officer in many camps because of the many negative effects it had on the inmates.

Most prisoners formed themselves into a combine. A group of men that pooled all their resources together, whether it be food, collecting of fire wood, cooking etc. for the collective good and survival of the group. I have attached the entry in my father's Red Cross Wartime Log that lists the men in his combine. The image that I have submitted are from my father's Red Cross "Wartime Log." In August of 1943 the Red Cross in Geneva Switzerland distributed throughout the P.O.W. camps, (both British and American) blank hard covered books that the prisoners recorded their daily thoughts and activities in. As you can imagine food was very much on their minds. I am fortunate that my father's Wartime Log has survived and I am now the proud owner of it.

As a Brit living in the U.S. it is unusual that I share any of this information with anyone this side of the pond! Most of the research I have been involved with, naturally, has been with people in the UK.

Chow, David.

Submitted by David Layne

Regimental Colors

Shortly after the December 8, 1941attack on Pearl Harbor Japanese forces moved against Clark Field in the Philippines. General Douglas MacArthur ordered his joint American and Filipino forces, about 75,000 men, to mass on the Bataan Peninsula in order to regroup and hopefully stop or slow the Japanese forces. For over three and a half months the Allies held onto Bataan and neighboring Corregedor. Soon they were completely cut off from the outside world. Despite this the Quartermasters of the 12th Quartermaster Regiment did everything possible to fight and serve the troops.

The caught fish, slaughtered water buffalo, brewed coffee so many times that the beans turned white, distilled sea water for salt and more in order to supply the fighting men as well as nurse, workers and more. As long as a scrap of food was available the effort was put forth. Even if it consisted of delivering a small amount of food by hand to a foxhole fighting as they went. Every effort was made to make use of every piece of working equipment and salvage parts to keep things going. There were several members of the Quartermaster Corps among the casualties of the infamous Death March.

Lieutenant Beulah Greenwalt, a Quartermaster Nurse, wrapped the regimental colors around her as if she were wearing a wrap like shawl. For the next 33 months, Lieutenant Greenwalt remained a prisoner of war with the other nurses in Manila where they were deprived of just about everything and survived on a starvation diet. When the war ended in 1945, and the surviving POWs were released, Lieutenant Greenwalt sought out and found the Regimental Commander, and presented him with the flag she had protected and cherished all that time.

Source U.S. Army Quartermaster Corps Historian Fort Lee, Virginia.

Cold Ham Sandwich

We generally have something decent to eat before a mission. I flew many times over Europe and we had all kinds of small rations, sandwiches, coffee and such most times. We either ate before or took a packed lunch. It depended on what was available. Sometimes it was flight packs with these small things like candy, crackers and such. Other times we had some very nice sandwiches with fresh bread. One night we were out it was pretty darned cold and we decided to break out some ham sandwiches and coffee. When I was handed my sandwich it was just about frozen. I stuffed it down my coat wrapped and all and let my body heat it up. Well, we got busy with some flak and ground fire and I didn't touch that sandwich until we almost landed. It was pretty mashed up but I ate it, I was hungry. For the next few days my coat smelled like a ham sandwich.

Submitted by Andrew R, USAF WWII.

Cooking for Jarheads

I was a cook during WWII in the Pacific. We did our best in every way. Sometimes things just don't go right. It's hard to cook things under some situations. But we all tried our best. Once we were cooking up some soup and stew and such in some huge pots and this Jap plane flew over shooting things up. I was outdoors brining in some supplies. We all scrambled to holes and cover and started filling the sky with light fire. I looked over and I was standing there with a marine and I said something like "Hope that son of a @#$%$ don't blast up my cooking!" The marine never blinked and said "Well… maybe he was trying to save me from eating it!" I could not think of anything to say.

You have to have a sense of humor with stuff like that. Now I look back and laugh because that guy was pretty funny. I think his name was Dan or Danny. Years later I was telling that story to an older Marine I met and he said "That's what happens when you're cooking for jarheads. We always like to have the last word. Even when it's chow!" All in all I think everyone appreciated the effort of a hot meal served up in a cup, helmet or a bowl.

Submitted by J.S.

Thanks to our Cooks

You never really appreciate what someone does until you do it yourself or have the work they do deprived from you for a period of time. They did everything possible to feed the men hot meals and provide us all with things we needed. But in France, the next thing you know we were out in front of everything and we survived on rations for days, weeks. We also ate what we could find. The Germans did the same thing. You can complain about your rations and then realize it looks like a feast to one of those guys who didn't eat for a long time. I had the best stew and bread served up with hot coffee and doughnuts after not eating a hot meal for about 3 or 4 weeks. Tasted like gold. I just wanted to say thanks to all the cooks.

Submitted by anonymous.

Peanut Butter A Welcome Addition

I was "Called-up" in October of 1942 and served as a Driver/Op (Wireless Operator) with the 49th LAA (78 Div) from April of 1943 to December of 1944 (North Africa, Sicily, Italy, Egypt). The Regiment was disbanded in December of 1944 and I was retrained (in Italy) by the RAC. I then served as Loader/Op with the 4th Queen's Own Hussars from March 1945 to January of 1946 (Italy, Austria, Germany) finally finishing up as Tech Corporal. for "A" Squadron. I was "De-mobbed" in April of 1947.

There were inevitably a few anomalies to the Ration system. Prior to being called up in October '42 I used to commute daily between Luton and Kings Cross and as everyone piled out at Kings Cross, one could see an almost permanent queue outside a small kiosk. Human nature being what it is, if the queue was not too long I always joined in to see what goodies were on offer. For some unknown reason Peanut Butter had missed being on the list of "Points only" and proved a welcome addition to my family's diet. Lucozade tablets were also to be found and on the very rare occasion a No.8 battery was also available, strictly one to a customer.

Submitted by Ron Goldstein, ex Royal Armoured Corps.

Dehydrated Meat Stampede

"Dear reader, I shall offer this "meal" we had served to us while we were in Algeria in 1943, and of which I wrote for the BBC War series in 2004, with a provision that you do not make this stuff—you do not eat this stuff under any duress —OR if so—I cannot be held liable for your Medical and Hospital charges!" -—Tom

It was decreed from on high in the Army Kitchens in the U.K. that we would enjoy the delights of a new development which had the main benefit of conserving space in the Merchant Navy ships to allow the storage of even more ammunition and guns in the sea passage from home. We would therefore have served a sufficient quantity of "Dehydrated Meat", true enough—this was "enjoyed " at least, the Orderly Officer heard NO complaints, but then he was a very big, burly, South African International Rugby player who never did get many complaints ! Major Christopher Newton-Thompson. M.C. died in May 2002.

Later that evening, when the sun was wending its way towards Morocco, it was noticed that our showcase latrine was quite busy and very soon became a veritable stampede with most trying "to get there in time"—many didn't, which was not too pleasant in the a.m. when it was very noticeable. This was the result of the "dehydrated meat dinner" was the general consensus and everyone suffered the main effects which quickly cleared. At that time the senior N.C.O.'s and Officers dined later in the day as only gentlemen should and thus they were all unaware of the problems attending the "dehydrated meat dinner".

It was much later therefore that the senior N.C.O.'s felt the need to visit the facilities of our showcase latrine which had been very busy until they made their visit with the result that the main supporting beam gave way with a mighty crack and the Squadron Sergeant Major, along with the Squadron Quartermaster Sergeant, the Squadron Sergeant Cook, and the Squadron Sergeant Mechanic/Fitter of A squadron, 145th regiment R.A.C. of 21st Tank Brigade, British 1st Army, landed , as they say.... in the mire.

It was extremely difficult to keep a straight face for some time after that incident; meanwhile no more dehydrated meat was ever served again.
—Cheers

Submitted by Trooper Tom Canning, ex British 21st Tank Brigade, Africa, Italy.

This crew is working on packing assorted supplies for an air drop in Burma-India during the war. Note the wide assortment of items and the parachute on the wrapped package to the left.
Photo from the collection of the National Archives.

CHAPTER NINE

Recipes From the Chow Line

An ad for The Great Atlantic and Pacific Tea Company, A&P Coffee, appeared in *Women's Day* in 1943.

An ad from 1943 for A1 Steak sauce combines a war time theme with a quick recipe and cooking tip. *From the Collection of the Hamilton Co. Bicentennial Library, Chattanooga, Tennessee.*

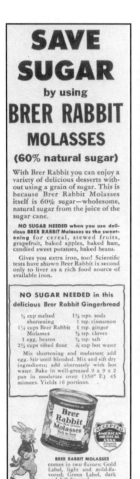

A 1945 ad for SPAM.
Photo courtesy of the Hormel Corporation.

The 1942 ad for Brer Rabbit New Orleans Molasses is a perfect example of advertisers combining war time tips for working with items in short supply.
From the Collection of the Hamilton Co. Bicentennial Library, Chattanooga, Tennessee.

A 1942 Camel Cigarette
advertisement by
R.J. Reynolds Tobacco.
From the Collection of S. Westley

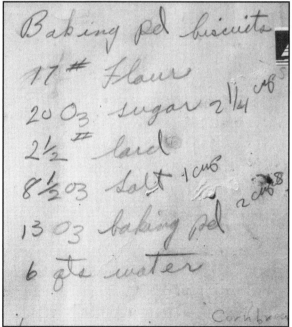

A hand written recipe
by Baker 1st Class Bob
Hall from his personal
cookbook used on the
USS Parche during
World War Two. Bob
wrote many recipes
on the inside of the
covers.
*Photo courtesy of Bob
Hall, USS Parche.*

227

F☾OD FACTS

6 different cakes from one simple recipe!

2½ oz. margarine; 3 oz. sugar; 2 dried eggs (dry); 4 tablespoons water; 2 level tablespoons household milk (dry); ½ lb. flour, 4 level teaspoons baking powder; water to mix (just under half-a-pint); flavouring.

Cream fat and sugar, adding dried eggs, dry. Beat in water gradually Sieve milk, flour, and baking powder together and add to creamed mixture. Mix to soft dropping consistency with the water, and put into greased tin. Bake in a moderate oven for 1—1½ hours. (This makes a good plain cake. Vanilla, lemon, or any other flavouring could be added.)

Fruit Cake

Bakewell Tarts

Marmalade Sandwich

Chocolate Cakes

THE advantage of a basic cake recipe like this is that once you've got the knack of making it, you can use the same recipe for almost any kind of cake. You can make little cakes and tart fillings, a jam sandwich, a fruit cake or a chocolate cake, merely by varying the recipe slightly.

Notice that you add the dried eggs dry to the creamed fat and sugar. And you add the household milk dry to the other dry ingredients. This is far easier than reconstituting both the eggs and milk before you begin. It's easier even than using shell eggs — and every bit as good!

This recipe with the variations is well worth cutting out and keeping. It's really very little trouble, with this recipe, to make a delicious cake for tea. And your family will certainly think it's a first-rate idea!

Variations

FRUIT CAKE. Add 2 level teasps. mixed spice to the dry ingredients before they are sieved, and add 2 to 4 oz. dried fruit to the creamed mixture with the dry ingredients. Baking-time as recipe.

BAKEWELL TARTS. Add ½ teasp. almond essence to creamed mixture, and use this as a filling. This mixture needs ¼ pint liquid. Line patty tins with pastry, put in a little jam, then the filling. (Makes about 24 small tarts.) Bake for 15 to 20 minutes.

MARMALADE SANDWICH. Add 2 level tablesps. marmalade and ½ teasp. almond essence to creamed mixture. Bake in sandwich tins in moderate oven for 25 to 30 minutes. Spread with marmalade when cold.

CHOCOLATE CAKES. Add 1 level tablesp. syrup to the creamed mixture and 3 level tablesps. cocoa to the dry ingredients. This mixture requires less water — about ¼ pint. (Makes about 18 small cakes.) Bake in patty pans about 15 to 20 minutes.

GINGER CAKE. (*Not illustrated*.) Add 3 level teasps. ginger and 1 level teasp. bicarbonate of soda to the dry ingredients, and 1 level tablesp. syrup to creamed mixture. Pour into flat tin, bake 15-20 minutes in a hot oven.

POINTS CHANGE—MATZOS reduced from 2 to 1 per lb. until the concluding day of the Passover. No other changes.

THIS IS WEEK 25 — THE FIRST WEEK OF RATION PERIOD No. 7 (JANUARY 7th TO FEBRUARY 3rd)

ISSUED BY THE MINISTRY OF FOOD, LONDON W.I.   FOOD FACTS No. 236

This London war time food tip was from the Ministry of Food and published in *The Times*, January 10, 1945.

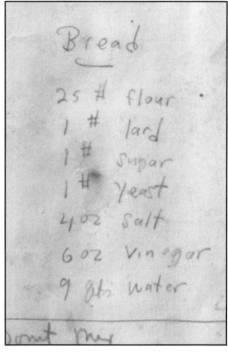

Bob Hall's hand written bread recipe is shown as it appears on the inside cover of his Navy cook book. Bob hand wrote many of his favorite recipes on the inside cover while serving on the USS Parche during World War Two.
Photos courtesy of Bob Hall, USS Parche.

While this is not a cook book in the normal sense of the term, it is a historical book about military cooking. All of the recipes in this chapter are from various World War Two military cooking manuals, museum collections, World War Two era cookbooks or pamphlets and similar sources. A few have been sent in by World War Two cooks, bakers or from their families. A few were sent in by people that wanted to share a recipe from a home front wartime kitchen.

A PRECAUTION about using these recipes should be noted. Many modern day cooks know their way around a kitchen well enough to adapt these recipes for use in today's kitchen if desired. However, cooking methods, ingredients, safety precautions have changed over the years. This requires, and obligates, me to say that these recipes are listed for historical reference only. If you do decide to try any of these recipes you are doing so at your own risk.

That being said, the recipes included in this book follow various formats. Some use abbreviated words such as Tbsp for tablespoon, or C for cup. Some spell everything out. Some of the recipes from military manuals or military museums are often written for enough portions to feed 100 men. That is a common portion count in many military recipes. Conversion calculators or methods to get smaller portion numbers would have to be used. The majority of recipes from pamphlets, cookbooks or other consumer sources of the day are most likely to be written for home use so portions would be more usable.

In some of the recipes you may run across a brand name or ingredient that is no longer made. Or you may come across ingredient spelling that is slightly off. As with the memory section of the book the recipes are shown as close to the way they were originally printed during the war. In order to preserve each recipes historical value no effort was made to standardize the recipe formatting, update ingredients, correct spelling and grammar or to convert measurements or portions for home use. The only thing done was to try and classify the recipes into sections similar to a regular cookbook such as breakfast foods, main courses etc.

While this is a historical look at recipes and foods from the World War Two era there are plenty of great dishes in the following pages. With the disclaimer and warnings in mind, many of these recipes seem modern enough that they could be safely converted to home use in your kitchen if done with common sense and caution. At the very least, they could inspire you to create your own version with a World War Two era recipe as your start. You would not be the first to do so.

While researching this book historian and researcher Luther Hanson, of the Fort Lee Quartermasters Museum, said that almost every day the phone would ring with someone looking for a military recipe. Callers range from veterans looking for a favorite dish to museums looking for info for a display or even a fundraising dinner that would feature military cooking from a particular era. Mr. Hanson also said some of the callers were even competition barbecue and chili cook-off teams looking for a military recipe or idea, from the Revolutionary War to the present, to use as a secret ingredient or recipe for contests.

Breakfast & Breads

Biscuits, Wartime Style
    2 cups sifted flour
    1 teaspoon salt
    3 teaspoons baking powder
    2 tablespoons fat (drippings, rendered pork, beef or lard)
    Milk to make soft dough (3/4 to one cup)
Sift the dry ingredients together and cut in the fat well. Stir in enough milk to make a soft dough. Drop the dough by the spoonfuls onto a baking sheet and bake in a hot oven (425° F.) for about 15 minutes or until lightly browned. This recipe makes about 12 biscuits. The fat may be reduced to 1 tablespoon in the above recipe but this makes a crisper and less tender biscuit. To make a "lid" for meat or vegetable pie, roll the dough out 1/2 inch thick, cover the stew, and bake in a hot oven.
From the pamphlet Fats in Wartime Meals, 1943.

Crackling Corn Bread
    2 cups cornmeal
    1/2 cup sifted flour
    4 teaspoons baking powder
    2 teaspoons salt
    1 egg beaten
    2 cups milk
    1 cup cracklings
Sift together the dry ingredients, add the milk, to which beaten egg has been added, and mix well. Stir in the cracklings cut into small pieces or ground through a food chopper. (Cracklings are crisp brown pieces left after fat is rendered.) Pour the mixture into a greased pan and bake in a hot oven (425° F.) 30 to 40 minutes or until well browned. Serve piping hot. If you use sour milk in the above recipe, add 1 teaspoon of soda and omit the baking powder.
From the pamphlet Fats in Wartime Meals, 1943.

Potato Pancakes

Grate 2 cups raw potatoes and mix immediately with 1/4 cup milk. Add 1 egg, beaten slightly, 2 tablespoons flour, 1 teaspoon salt, pepper, and 1 tablespoon finely, chopped onion. Drop from a tablespoon onto a greased frying pan. Cook until well browned and crisp on both sides. Serve hot.

From the pamphlet Potatoes in Popular Ways, 1944.

Military Potato Cakes

Form cold mashed potatoes into rounds 3 inches in diameter and 1/2 inch thick. Place in a hot skillet which contains a generous amount of fat. Brown on one side; turn and brown on other side. Serve hot. Allow 1 potato cake per serving. If desired, cooked potatoes may be put through the food grinder with parsley and molded into cakes. Brown as above, soaked break crumbs may be added to the potatoes to fill out the quantity for one meal.

From the Military Meals at Home Cookbook, 1943.

Army Cakes, wheat (hot cakes)

Please note that the word syrup is spelled "sirup" as in the original publication.

12 pounds flour
3 pounds sugar
4 ounces salt
12 ounces baking powder
36 eggs
1/2 pound fat, melted
1 can milk, evaporated
6 quarts water

Sift together the flour, sugar, salt, and baking powder. Beat the eggs and add to water and evaporated milk. Turn this mixture into the sifted flour and add the melted fat. Then beat into a smooth batter. If the batter seems too thick, add a little more water or milk. Grease a hot griddle iron or clean stove top with bacon rind or clean fat and pour out the batter, a spoonful at a time. Cook until nicely browned on both sides. Serve hot with butter or sirup, or both. Hot cakes should be cooked a few at a time.

232

If all the cakes for a meal are cooked before starting to serve, the first ones cooked will become tough and leathery.

From The Army Cook Training Manual 10-405, *April 24, 1942.*

Toast, French

Please note that the word syrup is spelled "sirup" as in the original publication. And that the title of the recipe is really French Toast. But when printed, in TM 10-405, this recipe was placed in the toast section. So French Toast became "Toast, french." The same happened with the "Toast, milk" recipe.

30 pounds bread, dry

5 cups milk, evaporated

7 pints water

36 eggs

1 pound flour

2 ounces salt

Slice the bread 1/2 inch thick, (be careful not to cut bread too thick). Mix milk, water, eggs, salt, and flour into a batter. Dip slices in the batter and fry in deep fat, or on a griddle. Serve hot with butter or sirup, or both.

From The Army Cook Training Manual 10-405, *April 24, 1942.*

Ration Muffins

1 cup water

2 tablespoons rendered fat or oil

1 teaspoon cinnamon

1 teaspoon ginger

1/2 teaspoon ground cloves

1 cup raisins

1 cup brown sugar

2 cups all-purpose flour

1 teaspoon baking soda

1/2 teaspoon baking powder

Large pinch of salt

Preheat oven to 350° degrees and grease two muffin pans. In a large mixing bowl, combine the flour, baking soda, baking powder and salt. In a saucepan over medium heat, bring the water, fat or oil, spices, raisins and brown sugar to a boil. Reduce heat and simmer for 5 minutes. Remove pan from heat and allow to cool. When cold mix with dry ingredients. Stir until everything is moist. Fill muffin pans equally and bake for 20 to 25 minutes.

Toast, Milk

Please note that the title of the recipe is Milk Toast, but when printed in TM 10-405 this recipe was placed in the toast section. So Milk Toast became "Toast, milk." The same happened with the "Toast, French" recipe.

20 pounds bread

4 pounds sugar

4 gallons milk, or 16 cans milk, evaporated, and 15 pints water Slices of left-over bread may be used. Place the bread in a large bake pan (not more than one-third full) and brown in a 15-count oven. Serve in vegetable dishes with hot sweetened milk poured over it.

From The Army Cook Training Manual 10-405, *April 24, 1942.*

Vegetable Omelet

To make an omelet that is "different" add a cooked green vegetable to the egg mixture before cooking. Or, spread the cooked vegetable on the top of the omelet after it has set but before it is rolled onto a hot, platter to serve. Have the vegetable drained and finely chopped, and use the vegetable juice in place of milk or water in mixing the omelet.

From the pamphlet Green Vegetables in Wartime Meals, 1943.

SPAM and Scrambled Eggs

I cooked this several times. Everybody got tired of SPAM but it was good. After the war I still ate it pretty often. Chop SPAM up and pan cook to warm. Add some sauces if you like. When browned pour in scrambled eggs. If you have it you can add some chopped onion of leftover items such as peppers and such for a omelet style egg.

Submitted by J.L. Reed.

Rumford Apple Corn Muffins

3/4 cup sifted flour

1/3 cup cornmeal

3 teaspoons Rumford Baking Powder

1/2 teaspoon salt

1/4 cup sliced raw apple

1 egg, well beaten

1/3 cup milk

1/4 cup honey

3 tablespoons melted shortening

SIFT together flour, cornmeal, Rumford Baking Powder and salt. Wash, pare and cut apple into eighths. Remove core and cut crosswise in very thin slices. Combine egg, milk and honey. Add to dry ingredients, stirring only enough to dampen well. Stir in melted shortening. Fold in apple. Fill well-greased muffin tins 2/3 full and bake in a moderately hot oven (400° F.) for 25 minutes. Makes 12 medium sized muffins.

Rumford Baking Powder, Sugarless Recipe Booklet World War II.

Quick Loaf Bread

3/4 cup sifted flour

3 1/2 teaspoons Rumford Baking Powder

3/4 teaspoon salt

1 1/2 cups whole wheat flour

1 cup corn syrup

2/3 cup milk

3/4 cup chopped nut meats (optional)

SIFT together flour, Rumford Baking Powder and salt. Mix with whole wheat flour. Blend corn syrup and milk, add to dry ingredients and mix well. Stir in nut meats, if used. Bake in a well-greased loaf pan (8 x 4 inches) in a moderate oven (350° F.) for 1 hour and 15 minutes. Cool before cutting.

Rumford Baking Powder, Sugarless Recipe Booklet World War II.

Basic Dough

2 cups milk, scalded

1/4 cup sugar

4 teaspoons salt

2 tablespoons shortening

2 cups water or milk

1 cake yeast

1/4 cup lukewarm water

12 cups sifted flour (about)

Scald milk. Add sugar, salt, shortening and water. Cool to lukewarm. Add yeast which has been softened in 1/4 cup lukewarm water. Add flour gradually, mixing it in thoroughly. When dough is stiff, turn out on lightly floured board and knead until smooth and satiny. Shape into smooth ball. Place in greased bowl. Cover and let rise in warm place (80° to 85° F.) until doubled in bulk. (If soft wheat flour is used, do not let dough quite double in bulk.) Punch down. (If soft wheat flour is used, shape at once.) Let rise again. When light, shape as desired.

Soft Bread Bun—Use Basic Dough recipe and shape into loaves. Place in greased bread pans. Let rise until doubled in bulk. Bake in moderately hot oven (400° F.) 40 to 45 minutes. Makes 4 (1-pound) loaves.

Raisin Bread—Add 2 cups seedless raisins to Basic Dough recipe. Dust raisins lightly with flour and fold into dough after it has risen the first time. Let rise again until doubled in bulk. Then divide and shape into loaves. Brush tops with melted butter. Let rise in greased bread pans until doubled in bulk. Bake in moderate oven (375° F.) 45 minutes. Makes 4 loaves.

From the Military Meals at Home Cookbook, 1943.

Oatmeal Fritters

1 1/2 cups rolled cats

3 1/2 tablespoons sugar

1 1/2 teaspoons salt

3 3/4 cups boiling water

2 1/4 teaspoons baking powder

2 tablespoons flour

Add oats and 1 1/2 tablespoons sugar gradually to boiling salted water. Cook, stirring constantly, until thickened. Continue cooking over low heat 30 minutes. Mix oatmeal mush with remaining sugar, baking powder and flour to make a stiff batter. With a tablespoon cut pieces about half the size of an egg and fry in hot deep fat (385° F.) until browned.

Drain on absorbent paper. Dust with confectioners' sugar or serve with sirup. If desired, add 1 egg to above recipe. Serves 6.

From the Military Meals at Home Cookbook, 1943.

WWII Carrot Buns

You will need

8 oz self-raising flour

3 oz margarine or cooking fat

3 oz sugar

4 tablespoons finely grated raw carrot

2 tablespoons sultanas or chopped dates

1 reconstituted dried or fresh egg

a little milk or water.

Method—Grease 2 baking trays. Sift the flour into a mixing bowl. Rub in the margarine or cooking fat. Add the sugar, carrot, sultanas and egg. Mix well, then add sufficient milk or water to make a sticky consistency. Divide mixture into 12 small heaps on baking tray and bake in a hot oven (gas mark7) for 12 to 15 minutes until firm and golden.

Recipe courtesy of the World Carrot Museum, www.carrotmuseum.co.uk

Hash Browned Potatoes

Add chopped cooked potatoes to a little fat in a fryng pan, Season with salt and pepper. Moisten with water-about 1/4 cup for 4 cups potatoes. Cook over low heat until brown on the bottom—don't stir. Serve folded in half.

Potato hash.—Add chopped cooked meat and enough gravy or hot water to moisten. Brown on both sides.

Potato Cakes.—Shape cold mashed potatoes into small cakes; roll in flour. Fry golden brown in a little fat. For variety, add to the mashed potatoes chopped cooked meat or fish, or grated cheese.

Potato Crust.—Line a baking dish with mashed potatoes. Fill center with vegetable stew and left-over bits of meat or fish. Cover with mashed potatoes. Bake in a hot oven (400° F.) until hot through and brown on top. If you have just a little potato, make only the upper crust.

From the pamphlet Potatoes in Popular Ways, 1944.

Meats and Main Dishes

The Art of S.O.S.

There are many stories about the famed S.O.S served up to troops during World War II. Veterans seem to fall into two camps. They either hated it, or they loved it. Here are a few military recipes for the dish along with one that does not require you cooking for 100 men.

Creamed Beef For 100
Yield: 100 men
Portion: not given
INGREDIENTS
Coarse ground beef 20 lb
Lard or butter 1 lb
Flour 2 lb
8 cans Milk, evaporated
2 gal Beef stock or water
Method:
Braise the meat. Make a gravy in a separate pan as follows: Melt the lard, add the flour, stirring constantly until thoroughly blended and browned. Stir in the liquid, a little at first, then enough to thin the mixture, and finally the remainder. Season to taste. Pour the gravy over the ground meat and simmer until the meat is tender.
From The Army Cook 1942.

Creamed Sliced Dried Beef For 100

Yield: 100 portions
Portion: 8 ounces (approx. 1 cup)
INGREDIENTS
Beef, dried, sliced 7 lb
Milk, liquid 5 gal
Fat, melted 2 lb
Flour 2 lb 8 oz
Pepper 1/2 oz
Method:
Cut beef into small pieces. Heat milk to boiling temperature. Blend

together fat and flour to a smooth paste. Stir into milk. Cook, stirring constantly, until thickened. Add pepper. Stir in beef. Let simmer about 10 minutes. Serve over toast.

Note: Soak meat in warm water 15 to 20 minutes if too salty.

1945 Cook Book of the United States Navy.

SOS For The Home

1 pound of ground beef browned
1 1/4 tablespoons of Worcestershire sauce
1 beef bouillon cubes dissolved in 1/2 cup of water
1 1/2 cups of flour
3 cups milk
l chopped onion
Garlic powder to taste
Salt and pepper to taste

Brown the ground beef and chopped onion; then drain. Break into small pieces. Return to pan and add remaining ingredients. Stir until thickened as desired. Serve over toast.

President Eisenhower's Recipe for Quail Hash

Quail
Good chicken stock
Salt and pepper
Flour

Put into sauce pan whatever number of quail seem sufficient for the company. Cover well with stock. Cook slowly for ten to fifteen minutes or until meat can be removed from bones easily. Remove from burner, strip and dice meat and season to taste. Add more stock if necessary to cover well. With small amount of additional stock make gravy with flour (browned or not as you choose) and pour over diced quail. Cover and simmer ten minutes longer.

The Dwight D. Eisenhower Presidential Library and Museum

Savory Bean Stew or Chili Con Corne

Soak and cook 1 1/2 cups of dry beans or peas in water in the usual way. In another pan fry 1/4 to 1/2 cup of diced salt pork until crisp. Then brown 1/2 cup chopped onion in the salt pork fat, add 1/2 pound ground lean meat stir and cook slowly for 5 minutes.

Combine meat, onion, salt pork, and 3 cups of cooked tomatoes with the cooked beans. Add salt and pepper and simmer until meat is tender and flavors well blended.

For Chile Con Carne

Add 2 to 4 teaspoons of chili powder and a bit of garlic, if desired, to the recipe for Savory Bean Stew. Red kidney or California Pink beans are favorites for chile con carne.

From the pamphlet Dried Beans & Peas in Wartime Meals, 1943.

Green Beans, Cabbage, or Squash Flavored With Meat

Meat flavors, especially the salted, smoked, or corned meats, add zest to any given vegetable. Cover the meat with water and simmer until almost tender. Use some of this liquid for cooking the vegetable—dilute if too salty. Simmer gently until the vegetable is tender, but not broken. Season to taste.

From the pamphlet Green Vegetables in Wartime Meals, 1943.

Sara Delano Roosevelt's (FDR's mother) Kedgeree

1 cup cooked flaked fish or crab, lobster or canned fish
1 cup cooked rice
1/4 cup cream or fish stock
2 tablespoons melted butter
1/2 teaspoon salt
1/4 pepper
2 hard cooked eggs

Mix the fish with the rice. Moisten with the cream and sauté lightly in butter. Do not press down-fish must be light and fluffy. Season with salt and pepper. Add the eggs, cut in quarters, sliced or chopped. Heat thoroughly. Serve with extra grating of freshly ground black pepper or dash of Worcestershire.

Courtesy of the Franklin D. Roosevelt Presidential Library. The Whitehouse Cookbook *by Janet Halliday Ervin.*

Sausage Rice Cake

12 1/2 Lbs. Meat.

6 Lbs. Rice.

12 ozs. Sausage Seasoning.

Method.—Cook rice, mix with minced meat and seasoning. Form into flat cakes. Brown lightly in hot, shallow fat, then cook slowly for 30 minutes. Serve with brown sauce. (Cakes should be 4 ozs.)

Submitted by the Royal Air Force Museum, London, R.A.F. Manual of Cooking and Dietary, Air Command, *April 1942. British Crown Copyright, RAF Museum. British Crown Copyright material is reproduced with the permission of the Controller of Her Britannic Majesty's Stationery Office.*

Vienna Steaks Recipe #109

25 Lbs. Meat (Dinner)

6 Lbs. Bread.

3 Lbs. Onion.

12 1/2 Lbs. Meat (for Tea Meal)

2 Lbs. Dripping

Salt, Pepper.

100 Eggs.

4 ozs. Parsley.

Method.—Prepare and cook the onions and allow to cool. Mince the raw beef. Soak the bread, squeeze out dry, and mix the meat, bread, onions and seasoning together. Mold into 100 portions (fish cake shape), dust with dry flour, fry in shallow fat, then finish off in the oven. Serve with fried egg on top of each Vienna Steak and serve with brown or tomato sauce.

Submitted by the Royal Air Force Museum, London, R.A.F. Manual of Cooking and Dietary, Air Command, *April 1942. British Crown Copyright, RAF Museum. British Crown Copyright material is reproduced with the permission of the Controller of Her Britannic Majesty's Stationery Office.*

Beef Fritters

8 slices bread

3 cups ground cooked beef

1 onion, minced

1/2teaspoon salt

1/8 teaspoon pepper

Flour

Soak bread in warm water. Press out excess water. Combine meat, bread, onion, salt and pepper and mix thoroughly. Shape into cakes, dredge with flour and fry in hot deep fat (365° F.) until browned. Serve hot with tomato sauce. Makes six medium fritters.

From the Military Meals at Home Cookbook, 1943.

Beef Rolls

1/4 cup chopped onions

1 tablespoon fat

1 cup dry bread crumbs

3 cups ground cooked meat

1/8 teaspoon chili pepper

1/4 teaspoon salt

1 recipe Plain Pastry

1 egg, slightly beaten

Brown onions in fat. Soak bread crumbs in water and press out excess water. Mix onions, crumbs, meat, chili pepper and salt together. Roll pastry into an oblong, having it 1/8 inch thick. Spread meat mixture about 1/2 inch thick cover pastry. Roll and place in baking pan. Brush top with egg. Bake in a slow oven (250° F.) or 1 hour. Serves 6.

From the Military Meals at Home Cookbook, 1943.

Corned Beef

3 pounds corned beef

3 peppercorns

Cover meat with cold water and add peppercorns. Cover kettle tightly and simmer 3 hours or until meat is tender. Add hot water from time to time so as to keep meat completely covered with water. If desired, carrots, parsnips and potatoes may be added about 45 minutes before meat is done. Serves 6,

From the Military Meals at Home Cookbook, 1943.

Beef hash

35 pounds potatoes

5 pounds onions

25 pounds meat scraps, fresh or cooked

10 quarts beef stock

1 clove garlic

Salt and pepper to taste

Chop the ingredients fine and add the beef stock until the mixture is of the consistency of ordinary mush and place about 3 inches deep in a well-greased pan. Smooth the top and grease lightly. Bake in a quick oven (400°-450° F.—9 to 12 counts) for 1 1/2 hours, or until done. Scraps of beef or pork, or a mixture of both, or corned beef may be used for making hash.

From The Army Cook Training Manual 10-405, April 24, 1942.

Beefsteak Potpie

35 pounds beefsteak, fresh or cooked, cut in small portions

3 gallons beef stock

4 pounds onion, (chopped and browned)

1 clove garlic

If fresh steak is used, season the meat with pepper and salt, roll the small pieces of steak in flour, and fry in fat. Remove the cooked steak, add 1 pound of flour to the frying fat, and brown. Add slowly the 3 gallons of stock to make a thin gravy, then add the onions. Pour this onion gravy over the steak. If cooked steak is used, the onion gravy is made by adding 2 pounds flour to 2 pounds hot fat, then adding the onions. Make a regular biscuit dough, using about 10 pounds of flour. Cut into biscuits, place them over the top of the steak and gravy, and allow them to brown in the oven. Serve hot.

From The Army Cook Training Manual 10-405, April 24, 1942.

Beefloaf

40 pounds beef, fresh

5 pounds bacon

2 pounds onions

1 clove garlic

25 eggs, beaten

1 pound flour

2 or 3 quarts beef stock

Salt and pepper to taste

Grind the meat, onions, and garlic together. Add beaten eggs, salt, and pepper. Mix well. Make into loaves about 4 inches wide by 3 inches high and as long as the pan is wide. A loaf of this shape can be cut into pieces of attractive size and about the proper size for the individual, and the pieces will hold their shape. Then make a batter of flour and beef stock, rubbing this over the loaves. Place in the oven (200°—250° F.-18 to 20 counts) and make for about 1 1/2 hours. A slice of bacon may be placed on top of each loaf to improve its flavor. Serve hot with gravy. Beefloaf may be served with tomato sauce if desired.

From The Army Cook Training Manual 10-405, April 24, 1942.

Beef Loaf

2 pounds beef, ground

1/8 pound bacon, ground

1 egg, slightly beaten

1/4 cup minced onion

1 slice garlic, minced

1 1/2 teaspoons salt

1/4 teaspoon pepper

1/2 cup beef stock

1/4cup flour

Mix first 7 ingredients thoroughly. Shape into loaf and place in greased baking pan. Mix stock and flour together and spread over loaf. Bake in moderate oven (350° F.) about 1 1/2 hours. Serve with tomato sauce. Serves 8. A slice of bacon may be placed on top of loaf before baking. Use half beef and half pork, Bake not less than 2 hours.

From the Military Meals at Home Cookbook, 1943.

Spaghetti Italian Style

1/4 cup salad oil or bacon drippings

2 onions, sliced

1 clove garlic, mashed

1 pound beef, ground

2 cups cooked tomatoes

1 1/2 cups tomato puree
1 teaspoon salt
1/4 teaspoon pepper
1/4 teaspoon paprika
1 pound spaghetti
Grated cheese

Heat oil in a deep pan. Add onions and garlic and brown in oil. Add meat (ground twice) and brown slowly. Add tomatoes, puree, salt, pepper and paprika. Simmer until sauce thickens. Boil spaghetti in salted water 20 minutes. Drain and wash in colander with hot water. Serve with sauce, topped with cheese. Serves 10.

From the Military Meals at Home Cookbook, 1943.

Rissoles

12 1/2 Lbs. Meat.
3 Lbs. Onions.
25 Lbs. Potatoes.
1 Packet mixed herbs.
Pepper and Salt.

Method.—Prepare and cook the potatoes, mince and allow to cool. Steam or boil the onions and leave to cool. Place the meat in a boiler with pepper, salt and stock; when cooked, strain and mince. Mix the meat, potatoes, onions and seasoning and shape into 100 equal portions. Dust with dry flour and pass through the oven on greased baking trays, or dip into the flour paste, roll in breadcrumbs and deep fry. The stock from the meat requires colouring and thickening before serving as a gravy with the rissoles. Note:—It must be understood that cooked meat and potatoes from the larder must be used before any fresh ingredients are used up in this way.

Submitted by the Royal Air Force Museum, London. R.A.F. Manual of Cooking and Dietary, Air Command, April 1942. British Crown Copyright, RAF Museum. British Crown Copyright material is reproduced with the permission of the Controller of Her Britannic Majesty's Stationery Office.

Ham, Baked

50 pounds ham, smoked

Wipe the ham with a damp cloth. Place in a pan with the fat side up. Roast in an uncovered pan at 325° F. (16 counts) allowing 25 to 30 minutes per pound. When the ham is done, remove it from -the oven and take, off the rind. With a sharp knife score fat covering in squares. Stick long-stemmed cloves into the intersections, spread brown sugar over the ham, and return to oven to brown.

From The Army Cook Training Manual 10-405, April 24, 1942.

Ham, Simmered

50 pounds ham, smoked

Wash and scape the ham. If the ham is very salty, let soak for several hours in fresh water. Then change the water. The water in which hams are cooked should never be allowed to reach the boiling point. Place hams in near-boiling water (enough to cover) and simmer until the hams are properly cooked. This process requires about 20 minutes to the pound. If two or more hams are simmered in the same vessel, the tine of cooking should be computed on the largest ham. Skim all the impurities from the water as they arise. Let the hams cool in the water in which they are cooked.

Mold, if present, may be removed from ham by wiping with a clean cloth dampened with vinegar. The water in which the ham was cooked may be used to cook cabbage, spinach, etc.

From The Army Cook Training Manual 10-405—April 24, 1942

Ham, smothered

50 pounds ham
1/4 ounce cloves, whole
1 pound sugar, brown
5 pounds bread crumbs
1 gallon milk
2 pounds onions, chopped

Trim off the rind or skin from hams and wipe with a clean cloth. Cut them into slices about one-fourth inch thick and put in a bakepan. Cover with boiling water and cook at a simmering temperature from 35 to 40 minutes. Drain off the water, place over the top the cloves, onions, and bread crumbs, and add the milk. Bake in a moderate oven (250°—325° F.-16 to 18 counts) for about 45 minutes or until the top is crisp and brown.

From The Army Cook Training Manual 10-405, April 24, 1942.

Hash, Chop Suey

7 pounds bacon, chopped fine

8 pounds onions, chopped fine

20 pounds beef, cooked, coarsely ground

17 pounds turnips, cooked and chopped

5 cans corn (No. 2 cans)

2 ounces chili powder

2 gallons beef stock

4 cans tomatoes (No. 3 cans)

4 pounds celery, diced

Salt and pepper to taste.

Place the bacon in a large bakepan and cook in the oven until well browned. Add the onions and fry, but do not allow to brown. Add the other ingredients and bake for 1 hour. The addition of Worcestershire sauce improves the flavor.

From The Army Cook Training Manual 10-405, April 24, 1942.

Georgie's Quail in Duffel Coat (George Patten)

One quail apiece

Clean a quail, or any small game bird, put a lump of butter inside of it. Sprinkle with salt, pepper and garlic salt. Cut a large Idaho potato in two and scoop out enough of each side to make a hollow for the bird. Tie the potato together tightly with string and bake 1 hour at 450 degrees.

The Rolling Kitchen, Ruth Patton Totten.

Chicken, creamed

60 pounds chicken (fowl) dressed, undrawn

10 pounds veal, diced

1 dozen eggs

2 cans pimento (No. 1/4 can)

4 pounds flour

10 cans milk, evaporated, diluted with 6 quarts water (preferably from the boiled chicken)

2 pounds butter, or 1 pound butter and
1 pound vegetable shortening
Salt and pepper to taste

Singe and draw the chickens, cut into fourths. Place in pan with the veal, cover with cold water, and boil until chicken meat falls off the bones. Remove bones (be careful not to leave splinters of bone in the finished product), dice the chicken meat and thoroughly mix with the diced veal. Hard-boil the eggs, dice, and add to the meat.

Make a cream sauce using the butter, flour, milk, and broth from the boiled chicken. Season to taste. Slice pimento into strips (thin), add to cream sauce, and pour the sauce over the meat and eggs.

Serve on toast or mashed potatoes.

NOTE.—The addition of two No. 1 can of mushrooms will improve this dish. Also, any left-over cooked chicken which may be on hand may, be used in place of fresh chicken.

From The Army Cook Training Manual 10-405, April 24, 1942.

Chicken Fricassee

70 pounds of chicken (fowl) dressed, undrawn
2 pounds butter or vegetable shortening
4 pounds flour
8 cans milk. Evaporated, diluted by 8 pints water or 8 quarts fresh milk
Salt and pepper to taste

Cut each chicken into about 12 pieces (natural divisions). Cover with water, season well with celery salt, and allow to simmer until tender. Remove the chicken and make a gravy, Using 1 pound butter, 1 pound flour, and the water in which the chicken as cooked. Pepper and salt the chicken well fry in shallow fat or roll in flour and fry in deep fat. Put into the gravy when fried. Before serving add the milk and the remainder of the butter. Care should be taken to break up the chicken as little as possible. Serve on a platter with or without ice. Old fowls may be utilized to advantage by this recipe.

From The Army Cook Training Manual 10-405, April 24, 1942.

Chicken, Fried

Please note that the actual recipe name is Fried Chicken, but due to the Army filing this recipe under various ways to cook chicken in TM 10-405 the recipe is listed as Chicken, Fried.

75 Pounds chicken (fryers or broilers) dressed, undrawn

12 eggs, beaten

10 pounds fat

4 cans milk diluted with 2 pints of water

4 pounds cracker meal, or flour, or bread crumbs

Fowls over 6 months old should not be fried. Remove pin feathers by singeing over hot blaze. Divide each chicken into 10 pieces. (natural divisions). Fry in shallow fat, or in deep fat. If fried in deep fat, dip each piece in the beaten eggs and then in the cracker meal. If the mixture does not adhere to the pieces sufficiently, repeat the operation. Drain well in a colander and keep hot until served. In case older chickens are used, which are large and possibly tough, fried pieces should be placed in a bakepan with about 2 inches of water, the pan covered, and placed in a slow oven to steam for about 40 minutes.

From The Army Cook Training Manual 10-405, April 24, 1942.

Chicken Salad

2 cups diced cooked chicken

1 cup diced celery

1 cup mayonnaise

Salt, Pepper, Paprika

Lettuce

Mix chicken with celery and mayonnaise. Season with salt, pepper and paprika. Serve on lettuce. Serves 6. If desired, veal may be used for 1/2 the chicken. If simmered with the chicken the veal will take on the chicken flavor.

From the Military Meals at Home Cookbook, 1943.

Curried Rabbit

This recipe is from the personal diary/cookbook of a British Army Chef who served in North Africa during World War Two. According to Nick Britten, journalist for the Telegraph newspaper the personal cookbook contained 118 recipes, all hand written by Harrison.

Rabbit 40 pounds

Curry powder 3 pounds

Fat 1 pounds

Rice 8 pounds

Method: Wash and joint rabbit, fry gently in hot fat, place into hot curry sauce and cook gently until tender (approximately 13/4 hours) serve with border of plain boiled rice.

From the personal cookbook of British Army Chef, Cpl James Abraham Harrison.

Campbell's Salmon Patties

This recipe is actually one of my grandfathers war ration recipes. The basic ingredients are canned salmon, some salmon juice from the can and a whole lot of crushed crackers. After those basic ingredients, eggs, salt and pepper are optional if you don't have any.

1 can salmon

4 cups crushed crackers

1 egg

salt & pepper

Oil for frying

Remove bones etc from salmon saving the meat and some of the liquid. Combine with remaining ingredients and form patties. Fry in hot oil until golden, dry on a paper towel and serve hot.

Kent Whitaker, from the kitchen of Angus Campbell

WWII Mock Fish

My mother used to make fritters called "Mock Fish" which were a meal from the days of the depression and eaten during the World War Two. Ingredients were from the vegetable garden or very cheap.

Plain Flour

Water

Salt

Grated Potato

Grated Onion

Egg (if available)

Spoon the mixture into pan and shallow fry. Serve hot with vegetables or salad. Funnily enough, my two daughters love it! Hasn't done them any harm.

From the kitchen of Geoff Swallow in honor of his mother Marg Swallow, Melbourne, Australia.

Mock Goose

Please keep in mind any resemblance to Goose is purely an illusion! This recipe is from My Royal British Legion Branch which produced a small book last year in aid of our Poppy Appeal. It's called Ration Book Recipes with a collection derived from the memories of our WW2 Veterans and their wives. It reminded me that in 1941 the One Week Ration per person was; 4oz Bacon or Ham, 8oz Sugar, 2oz Butter, 10cents-worth of Fresh Meat, 2oz Tea, 1oz Cheese, 2oz Jam (Jello?), and the equivalent of 1 small tin of Spam (or similar tinned item, as available). Here is what you'll need to make Mock Goose. —Les

1/2 pound of spuds
2 cooking apples
4 ounces cheese
1/2 tablespoon dried sage
225mL vegetable stock
1 tablespoon flour
Salt & pepper

Grate cheese, and wash and slice apples. Layer the spud, apple, cheese and sage alternately into greased dish, finishing with spud and cheese. Pour in 150mL of the Stock and bake for 45 minutes until brown. Blend remainder of stock with the flour and add to dish which is returned to oven for further 15 minutes. This dish serves four people, preferably with some decent vegetables. Bon appétit. —Les.

Recipe submitted by Les, WWII Veteran, RAF.

Salmon Cakes

2 cups hot mashed potatoes
2 cups flaked salmon
1 egg, well beaten
1 teaspoon salt
1/8 teaspoon pepper

251

Flour

Mix first 5 ingredients together thoroughly. Shape into cakes about 3 inches in diameter; roll in flour and fry in hot deep fat (375° F.) 2 to 5 minutes. Serve with tomato sauce. Serves 6.

From the Military Meals at Home Cookbook, 1943.

Salmon Hash

    2 cups flaked salmon

    1 1/2 cups mashed potatoes

    1/2 cup beef stock

    1 large onion, chopped

    1 teaspoon salt

    1/8 teaspoon pepper

Combine all ingredients and mix thoroughly. Place in a greased baking dish and bake in a moderate oven (350° F.) about 40 to 60 minutes. Serves 6.

From the Military Meals at Home Cookbook, 1943.

Baked Fish

    2 to 3 pounds fish

    Salt

    Sliced bacon

Clean fish, dry and rub inside and out with salt. Place on piece of heavy paper on baking sheet Place slices of bacon over lean fish. Bake in moderate oven (350° F.) 25 to 35 minutes. Baste lean fish every 10 minutes. Do not baste fat fish. To serve, lift fish with paper and slide fish onto platter. Serves 6. Fish may be stuffed, if desired. MUSHROOM STUFFING— Cook 1 cup sliced mushrooms in 3 tablespoons melted butter. Combine with 2 cups fine, soft bread crumbs, 1 teaspoon grated onion, 1/2 teaspoon salt and 2 tablespoons water. Mix lightly, but thoroughly. Will stuff 3 to 4 pound fish.

From the Military Meals at Home Cookbook. 1943.

Fresh Fried Fish

    2 pound fish

    Salt, pepper, flour and corn meal

Clean fish, leaving heads and tails on small fish. Cut large fish into 1 inch slices of fillets. Season with salt and pepper, then roll in flour and corn meal. Fry in hot deep fat (365° F.) 5 to 7 minutes or until tender. Serves 6.

TOMATO SAUCE—Brown 1 sliced onion in 2 tablespoons butter. Remove onion, Blend 2 tablespoons flour with butter. Add 1 1/2 cups strained cooked tomatoes gradually. Boil 3 minutes, stirring constantly. Season and serve hot. Makes 1 1/4 cups.

From the Military Meals at Home Cookbook, 1943.

Fried Oysters
    36 large shucked oysters
    2 eggs
    3/4 teaspoon salt
    1/8 teaspoon pepper
    2 tablespoons cold water
    1 1/2 cups cracker dust

Drain oysters. Beat eggs with seasonings, add water and mix. Dip oysters into egg mixture, then into cracker dust. Let stand 5 minutes before frying. Fry in hot deep fat (375°-380° F.) until browned. Serve hot, Serves 6.

From the Military Meals at Home Cookbook, 1943.

Fried Hot SPAM
    Slice SPAM in sandwich slices and cook in a skillet with butter and pineapple juice or some type of sauce like ketchup or what ever you have. Sprinkle with hot sauce. When browned serve with bread and cheese if you have it.

Submitted by J.L. Reed

SPAM n Potatoes
    Chop SPAM up and pan cook to warm. Add some sauces if you like. When browned stir in some onions and mix with mashed potatoes. You can add green peas if you desire.

Submitted by J.L. Reed.

Vegetables and Side Dishes

Carrot Croquettes
> 6 carrots
> 1 gill of milk
> 1 oz. margarine
> 1 oz. corn flour
> Seasoning to taste
> Fat for frying
> Oatmeal
> Form into patties and fry.
> *Recipe courtesy of the World Carrot Museum,* www.carrotmuseum.co.uk

Meatless Bean Recipe Ideas
For a tasty tomato sauce to go with beans, cook a sliced onion in 2 tablespoons of fat. Blend in 2 tablespoons of flour and brown slightly. Stir in 2 cups of cooked tomatoes, season, and cook until thickened. If desired, add green or red sweet peppers, chopped fine. Serve hot over the hot beans.

For bean "sausages," mash 3 cups of cooked beans. Mix well with a cup of bread crumbs, 1 beaten egg, 1 teaspoon of sage, if desired, and salt and pepper to taste. Moisten with milk or bean liquid. Shape into the form of sausages, dip in raw egg beaten with a little water, then roll in bread crumbs. Brown in a little melted fat.

To make a bean loaf, use the above recipe. Add a chopped onion, finely chopped celery, or some dried herbs if you like. Shape into a loaf, place in a shallow pan, pour a little melted fat over the top, and bake until well browned. Serve with hot tomato sauce.

From the pamphlet Dried Beans & Peas in Wartime Meals, 1943.

Meatless Monday Bean Loaf
Meatless meals were part of World War One and the concept continued on during World War Two. Homemakers were encouraged to try recipes that concentrated on vegetables, or that included a main faux dish that mimicked the flavor and texture of a traditional meat dish.

> One cup uncooked navy beans or three cups cooked navy beans
> 1 cup bread crumbs

1 small onion, diced

3 tablespoons cooking fat

1 egg

1 1/2 teaspoons salt

1 cup evaporated milk

In a bowl, mash cooked beans. Add other ingredients in the order listed and stir until well blended. Turn into a well greased 2-quart baking dish. Shape into a loaf. Bake in a moderate oven (375° F.) 45 minutes.

From Chattanooga News Free Press, *January 1944.*

Kale and Rice Ring

Cook 2 quarts of kale, drain if necessary, and add one-quarter cup of meat drippings. Make a ring with 3 cups of hot cooked rice and fill the center of the ring with the vegetable. Or mix the seasoned vegetable and the rice together and serve. Hot, fluffy mashed potatoes may be used for the ring instead of the rice.

From the pamphlet Green Vegetables in Wartime Meals, 1943.

Harvard Beets

1/3 cup sugar

1 tablespoon cornstarch

1/4 teaspoon salt

1/2 cup vinegar

3 cups cubed cooked beets

2 tablespoons butter

Combine sugar, cornstarch and salt; add vinegar and boil 5 minutes, stirring constantly, Add beets and butter; cook over boiling water until beets are heated through. Serves 6.

From the Military Meals at Home Cookbook, 1943.

Wilted Greens

First cousin to panned vegetables is the old-fashioned way of wilting garden lettuce and

other greens. To every 2 quarts of the greens, measured after they are looked over and washed, allow one-fourth cup meat drippings, one-half cup vinegar, and if desired a small onion chopped.

255

Cook the onion in the fat until it turns yellow. Add the vinegar, and when it is heated add the

greens. Cover and cook until wilted. Season with salt and pepper and serve hot. Or let cool and serve as a salad.

From the pamphlet Green Vegetables in Wartime Meals, 1943.

Peas and Potatoes

Cook 2 cups of peas and 2 cups of diced potatoes, new or old, with a little chopped onion, until all are tender. Add a little fat and seasoning and serve at once.

From the pamphlet Green Vegetables in Wartime Meals, 1943.

Spinach Loaf

Spinach and kale are especially good in a vegetable loaf. Prepare exactly as for creamed vegetables, adding a little chopped onion for flavor. Remove the center of a loaf of stale bread, leaving a shell for the creamed vegetable. (Use the crumbs in puddings or other baked dishes.) Fill with the hot vegetable mixture and moisten the sides and top of the loaf. Bake until hot and crisp, then cut in slices and serve.

From the pamphlet Green Vegetables in Wartime Meals, 1943.

Scalloped Asparagus and Spaghetti

1 1/2 cups spaghetti

2 cups cooked asparagus

1 cup thin white sauce

Cook the spaghetti in salted, boiling water until tender, and drain. Place layers of the spaghetti and cooked asparagus in a greased baking dish. Add 3 or 4 drops of table sauce to the white sauce, and pour over the contents of the baking dish. Sprinkle with fine bread crumbs, and bake until golden brown in a moderate oven. Cabbage combines well with spaghetti, too, in a scalloped dish—or try noodles for a change. Melt a little cheese in the white sauce if you wish, to add more flavor and food value.

From the pamphlet Green Vegetables in Wartime Meals, 1943.

5-Minute Cabbage

Heat 3 cups of milk, add 2 quarts of shredded cabbage, and simmer for about 2 minutes. Mix 3 tablespoons of flour with 3 tablespoons of melted fat Add to this blended flour and fat, a little of the hot milk. Stir into the cabbage and cook for 3 or 4 minutes, stirring all the while. Season to taste with salt pepper and serve at once.

From the pamphlet Green Vegetables in Wartime Meals, 1943.

Stewed Okra and Tomatoes

Add about 3 cups each of diced okra and tomatoes to 3 tablespoons of melted fat in a saucepan. Sprinkle with salt and pepper. Cover and cook for 10 or 15 minutes at moderate heat. Remove the cover and cook a little longer for the liquid to evaporate. Serve piping hot. Squash used instead of okra makes another interesting combination . . . follow the same recipe as for okra and tomatoes.

From the pamphlet Green Vegetables in Wartime Meals, 1943.

Heinz Panama Radish Salad

This recipe comes from a Heinz advertisement during World War II. Mix about 2 doz. medium-sized radishes (sliced) with

1/2 teaspoon salt

1/2 teaspoon minced onions

1/2 teaspoon chopped mint or parsley leaves

A large tomato, chopped fine (if you have it)

Add 1/4 cup Heinz Pure cider vinegar

2 teaspoon Heinz Olive Oil (optional)

Garnish with tender radish tops and garden lettuce.

Heinz Victory Garden Advertisement

Heinz Old-Fashioned Potato Salad

This is another great Heinz War era recipe from an advertisement. Heinz, like many companies used their advertising to promote easy recipes using their products that could be prepared on a budget and with rationed items and items from a Victory Garden.

Made from any kind of potatoes, this salad is delicious—but, if possible, do try it with tiny new potatoes from your garden.

To serve 4 you need 4 cups cubed boiled potatoes
1 small onion, chopped
For dressing . . . heat 3 tablespoon bacon droppings
2 tablespoons Heinz Cider Vinegar
2 tablespoon water
1 tablepsoon Heinz Worcestershire Sauce

Pour on potatoes. Salt to taste. Sprinkle with chopped onion tops. Serve hot. Surround potato salad with tender young beet tops or dande- lions, shredded. Save a little of the bacon dressing to pour over greens.
Heinz Victory Garden Advertisement

Fried Cabbage

1/4 cup bacon drippings
3 cups chopped cooked cabbage
1/2 teaspoon salt
1/8 teaspoon pepper

Melt bacon drippings, add cabbage, salt and pepper. Cover and cook over low heat 20 to 30 minutes, stirring frequently to prevent scorching. Serves 6.
From the Military Meals at Home Cookbook, 1943.

Baked Carrots

1 1/2 pounds carrots
1/4 cup boiling water
4 tablespoons bacon drippings
1/2 teaspoon salt
1/8 teaspoon pepper

Scrape carrot and cut into 1/2 inch slices. Add water, cover tightly and cook 20 minutes, or until tender. Melt drippings in a baking dish, add car- rots, salt and pepper, cover and bake in a moderate oven (350° F.) about 15 minutes. Serves 6.

MINT GLAZED CARROTS—To cooked carrots add 1/2 cup mint leaves and boiling water. Boil 5 minutes. Drain, add salt, pepper, 1/2 cup butter and 1/2 cup sugar. Set in oven until sugar melts.

TOASTED CARROTS—Scrape and boil. Drain, add seasoning, roll in butter, then in corn flakes and brown in oven at 350° F.
From the *Military Meals at Home Cookbook, 1943.*

Asparagus

    1 1/2 pounds asparagus

    1 teaspoon salt

    Hot toast

Wash asparagus thoroughly and tie into 6 individual bundles. Place bundles upright, with stems down, in boiling water to cover thick part of stalks; add salt, cover and cook 20 to 25 minutes, or until stalks are tender. Drain, season with pepper and butter and serve on hot toast. Serves 6.

    CREAMED—Serve with cream sauce using asparagus water for one-half of the liquid.

From the Military Meals at Home Cookbook, 1943.

Simmered Dry Beans

    1 1/4 pounds dry beans

    1/4 pound sliced bacon or salt pork

    1 teaspoon salt

    1/8 teaspoon pepper

Wash beans thoroughly, cover with cold water, heat to boiling and simmer until tender, about 4 hours. Add water as necessary. After 2 hours add meat, salt and pepper. Serves 6. Dried Limas are prepared in the same way. To shorten cooking time soak beans overnight. Drain and cook in boiling salted water with bacon until beans are tender, about 1 to 1 1/2 hours.

From the Military Meals at Home Cookbook, 1943.

Fresh String or Snap Beans

    1 1/2 pounds string or snap bears

    3/4 teaspoon salt

Wash beans and remove ends and strings. Cut into 1-inch pieces. Add boiling water to 1/3 cover beans; add salt, cover tightly and cook 30 to 35 minutes, or until just tender. Drain, saving liquid for soups and gravies. Season with pepper and butter. Serves 6.

    STRING BEANS WITH CHEESE—Arrange beans in greased baking dish, season with salt and cayenne, add 1/2 cup cheese, 1 tablespoon butter and 1/3 CUP cream. Stir until well mixed. Cover with 1/4 cup cheese and 1 tablespoon butter. Bake in hot o.ven (400° F.) 20 minutes.

From the Military Meals at Home Cookbook, 1943.

Canned beans

    3 cups canned baked beans

    1/4 cup tomato catchup

    2 tablespoons minced onion

    1 tablespoon minced pickle

    1 tablespoon molasses

    1/2 teaspoon prepared mustard

    6 slices bacon

Mix all ingredients together, except bacon, and place in baking dish. Cover top with bacon slices. Bake in a moderate oven (350° F.) 40 minutes. Serves 6.

From the Military Meals at Home Cookbook, 1943.

Sweet-Sour Green Beans

A little vinegar and sweetened cream or evaporated milk added to cooked green beans gives that different flavor that your family will enjoy as a change.

From the pamphlet Green Vegetables in Wartime Meals, 1943.

Quick Mashed

Peel 6 medium-sized hot cooked potatoes. Mash thoroughly and quickly. Beat in hot milk a little at a time until potatoes are fluffy and smooth. Season with salt and pepper. If desired, add fat, finely chopped green pepper, pimiento, chives, or onion.

From the pamphlet Potatoes in Popular Ways, 1944.

Creamed Potatoes

    4 tablespoons fat

    4 tablespoons flour

    1/2 teaspoon salt

    1/4 teaspoon pepper

    1 cup hot beef stock

    1 cup evaporated milk

    3 cups diced cooked potatoes

    1/4 cup minced parsley

Melt fat, add flour, salt and pepper. Stir until blended. Add beef stock and milk gradually, Heat to boiling and cook slowly until thickened, stirring constantly. Add potatoes and heat thoroughly. Sprinkle with parsley. Serves 6.

From the Military Meals at Home Cookbook, 1943.

Potato Hot Pot

>3 cups sliced or diced potatoes
>1 medium-sized onion, sliced
>2 tablespoons fat
>3 1/2 cups tomatoes
>1 1/2 teaspoons salt
>Pepper

Cook the potatoes and onion in the fat 10 minutes. Add the tomatoes, salt, and pepper. Cover and simmer 25 to 30 minutes, or until potatoes are tender.

For variety, add a cup of cooked green beans during the last 10 minutes of cooking, or add a dash of chili powder or a few sprigs of thyme, or sprinkle with a little grated cheese, just before serving.

From the pamphlet Potatoes in Popular Ways, 1944.

Boiled in Jackets

First of all scrub the potatoes, then drop them into a kettle of boiling water . . . enough to cover them. Cook covered until tender; drain at once so the potatoes won't get waterlogged. Peel and season with table tat, meat drippings, or gravy, salt and pepper to taste. Or eat skins and all if they are small new potatoes.

From the pamphlet Potatoes in Popular Ways, 1944.

The Perfect Baked Potato

Wash and dry potatoes of uniform size. Bake in a hot oven (425° F.) 40 to 60 minutes or until tender. If you want the skin to be soft, rub a little fat on the potato before baking.

Cut crisscross gashes in the skin of the baked potato on one side. Then pinch the poato so that some of the soft inside pops up through the opening. Drop in meat drippings, bits of crisp-cooked salt pork, or table fat.

Save fuel by baking potatoes when you oven-cook other food. If a moderate oven is called for, allow a little extra time for the potatoes to bake.

Stuffed.—For an extra special, cut large baked potatoes in half lengthwise. Scoop out the inside. Mash; add fat and seasonings. Stir in hot milk and beat until fluffy and smooth. Stuff back into potato shells, brush top with melted fat,, and brown in a hot oven.

For a main dish, add chopped left-over cooked meat or grated cheese. *From the pamphlet* Potatoes in Popular Ways, 1944.

Potatoes Au Gratin
3/4 cup grated cheese
1 1/2 cups medium white sauce
6 hot cooked potatoes

Add cheese to white sauce and stir until melted. Cut potatoes into 3/4-inch cubes and add to sauce. Mix carefully so as not to break the cubes of potato. Bake in hot oven (450° F.) until browned. Serves 6.
From the Military Meals at Home Cookbook, 1943.

Lyonnaise Potatoes
3 cups diced cooked potatoes
2 tablespoons minced onion
3 tablespoons fat
1/2 teaspoon salt
1/4 teaspoon pepper

The potatoes should be rather underdone to produce the best results. Sauté onions in fat until yellow, add diced potatoes, salt and pepper. Spread on bottom of greased baking pan and bake in quick oven (400° F.) 15 minutes, or until browned. Serves 6. Fry potatoes, adding chopped green pepper and pimiento.
From the Military Meals at Home Cookbook, 1943.

Candied Sweet Potatoes
6 sweet potatoes
1 tablespoon butter
1/2 cup sugar
3/4 cup beef stock

Cook sweet potatoes or yams until tender, peel and cut into halves lengthwise. Arrange in layers in greased baking pan, dotting each potato with butter and sugar. Add beef stock and bake in moderate oven (350° F.) 30 minutes, or until browned, Serves 6.

From the Military Meals at Home Cookbook, 1943.

French Fried Potatoes

Wash and pare potatoes and cut into 1/2-inch slices. Dry between towels and fry in deep fat (380° F.). Drain on soft paper, sprinkle with salt and serve. Allow 1 potato. per serving.

From the Military Meals at Home Cookbook, 1943.

Macaroni & Cheese

2 cups macaroni, broken into short lengths

8 cups boiling water

2 teaspoons salt

1/4 pound cheese, diced Paprika

Add macaroni to rapidly boiling salted water and cook until tender, 12 to 15 minutes. Drain. Spread 1/3 of macaroni in greased baking dish, cover with 1/3 of cheese, continue until all are used. Bake in a moderate oven (350° F.) 25 minutes. Sprinkle with paprika. Serves 6. If desired, add 1 1/2 cups cooked tomatoes to mixture and cover with bread crumbs.

From the Military Meals at Home Cookbook, 1943.

Potato Salad

Hot. —Cook 3 1/4 cup diced salt pork until crisp. Add 1/4 cup vinegar, 1/4 cup water, 1 medium-sized chopped onion, and 1 quart cubed cooked potatoes. Season with salt and pepper. Heat well.

Cold.—Slice or dice cold cooked potatoes. Season with salt, chopped onion, and salad dressing. lf desired, add sliced hard-cooked eggs.

From the pamphlet Potatoes in Popular Ways, 1944.

Potato Puff

To 3 cups mashed potatoes add 1 egg yolk, hot milk to moisten, 2 tablespoons melted fat, salt, and any other seasoning you like.   Beat well. Then fold in 1 stiffly beaten egg white. Pile lightly into a greased baking dish. Bake in a moderately hot oven (375° F.) 30 minutes or until puffy and brown.

From the pamphlet Potatoes in Popular Ways, 1944.

Potato Scallop

    6 medium-sized potatoes
    2 tablespoons flour
    1 1/2 teaspoons salt
    Pepper
    2 tablespoons fat
    2 cups hot milk

Peel and slice the potatoes. Put a layer of potatoes in a greased baking dish. Sprinkle with part of flour, salt, and pepper. Dot with fat. Repeat until all the potatoes are used. Pour in the milk-use very fresh milk or it may curdle. Bake in a moderate oven (350° F.) for 1 hour or until the potatoes are tender and browned on top. Add more milk if the potatoes get dry.

From the pamphlet Potatoes in Popular Ways, 1944.

Fried, Country Style

Peel, and slice thin, enough raw potatoes to make 1 quart. Put in a frying pan with 2 tablespoons of melted fat or meat drippings. Cover closely. Cook over medium heat 10 to 15 minutes or until browned on the bottom. Turn and brown on the other side. If desired, brown a little chopped onion in the fat before adding the potatoes.

From the pamphlet Potatoes in Popular Ways, 1944.

Roast Potatoes

Peel medium-sized potatoes and place around meat in roasting pan during the last hour or hour and a half of cooking the meat. Turn and baste potatoes occasionally with meat drippings.

From the pamphlet Potatoes in Popular Ways, 1944.

Boston Baked Beans

To bake beans rich and brown in the Boston style, long slow cooking is necessary. Soak 2 cups of beans overnight in 1 1/2 quarts of cold water. In the morning simmer for 45 minutes, or until the beans begin to soften.

Score a 1/4-pound piece of salt pork and put half of the pork in the bottom of the bean pot. Add the beans and bury the other half of the pork in the top portion of the beans, with only the scored rind exposed. Mix 4 tablespoons of molasses, 1 to 2 teaspoons of salt, and 1/2 teaspoon of mustard if desired, with a little hot water. Pour over the beans. Cover with hot water.

Put a lid on the pot and bake in a slow oven for 6 or 7 hours. Add a little hot water from time to time. During the last hour of baking remove the lid to let the beans and pork brown on top.

For Variety in Flavor.—Place a peeled onion in the bottom of the bean pot, or add the onion plus tomato catsup. Some New Englanders use maple syrup or maple sugar in place of the molasses to sweeten their baked beam.

From the pamphlet Dried Beans & Peas in Wartime Meals, 1943.

Beans Baked the Michigan Way

To 1 quart of beans that have already been cooked tender in water with a 4-ounce piece of salt pork, add 4 tablespoons of molasses or brown sugar and salt to season. Place in a shallow pan with enough of the bean liquid to moisten well. Slice the salt pork over the top. Brown in the oven.

From the pamphlet Dried Beans & Peas in Wartime Meals, 1943.

Beans Western

Brown a chopped onion in a little fat. Add 2 cups of tomatoes. Season with salt and pepper. Bring to a boil and add 1 quart of cooked beans. Simmer 15 to 20 minutes. Sprinkle with parsley and serve hot.

From the pamphlet Dried Beans & Peas in Wartime Meals, 1943.

Mexican Style Beans

Soak 2 cups of beans (pintos preferred) overnight in 1 1/2 quarts of water. The next day, bring them to a boil and simmer for about 3 hours. When the beans start to simmer, add a few bacon rinds. After 2 hours, add a minced clove of garlic and a dried red chili pepper, or chili powder, and salt to taste. The cooked juice should be thick. If desired, mash the beans and add grated cheese.

From the pamphlet Dried Beans & Peas in Wartime Meals, 1943.

Hot Bean Salad

Cut 2 strips of bacon or salt pork into half inch pieces and fry to a light brown. Add a third of a cup of chopped onion and brown lightly. Add 3 cups of boiled or baked beans, 1/2 teaspoon of mustard, 1/4 cup each of vinegar and water, and a dash of pepper. Simmer until the beans absorb the vinegar and the water. Serve hot.

Double the recipe if you wish to serve hot bean salad as the main dish.
From the pamphlet Dried Beans & Peas in Wartime Meals, 1943.

Succotash

Chop and brown an onion in a little fat. Add 2 cups each of cooked com and beans. Simmer for a few minutes. Season with salt and pepper and serve hot. If desired, add chopped green pepper for more flavor and color.

From the pamphlet Dried Beans & Peas in Wartime Meals, 1943.

Hopping John, Southern Style

Cook a ham bone or knuckle in 2 quarts of water for 2 hours. Then add 1 cup of dried peas or beans that have been soaked overnight in cold water and cook until almost tender. Remove the ham bone, add a cup of washed rice, and salt and pepper. Boil gently about 20 minutes, or until the rice is soft and the liquid almost cooked away. Serve hot.

From the pamphlet Dried Beans & Peas in Wartime Meals, 1943.

Spanish Rice

1 cup rice
2 tablespoons fat
3 slices bacon
2 onions, minced
1/2 cup minced green pepper
2 cups cooked tomatoes
1 teaspoon salt
1/4 teaspoon pepper
1/2 teaspoon chili powder
3 cups beef stock
Wash rice and drain thoroughly, Fry rice in fat until browned. Fry

266

bacon, onions and green pepper in skillet until browned. Add tomatoes and cook slowly for 10 minutes, Combine rice and tomato mixtures in double boiler; add salt, pepper, chili powder and beef stock. Simmer until rice is tender. Serves 6.

From the Military Meals at Home Cookbook, 1943.

Apple and Celery

1 cup diced celery

2 cups diced apples

1 cup mayonnaise

Combine all ingredients, chill serve in lettuce cups. Serves 6.

From the Military Meals at Home Cookbook, 1943

Coleslaw

4 slices bacon, diced and browned

1 cup vinegar

3 onions, chopped fine

2/3 cup sugar

1/2 teaspoon salt

1 small head Cabbage, chopped fine

Mix bacon, vinegar, onions, sugar and salt together and heat to boiling. Remove from heat and pour over chopped cabbage. Serve hot or cold. Serves 6.

From the Military Meals at Home Cookbook, 1943.

Cucumber and onion Salad

2 medium cucumbers

3 onions, sliced

1 cup vinegar

1 teaspoon salt

1/8 teaspoon pepper

Pare cucumbers and slice thin. Add onions and season. Serves 6. If cucumbers are very tender they need not be pared. The green rind is decorative. Cucumbers are attractive when scored lengthwise with a fourtined fork before slicing,

From the Military Meals at Home Cookbook, 1943.

Pimiento Salad

    1 canned pimiento, chopped

    1 small head cabbage, shredded

    1/2 cup diced celery

    3 sweet pickles, chopped

    1/8 cup mayonnaise, lettuce

    Toss first 4 ingredients together with mayonnaise. Serve cold on
       lettuce. Serves 6.

    From the Military Meals at Home Cookbook, 1943.

Mrs. Truman's Bing Cherry Mould (Salad)

    1 large can bing cherries

    2 packages cream cheese

    1 package cherry Jello (or any red gelatin)

    1 package lime Jello

Measure the juice from the cherries and add water to make two cups. Heat and dissolve cherry Jello in this. When partly set, add cherries. Make lime Jello with water. When partly set, beat in cheese. Put cheese Jello in bottom of mould; let set; then put cherry mixture on top. Serve with mayonnaise.

    Harry S. Truman Library & Museum

Salad Dressing

    1/4 cup fat (drippings or rendered trimmings)

    3 tablespoons flour

    1/4 teaspoon mustard

    1 1/2 teaspoons salt

    1 tablespoon sugar

    1 cup milk

    1 egg

    1/3 cup vinegar

Blend the melted fat and flour mixed with the seasonings. Add the cold milk. Heat and stir constantly until thickened. Cover and cook over boiling water for 5 minutes longer. Add part of the sauce slowly to the beaten egg while stirring. Combine with the rest of the sauce. Stir and cook a few minutes. Add the vinegar slowly and continue to cook until thick.

    From the pamphlet Fats in Wartime Meals, 1943.

World War II Mayonnaise

My mother made this during the war. She continued to make it for years after. I guess we just got used to the flavor. She never did go back to store bought until later in life.

2 raw egg yolks
1/2 teaspoon salt
1/4 teaspoon pepper
1/4 teaspoon paprika
1/8 tsp. dry mustard
1 cup salad oil
2 tablespoon vinegar or lemon juice

Add the dry seasonings to the egg yolks, beating thoroughly. Add vinegar or lemon juice and beat again. Add the oil gradually, drop by drop, constantly beating. The mixture should become thick and creamy. If the mixture breaks or curdles, start with another clean bowl and add another egg yolk and a small quantity of oil to the yolk; then, by very small quantities, add the curdled mixture. This third egg process should restore the consistency.

Submitted by Carol F.

Soups Stews & Chowders

Barley Soup

7 gallons beef stock
3 pounds barley, pearled
2 pounds onions, chopped
Salt and pepper to taste

Thoroughly mix all ingredients and boil for 1 hour. Ten minutes before serving add enough beef stock to make 10 gallons of soup. Season to taste with salt and pepper.

From The Army Cook Training Manual 10-405, April 24, 1942.

Bean soup

3 pounds beans, dry
7 gallons water or beef stock
10 pounds soup bone

1 1/2 pounds bacon, diced and browned
2 cans tomatoes (No. 21/2 or No. 3 cans)
Salt and pepper to taste

Thoroughly clean and wash the beans. Place them and the soup bone and the beef stock and allow to simmer for about 5 hours, or until the beans have gone to pieces and will pass through a colander. Ten minutes before serving add the tomatoes, the diced and browned bacon, and enough beef stock to make 10 gallons of soup. Thicken with a flour batter and season to taste with salt and pepper. Serve hot with crackers or croutons.

From The Army Cook Training Manual 10-405, April 24, 1942

Beef soup

7 gallons beef stock
5 pounds beef (shank, neck, etc.)
2 cans tomatoes (No. 3 cans)
2 pounds rice, if desired
1 bunch parsley, if desired
Salt and pepper to taste

This soup may be made to best advantage on days when simmered beef is served. After simmering the beef until done. Take it out and skim off the grease. Dice the beef very fine and add the stock and tomatoes to the water in which the beef was boiled; if desired, a little rice maybe added. Ten minutes before serving, add enough beef stock to make 10 gallons of soup. Season to taste with salt and pepper and serve hot. Sprinkle with chopped parsley.

From The Army Cook Training Manual 10-405, April 24, 1942

Bean Chowder

1 cup dry beans
1 cup diced carrots
1 cup tomatoes
1/2 cup shredded green pepper
1 onion, chopped fine
2 teaspoons salt
2 tablespoons uncooked cracked wheat or 1 tablespoon flour

2 cups milk

Pepper to taste

Soak the beans overnight in 1 1/2 quarts of cold water. Cook in a covered pan until the beans begin to soften, then add the vegetables and cook until tender. Add salt and cracked wheat or flour mixed with a little cold water. Stir. Cook about 30 minutes. Add the milk and pepper, heat to boiling, and serve.

From the pamphlet Dried Beans & Peas in Wartime Meals, 1943.

Quick Potato Soup

3 cups tubed potatoes

2 tablespoons chopped onion

2 tablespoons fat

1 1/2 cups boiling water

4 cups milk

1 1/2 teaspoons salt

Pepper

Cook the potatoes, onion, and fat in the water until the potatoes are tender. Add the milk, salt, and pepper. Heat and serve.

From the pamphlet Potatoes in Popular Ways, 1944.

Potato Soup With Oatmeal

4 cups meat stock, or use bouillon cubes

2 cups diced potatoes

1/2 cup sliced onions

1 cup sliced carrots

1/2 cup chopped celery

1/2 cup rolled oats

1/2 to 1 cup cooked tomatoes

Salt and pepper

To meat stock add potatoes, onions, carrots, and celery. Bring to boiling point. Gradually stir in the rolled oats. Simmer 20 minutes or until vegetables are tender. Add the tomatoes. Season with salt and pepper and heat.

From the pamphlet Potatoes in Popular Ways, 1944.

General Eisenhower's Recipe For Vegetable Soup

The best time to make vegetable soup is a day or so after you have had fried chicken and out of which you have saved the necks, ribs, backs, uncooked. (The chicken is not essential, but does add something.) Procure from the meat market a good beef soup bone—the bigger the better. It is a rather good idea to have it split down the middle so that all the marrow is exposed. In addition, buy a couple pounds of ordinary soup meat, either beef or mutton, or both.

Put all this meat, early in the morning, in a big kettle. The best kind is heavy

Aluminum, but a good iron pot will do almost as well. Put in also the bony parts of the chicken you have saved. Cover it with water, something on the order of 5 quarts. Add a teaspoon of salt, a bit of black pepper and, if you like a touch of garlic (one small piece). If you don't like garlic put in an onion. Boil all this slowly all day long. Keep on boiling till the meat has literally dropped off the bone. If your stock boils down during the day, add enough water from time to time to keep the meat covered. When the whole thing has practically disintegrated pour out into another large kettle through a colander. Make sure that the marrow is out of the bones. Let this drain through the colander for quite awhile as much juice will drain out of the meat. (Shake the colander well to help get out all the juice). Save a few of the better pieces of meat just to cut up a little bit in small pieces to put into your soup after it is done. Put the kettle containing the stock you now have in a very cool place, outdoors in the winter time or in the ice box; let it stand all night and the next day until you are ready to make your soup.

You will find that a hard layer of fat has formed on top of the stock which can usually be lifted off since the whole kettle full of stock has jelled. Some people like a little bit of the fat left on and some like their soup very rich and do not remove more than about half of the fat.

Put the stock back into your kettle and you are now ready to make your soup. In a separate pan, boil slowly about a third of a teacupful of barley. This should be cooked separately since it has a habit, in a soup kettle of settling to the bottom and if your fire should happen to get too hot it is likely to burn. If you cannot get barley use rice, but it is a poor substitute. One of the secrets of making good vegetable soup is not to cook any of the vegetables too long. However, it is impossible to give you an exact measure of the vegetables you should put in because some people like their vegetable soup almost as thick as stew, others like it much thinner. Moreover, sometimes you can get exactly the vegetables you want; other times you have to substitute. Where you use canned vegetables, put them in only a few minutes before taking the soup off the fire. If you use fresh ones, naturally they must be fully cooked in the soup. The things put into the soup are about as follows:

1 qt. can of canned tomatoes

1/2 teacup full of fresh peas. If you can't get peas, a handful of good green beans cut up very small can substitute.

2 normal sized potatoes, diced into cubes of about half-inch size.

2 or 3 branches of good celery.

1 good-sized onion. (sliced)

3 nice-sized carrots diced about the same size as potatoes.

1 turnip diced like the potatoes.

1/2 cup of canned corn.

A handful of raw cabbage cut up in small pieces.

Your vegetables should not all be dumped in at once. The potatoes, for example, will cook more quickly than the carrots. Your effort must be to have them all nicely cooked but not mushy, at about the same time. The fire must not be too hot but the soup should keep bubbling. When you figure the soup is about done, put in your barley which should not be fully cooked, add a tablespoonful of prepared gray seasoning and taste for flavoring, particularly salt and pepper, and if you have it, use some onion salt, garlic salt and celery salt. (If you cannot get the gravy seasoning, use one teaspoonful of Worcestershire sauce.) Cut up the few bits of the meat you have saved and put about a small handful into the soup. While you are cooking the soup do not allow the liquid to boil down too much. Add a bit of water from time to time. If your stock was good and thick when you started, you can add more water than if it was thin when you started.

As a final touch, in the springtime when nasturtiums are green and tender, you can take a few nasturtium stems, cut them up in small pieces, boil them separately as you did the barley, and add them to your soup. (About one tablespoonful after cooking.)

The Dwight D. Eisenhower Presidential Library and Museum

Clam chowder

    6 quarts clams, husked, diced

    2 pounds bacon, diced and browned

    12 pounds potatoes, diced, raw

    7 gallons beef stock

    2 pounds onions, chopped, browned

    2 pounds flour

    Salt and pepper to taste

Boil the potatoes, clams, bacon, and onions in the beef stock until well done. If fresh clams are used, wash thoroughly to remove sand. Thicken slightly with a flour batter and serve hot. Season to taste with salt and pepper and add enough beef stock 10 minutes before serving to make 10 gallons.

From The Army Cook Training Manual 10-405, April 24, 1942.

Corn Chowder

    5 cans corn (No. 2 cans)

    2 pounds bacon, diced

    2 pounds onions

    6 pounds potatoes, diced

    8 gallons beef stock

    4 cans milk, evaporated

    2 pounds bread, diced

    Salt and pepper to taste

Brown the bacon and onions in a bakepan, then transfer to a boiler and add the potatoes and beef stock. Boil until done (about 20 minutes). Add enough beef stock 10 minutes before serving to make 10 gallons. Toast sliced bread (preferably dried-out bread) in the oven and add it to the chowder after, the potatoes are done. Add the milk and corn but do not allow to boil. Season to taste with salt and pepper.

From The Army Cook Training Manual 10-405, April 24, 1942

General Eisenhower's Old-Fashioned Beef Stew

    For 60 portions, use the following ingredients:

    20 pounds stewing meat (prime round)

    8 pounds small Irish potatoes

    6 bunches small carrots

    5 pounds small onions

15 fresh tomatoes
1 bunch bouquet garniture
3 gallons beef stock
Salt, pepper, and Accent

Stew the meat until tender. Add the vegetables and bouquet garniture (thyme, bay leaves, garlic, etc. in cloth bag). When vegetables are done, strain off 2 gallons of stock from the stew and thicken slightly with beef roux. Pour back into stew and let simmer for one-half hour.

For A Family

To adapt above recipe to average family use (6 portions), use one-tenth of the ingredients listed. This would be approximately as follows:

2 pounds stewing meat (prime round)
1 pound small Irish potatoes
1 bunch small carrots
3/4 pound small onions
2 fresh tomatoes
Assorted spices
2 1/2 pints beef stock
Salt, pepper, and Accent

Cook as in above recipe, straining off 1 cup of stock from stew instead of the 2 gallons.

The Dwight D. Eisenhower Presidential Library and Museum

Mutton Stew

35 pounds mutton
40 pounds potatoes
7 pounds onions
3 gallons beef stock or water
1 pound flour

Cut the Mutton into 1 inch cubes. Add sufficient beef stock or cold water to just cover the mutton, and allow to simmer slowly for 1 1/2 hours or until the mutton is done. Add vegetables and cook until done. Season to taste with pepper and salt and thicken slightly with a flour batter. Serve hot with or without dumplings (recipe 80). If dumplings are added, use only 20 pounds of mutton and 30 pounds of potatoes.

From The Army Cook Training Manual 10-405, April 24, 1942.

Dried Bean or Pea Soup

Soak 1 cup of dried beans or peas overnight in a quart of water. In the morning, add another quart of water, 1/4 pound of salt pork, an onion, and a few stalks of celery, if desired.

Simmer until the beans or peas are tender. Remove the salt pork and rub the rest through a strainer if a smooth soup is wanted. Cut the salt pork into tiny pieces and return to the soup. Add a tablespoon of flour mixed well with a little water to keep the bean pulp from settling to the bottom Stir, reheat, and season with salt and pepper.

With Meat Leftovers.—In place of the salt pork in the recipe above, cook the beans with a ham bone, or add some chopped leftover meat, or a frankfurter cut into thin slices.

Add Roasted Peanuts—Finely chopped or ground peanuts are good in bean soup, also.

With Tomato or Carrots. —These add a touch of color and a few more vitamins to bean or pea soup.

For a "Hot" Soup.—Add a clove of garlic, half a chopped onion, 1 tablespoon oregano, and 2 chili peppers. Strain after cooking. Heat again and serve.

From the pamphlet Dried Beans & Peas in Wartime Meals, 1943.

USS Alabama Beef Stew for 2500 Men

Ingredients Weights per 2,500 portions
Beef (Bone In) 1,000 lbs.
Beef (Boneless) 700 lbs.
Salt 9 lbs.
Pepper 12 1/2 oz.
Flour 37 lbs.
Fat 37 lbs.
Beef Stock (or water) 100 gallons
Peas, fresh or frozen 125 lbs.
Tomatoes 318 lbs.
Onions, small, quartered 150 lbs.
Carrots, sliced or cubed 150 lbs.
Potatoes, cubed 300 lbs.
Celery 125 lbs.

Flour for gravy 25 lbs.

Cold Water for gravy 13 quarts

Salt & Pepper for gravy As desired

1—Cut meat into 1 to 2 inch cubes.

2—Mix together salt, pepper, and flour. Dredge meat in flour. Cook in fat until browned, stirring constantly.

3—Add 100 gallons stock or water. Cover. Let simmer for 2 1/2 to 3 hours or until tender.

4—Cook peas in small amount of water 10 to 15 minutes. Drain.

5—Add remaining vegetables to meat mixture. Cook 40 to 45 minutes.

6—Blend together flour and water to a smooth paste. Drain stock from meat and vegetables, and then thicken with paste. Heat to boiling temperature, stirring constantly. Add salt and pepper as desired.

7—Pour gravy over meat and vegetables. Reheat.

8—Garnish with cooked peas and serve.

Courtesy of USS Alabama Battleship Memorial Park.

DESERTS COOKIES ETC.

World War II Faux Whipped Topping

2 egg whites

1/2 cup confectioners' sugar

1 cup grated apple

1 teaspoon lemon juice

Beat egg whites until stiff. Add half the sugar while beating. Then add the grated apple and rest of sugar alternately while continuing to beat. Stir in lemon juice quickly. Plop dollops onto fruit or desserts.

Submitted by Carol F.

Mom's Sugarless Apple Dessert

I remember mom making this recipe in several versions. She saw it in a newspaper or magazine. But it was always different depending on what we had. Today I add in mini marsh mellows.

Crushed RITZ crackers

Cooking apples

Condensed milk

Orange juice

Nuts or grated chocolate

Arrange crushed crackers at bottom of dish. Grate raw cooking apple. Whip together with the condensed milk. Add a little orange juice. Arrange in dishes with nuts or grated chocolate on top.

From the collection of R.T. Wilsom

Red Cross Doughnuts

During the war the Red Cross touched lives by providing care and services across the world. Besides care packages and clothing millions of hungry people enjoyed a cup of coffee and a famous Red Cross doughnut.

1 1/2 cups sifted flour

1/4 teaspoon baking soda

1/4 teaspoon salt

1/4 teaspoon butter or substitute, melted

1/4 teaspoon ginger

1/4 cup molasses

1/4 cup sour milk

1 egg, well beaten

Combine half of the flour with the soda, salt, and ginger. Combine egg, molasses, sour milk, and melted butter or substitute. Blend with flour mixture and stir until thoroughly mixed and smooth. Add remaining flour to make dough of sufficient body to be rolled. Roll, on floured board, to thickness of 1/4 inch. Cut with donut cutter. Fry in deep hot fat (360° degrees) until lightly browned, about 2 to 3 minutes. Drain on brown paper.

Recipe from the Red Cross media kit.

WWII Butterscotch Sugarless Cake

This recipe was one of my father's favorites. My mom used to make these for him during the war. She often still used natural things like honey for sugar. She seemed to learn how to cook with very little and everything tasted great. She used to say that "rationing" could teach you a lot about how much you could do with so little.

1/2 cup solid shortening

1 cup white corn syrup

2 eggs, beaten

1 package butterscotch pudding mix

1/2 teaspoon salt

2 /3 cup sour milk or buttermilk

2 cups flour

1 teaspoon baking powder

1/2 teaspoon baking soda

1 teaspoon vanilla extract

Preheat oven to 350°

Beat together shortening and corn syrup in bowl. In a different bowl, combine the eggs, pudding mix and salt. Mix with shortening mixture. Next, add sour milk alternately with combined flour, baking powder, and baking soda. Mix well and add vanilla. Divide batter evenly between two greased and floured 9-inch cake pans. Bake in a 350° pre-heated oven 30 to 35 minutes or until done Check often as they may burn. Remove early if needed. Remove from oven, cool completely then fill and/or frost as desired. I use plain vanilla frosting with chocolate sprinkles.

Submitted by Carol Anderson.

Swans Down 1943 Eggless Chocolate Cake

This recipe comes from an advertisement published in 1943 for Swans Down Cake

Flour. Swans was a well known source for budget minded and creative recipes during the war.

2 squares Baker's Unsweetened Chocolate

1 cup milk

1 3/4 cups sifted Swans Down Cake Flour

3/4 teaspoon soda

3/4 teaspoon salt

1 cup sugar

1/3 cup shortening

1 teaspoon vanilla

Combine chocolate and milk in top of double boiler and cook over rapidly boiling water 5 minutes, stirring occasionally. Blend with rotary egg beater; cool. Sift flour once, measure, add soda, salt, and sugar and sift together three times. Cream shortening; add flour mixture, vanilla, and chocolate mixture, and stir until all flour is dampened. Then beat vigorously 1 minute. Bake in two greased and lightly floured 8-inch layer pans in moderate oven (375° F.) 20 minutes, or until done.

Swans Down Cake Flour advertisement recipe, 1943.

World War Two Cake

1 cup shortening
1/4 cup sugar
1 cup corn syrup
2 eggs, beaten
2 cup cake flour
1 teaspoon salt
2 teaspoon baking powder
1/2 teaspoon baking soda
1/4 cup butter milk
1/4 cup sour cream
2 teaspoon vanilla

Cream together shortening and sugar. Add corn syrup and beaten eggs. Sift together the dry ingredients and mix alternately with the sour milk and sour cream. Add vanilla. Bake in greased 9"x13" pan at 350° for 35 to 40 minutes.

Rumford Special Cake

(Three eggs-Corn Syrup)

A cake for a party—particularly good in seasons when eggs are plentiful, though not too demanding at any time. Frost it with the sugarless frosting, flavored with orange!

3 cups sifted cake flour
4 teaspoons Rumford Baking Powder
1/2 teaspoon salt
1/2 cup shortening
1 1/2 cups corn syrup
3 egg yolks
2 teaspoons grated orange rind
1 cup milk
3 egg whites

SIFT together flour, Rumford Baking Powder and salt. Cream shortening, add 1 cup of the corn syrup gradually, and cream until fluffy. Add egg yolks, one at a time, and beat well. Add sifted dry ingredients alternately with milk, stirring well after each addition. Add grated orange rind. Then, beat egg whites until stiff, and add to them the remaining 1/2 cup corn syrup gradually, beating until mixture stands in stiff peaks. Fold into batter until well-blended. Bake in 2 greased 9-inch layer cake pans in a moderate oven (375° F.) for 25 to 30 minutes. Cool and frost as desired. (See recipe for sugarless frosting in this folder.)

Rumford Baking Powder, Sugarless Recipe Booklet World War II.

Sugarless Frosting

This is one of the variations possible by adding different flavorings and colorings, chocolate shot, coconut, or whatever!

1 1/4 cups corn syrup

3 egg whites

2 teaspoons flavoring (vanilla or other flavoring)

1 teaspoon Rumford Baking Powder

BOIL corn syrup in a saucepan over direct heat until it spins a thread when dropped from a spoon. Beat egg whites foamy, add Rumford Baking Powder and beat until stiff. Add corn syrup slowly, beating vigorously while adding. Add flavoring and continue beating until frosting is stiff and stands in peaks. This makes frosting for two 9-inch layers; one medium loaf cake; or 16 large cup cakes.

Rumford Baking Powder, Sugarless Recipe Booklet World War II.

Rumford Honey Cake

Any nutrition expert will tell you about honey's qualifications as a pure natural sweetening-and you'll find out that it helps a cake stay fresh longer!

2 cups sifted cake flour

3 teaspoons Rumford Baking Powder

1/4 teaspoon salt

1/2 cup shortening

2 egg yolks

1 cup honey

1/2 cup milk

2 egg whites

1 teaspoon vanilla

SIFT together flour, Rumford Baking Powder and salt. Cream shortening until light. Beat egg yolks until lemon colored, gradually adding 1/2 cup of the honey while beating. Add the egg-honey mixture slowly to the creamed shortening, creaming while adding. Add sifted dry ingredients alternately with milk, mixing well after each addition. Beat egg whites until stiff; gradually beat in remaining 1/2 cup of honey until mixture stands in stiff peaks. Fold into cake batter until well-blended. Bake in 2 greased 9-inch layer cake pans in a moderate oven (375° F.) for 30 minutes. Cool and frost as desired.

Rumford Baking Powder, Sugarless Recipe Booklet World War II.

White Cake

2 cups sifted flour

1/4 teaspoon salt

2 1/2 teaspoons baking powder

1/2 cup shortening

1 cup sugar

2 eggs, separated

2/3 cup milk

1 teaspoon vanilla

Sift flour, salt and baking powder together. Cream shortening with sugar until fluffy. Add beaten egg yolks and beat thoroughly. Add sifted dry ingredients alternately with milk and vanilla in small amounts, beating well after each addition. Fold in stiffly beaten egg whites. Pour into greased pans and bake in moderate oven (350° F.) about 25 minutes. Cool, fill and frost as desired. Makes 2 (8-inch) layers.

From the Military Meals at Home Cookbook, 1943.

Uncooked Icing

2 cups confectioners' sugar

1/2 cup cold water (about)

2 teaspoons vanilla

4 tablespoons butter

Mix sugar with enough cold water to make a spreading consistency.

Add vanilla and butter and mix well. Spread on cake and let stand 30 minutes before serving. Will cover 2 (8-inch) layers.

From the Military Meals at Home Cookbook, 1943.

Quick Cake

2/3 cup shortening

1 1/4 cups brown sugar, firmly packed

3 eggs, separated

2 cups sifted flour

1/4 teaspoon salt

3 teaspoons baking powder

2 teaspoons cinnamon

1/2 teaspoon nutmeg

1/2 cup milk

Cream shortening and sugar together until fluffy, add beaten yolks. Sift dry ingredients together 3 times and add alternately with milk to first mixture, beating thoroughly after each addition. Fold in stiffly beaten egg whites. Fill into greased cupcake pans 213 full and bake in moderate oven (350° F.) about 25) minutes. Makes 30 cupcakes.

From the Military Meals at Home Cookbook, 1943.

Foundation Cake

1/2 cup fat

1 cup sugar

1 teaspoon flavoring

2 eggs beaten

2 cups sifted cake flour (or 1 3/4 cups all purpose flour)

3 teaspoons baking powder

1 teaspoon salt

3/4 cup milk

Cream the fat and the sugar gradually, and then the flavoring. Beat in the eggs. Add the sifted dry ingredients and milk alternately and beat until mixture is smooth. Pour into lightly greased pans. For a layer cake, bake in a moderate oven (375° F.) for 25 minutes. For a loaf cake, cook in a very moderate oven (325° F.) for 40 to 45 minutes. For cup cakes, cook in a moderate oven (375° F.) for 20 minutes.

If you plan to eat the cake soon after baking, you can reduce the fat in the above recipe to 1/4 cup.

Quick Mix Cake—When time is short, use very soft or melted fat or oil and mix the quick way. Sift all dry ingredients together and combine milk, eggs, fat, and flavoring. Add the dry ingredients to the liquid all at once and stir until the mixture is smooth. Bake as above, and serve while hot.

From the pamphlet Fats in Wartime Meals, 1943.

Corn Cake

2 eggs, slightly beaten

1 cup milk

1/4 cup melted shortening

1/4 cup yellow corn meal

1 cup sifted flour

1 teaspoon salt

1/3 cup sugar

2 1/2 teaspoons baking powder

Beat eggs, add milk and shortening. Sift remaining ingredients together; add to egg mixture and beat well, Pour into greased shallow pan. Bake in hot oven (400° F.) until it shrinks from the sides of the pan, about 20 to 25 minutes. Serves 6.

From the Military Meals at Home Cookbook, 1943.

Piecrust

5 tablespoons fat (commercial oil or fat, or home-rendered poultry or meat fat)

1 1/2 cups sifted flour

1 teaspoon salt

2 1/2 to 4 tablespoons water

Work the fat into sifted flour and salt, with finger tips or a fork, until mixture is granular. Sprinkle some of the water over the surface, combining each dampened part into a dough. Add more water sparingly until mixture is a stiff dough. Divide the dough in half to make two crusts and roll on a lightly floured board.

If you make the pastry with oil, mix the oil with the 2 1/2 tablespoons of water, then combine it with the flour. Roll out as directed above.

If you are using a rendered beef fat or other hard fat, cut it thoroughly into the flour, and warm the water before you add it, to soften the fat. Use 6 tablespoons of a hard fat in the above recipe.

Eisenhower Deep Dish Apple Pie

6 tart apples
1/2 cup sugar
1/2 cup brown sugar
1/2 teaspoon nutmeg
Grated rind of 1 lemon
Grated rind of 1 orange
3 tablespoons butter or margarine
1/2 pastry recipe (below)

Pare and core apples; cut into eights. Place in deep, greased baking dish. Combine sugar, brown sugar, nutmeg, lemon rind and orange rind. Sprinkle over apples. Dot with butter or margarine. Top with thin sheet of pastry, pricked in a design. Bake in hot oven. (425°) Serves six.

Pastry:
2 cups flour
3/4 teaspoon salt
2/3 cup shortening
Cold water

Sift flour; measure. Mix and sift flour and salt. Cut in shortening with 2 knives or pastry blender until flour shortening particles are about the size of small peas. Sprinkle 1 tablespoon cold water over mixture and mix in lightly with a fork. Continue adding water in this fashion until pastry gathers around fork in a soft ball. Divide pastry in half and roll each half separately on lightly floured board to 1/8" thickness. Handle rolling pin very lightly. Makes enough for two crust 9" pie. Note: Make 1/2 this recipe for deep dish or one crust pies.

The Dwight D. Eisenhower Presidential Library and Museum

RITZ® Mock Apple Pie

This recipe is a variation of a cracker pie recipe that American pioneers are said to have used when short on apples or other pie fillings. Soda crackers were used. During the depression years Ritz Crackers came out with an updated version of the cracker pie. It has become something of a legend since those days, and during the World War II years it was a staple for many families.

RITZ® Mock Apple Pie
Pastry for 2-crust 9-inch pie
36 RITZ Crackers, coarsely broken (about 1-3/4 cups crumbs)
2 cups sugar
2 tsp. cream of tartar
Grated peel of 1 lemon
2 Tbsp. lemon juice
2 Tbsp. butter or margarine
1/2 tsp. ground cinnamon

Preheat your oven to 425° F. Roll out half of the pastry and place in 9-inch pie plate. Place cracker crumbs in crust; set aside.

MIX sugar and cream of tartar in medium saucepan. Gradually stir in 1-3/4 cups water until well blended. Bring to boil on high heat. Reduce heat to low; simmer 15 minutes. Add lemon peel and juice; cool. Pour syrup over cracker crumbs. Dot with butter; sprinkle with cinnamon. Roll out remaining pastry; place over pie. Trim; seal and flute edges. Slit top crust to allow steam to escape. BAKE 30 to 35 minutes or until crust is crisp and golden. Cool completely.

Submitted by D. Paterson WWII veteran.

Custard Pie
4 eggs, slightly beaten
1/4 teaspoon salt
1/2 cup sugar
3 cups milk, scalded
1/2 teaspoon vanilla
1/2 recipe Piecrust and nutmeg

Combine eggs, salt and sugar; add milk and vanilla slowly. Line pie pan with piecrust, pour in filling and sprinkle with nutmeg. Bake in very hot oven (450° F.) 10 minutes. Reduce temperature to moderate (350° 'F.) and bake 30 minutes longer, or until a knife inserted comes out clean.

Makes 1 (9-inch) pie.

CRANBERRY CUSTARD PIE—Cook 2 cups cranberries in 1 cup

water until skins pop. Force through sieve. Add to custard.

COCONUT CUSTARD—Add 1 1/2 cups moist shredded coconut to filling. *From the* Military Meals at Home Cookbook, 1943.

Banana Cream Pie
1/2 cup sugar
5 tablespoons flour
1/4 teaspoon salt
2 cups milk
2 egg yolks, slightly beaten
1 tablespoon butter
1/2 teaspoon vanilla
3 ripe bananas
1 baked pie shell
1 recipe Meringue

Combine sugar, flour and salt in top of double boiler. Add milk slowly, mixing thoroughly. Cook ever rapidly boiling water until well thickened, stirring constantly. Stir small amount of hot mixture into egg yolks; then pour back into remaining hot mixture while beating vigorously. Cook 1 minute longer. Remove from heat and add butter and vanilla. Cool. Peel and slice bananas into pie shell and cover immediately with filling. Top with meringue and bake. Makes 1 (9-inch) pie.

From the Military Meals at Home Cookbook, 194.

Chocolate Meringue Pie
1 cup sugar
3 tablespoons cornstarch
3 tablespoons flour
1/2 teaspoon salt
2 1/2 cups hot milk
2 ounces (2 squares) chocolate
2 egg yolks, well beaten
1 teaspoon vanilla
1 tablespoon butter
1 baked pie shell
1 recipe Meringue

Blend sugar, cornstarch, flour and salt. Stir in hot milk and cook over boiling water until thickened. Add chocolate broken into small pieces; stir until smooth. Add a small amount of the mixture to egg yolks, blending thoroughly; return to remaining mixture and cook 2 minutes longer. Cool; add vanilla and butter. Pour into baked pie shell. Top with meringue and bake as directed. Makes 1 (9-inch) pie.

From the Military Meals at Home Cookbook, 1943.

Meringue

2 egg whites

4 tablespoons sugar

1/8 teaspoon salt

1/4 to 1 teaspoon flavoring

Beat egg whites until stiff, add sugar, salt and flavoring gradually and beat until well blended. Spread over filling and bake in a slow oven (325° F.) until a delicate brown, 15 to 20 minutes. In placing meringue on pie or cake, be sure that pie is completely covered with meringue all the way around. It is less likely to shrink.

From the Military Meals at Home Cookbook, 1943.

Brown Sugar Meringue

2 egg whites

4 tablespoons brown sugar

1/2 teaspoon vanilla

Beat egg whites until frothy. Add sugar gradually and beat until stiff. Add vanilla and pile on pie. Bake as directed above. Topping for 1 (9-inch) pie.

From the Military Meals at Home Cookbook, 1943.

Mrs. Truman's Frozen Lemon Pie

2 eggs, separated

1/3 cup fresh lemon juice

1 tablespoon grated lemon rind

1 cup whipped cream

1/2 cup sugar

1/2 cup crumbled graham crackers

Beat egg yolks. Add lemon juice, rind and all, with two tablespoons of sugar. Cook over low heat, stirring constantly. Cool. Beat egg whites, add two more tablespoons of the sugar, fold into cooked mixture; then fold in whipped cream. Line greased pie or refrigerator pan with graham cracker crumbs. Save some to sprinkle on top. Pour filling into pan and freeze.

Harry S. Truman Library & Museum

Oatmeal Cookies

1 1/2 tablespoon flour
1/2 teaspoon salt
1 teaspoon baking powder
1/2 cup sugar
1 1/4 cups oatmeal
1 egg
1/4 cup milk
1/2 teaspoon flavoring

Sift together flour, salt, and baking powder. Mix in the sugar and oatmeal, and add to the lightly beaten egg and milk. Add the flavoring and mix until well blended. Drop by spoonfuls onto a greased cooky sheet and bake in a moderate oven (350° F.) This makes a crisp chewy cooky with a nutty flavor.

NOTE: the original pamphlet spelling of "cooky" is kept as found in the original pamphlet.

From the pamphlet Fats in Wartime Meals, 1943.

Rumford Drop Cookies

War-time way to keep the cookie jar full-with easily digested honey as the sweet-tooth ingredient!

2 1/2 cups sifted flour
3 teaspoons Rumford Baking Powder
1/4 teaspoon salt
2/3 cup shortening
1 1/4 cups honey
1 egg, well beaten
1 1/2 teaspoons vanilla

SIFT together flour, Rumford Baking Powder and salt. Cream shortening,

289

add honey slowly and cream until fluffy. Stir in well-beaten egg and vanilla. Add sifted dry ingredients, a little at a time, blending well after each addition. Drop by teaspoonfuls on lightly greased cookie sheet and bake in a moderately hot oven (425° F.) for 12 to 15 minutes. Makes about 4 dozen cookies.

Rumford Baking Powder, Sugarless Recipe Booklet World War II.

Mamie's (Eisenhower) Sugar Cookies

1/2 cup butter
1 cup sugar
2 egg yolks
1 Tbs. cream
1 tsp. vanilla
1/2 tsp. salt
1 tsp. baking powder
1 1/2 cup flour

Mix and sift flour, baking powder and salt. Cream butter, add sugar slowly and cream until fluffy. Stir in well-beaten egg yolks and vanilla extract. Add sifted dry ingredients alternately with the cream. Chill for one hour, roll and cut in any desired shape. Sprinkle with sugar before baking. Bake in a moderate oven (350° or 375° degrees) for 10 to 12

The Dwight D. Eisenhower Presidential Library and Museum.

WWII Carrot Cookies

You will need
1 tablespoon margarine
2 tablespoons sugar
1 to 2 teaspoons of vanilla essence
4 tablespoons grated raw carrot
6 tablespoons self- raising flour (or plain flour with 1/2 teaspoon baking powder added)
1 tablespoon of water.

Method—Cream the fat and the sugar together with the vanilla essence. Beat in the grated carrot. Fold in the flour. If mixture very dry then add a little water. Drop spoonfuls onto greased tray and press down just a little. Sprinkle tops with sugar and cook in an oven at 200° centigrade for about 20 minutes.

Recipe courtesy of the World Carrot Museum, www.carrotmuseum.co.uk

Potato Griddle Scones

    2 cups sifted flour

    1 teaspoon salt

    3 teaspoons baking powder

    3 tablespoons fat

    1 cup cold mashed potatoes

    1 egg, beaten

    1/3 cup milk (about)

Sift together flour, milt, and baking powder. Cut in fat with 2 knives or a pastry blender. Blend in the potatoes. Mix egg and milk; add to first mixture. Mix slightly. Roll 3/8 inch thick and cut into squares. Bake slowly on a hot greased griddle or frying pan. Turn several times to cook through. Makes 10 to 12.

For a main dish, pour creamed left-over meat or fish or vegetables over the scones.

From the pamphlet Potatoes in Popular Ways, 1944.

WWII Mock Apricot Tarts

    1 pound young carrots

    A few drops almond essence

    4 round tablespoons plum jam

    About 6 tablespoons cold water

    1 pound short crust or potato pastry

    2 teaspoons jam more if it can be spared

A 9 inch pie plate or flan dish, Flour dredger, Rolling pin, Greaseproof paper, Baking beans, Baking tray, Medium saucepan, Potato peeler, Grater, Tablespoon, Palette knife. Oven set at 190° C / gas mark 5, Shelf near the top, Time: 15-20 minutes.

    1. Line plate or flan dish with pastry and neaten carefully,

    2. Prick base with a fork,

    3. Add crumpled greaseproof paper and backing beans,

    4. Bake blind for 15 minutes,

    5. Remove paper and dry out 5 minutes more,

6. Cool,

7. While cases are cooking, peel, wash and dry the carrots,

8. Grate into saucepan,

9. Add jam, essence and water and cook slowly until a pulp forms,

10. Stir regularly and check it's not drying up,

11. Spread over the pastry case and top with a little more jam if available,

12. Could be served with mock cream.

Recipe courtesy of the World Carrot Museum, www.carrotmuseum.co.uk

Ice Cream

1/2 cup sugar

1/4 cup flour

2 eggs

2 cups milk

1/8 teaspoon salt

1 1/2 teaspoons vanilla

2 cups cream

Combine sugar and flour in top of double boiler. Beat eggs, add milk and salt, add gradually to dry ingredients, stirring to prevent lumping, Cook until mixture begins to thicken. Chill. Add vanilla and cream. Freeze in crank freezer. Makes 1 quart. Any flavoring extract may be used for flavor in place of vanilla, or any fruit may be added. This ice cream may be used as a base for chocolate, coffee, peach, strawberry ice cream, etc.

CHOCOLATE—Add 2 squares (2 ounces) melted chocolate to the hot milk custard.

COFFEE—Scald 1/4 cup ground coffee with the milk, strain through cheesecloth and cool before adding to eggs.

From the Military Meals at Home Cookbook, 1943.

Mrs. Truman Coconut Balls

This recipe for Coconut Balls was served by Mrs. Truman for White House Teas.

1 1/2 c. coconut

2/3 c. sweetened condensed milk

Dash of salt

1 tsp. vanilla

1/4 tsp. almond extract

Combine ingredients and make into balls. Bake on greased sheet at 350° degrees for 15 minutes, or until brown. Makes about 18 balls.

Harry S. Truman Library & Museum

Gingerbread

2 cups sifted flour

1/2 teaspoon soda

I teaspoon baking powder

1/2 teaspoon soft

1 teaspoon ginger

l egg

1/2 cup milk

1/4 cup malted lot (drippings, rendered meat or poultry fat, lard)

Sift together the flour, soda, baking powder, salt, and ginger. Combine the beaten egg, milk, and melted far, and add to the dry ingredients, stirring in the molasses last. Beat well. Bake in a shallow pan in a moderate oven (350° F.) about 30 minutes or in muffin pans in a hot oven (400° F.) for 20 to 25 minutes. Serve hot with applesauce or lemon sauce.

From the pamphlet Fats in Wartime Meals, 1943.

Rice and Pear pudding

NOTE: This recipe is from the personal diary / cookbook of a British Army Chef who served in North Africa during World War Two. According to Nick Britten, journalist for the Telegraph newspaper the personal cookbook contained 118 recipes, all hand written by Harrison.

Rice 6 1/2 lbs

Pears 6 1/2lbs

Nut Meg (SIC) 2oz

Cloves 1/2 oz

Sugar 1 1/2 lbs

Milk 25pts

Margarine 3/4 lb

Bring the milk to a boil, add rice, sugar, spices and margarine, cook till soft. Add peeled and chopped pears and cook for few minutes.

From the personal cookbook of British Army Chef, Cpl James Abraham Harrison.

Sweet Potato Pudding
>   4 tablespoons butter
>   1/4 teaspoon salt
>   1/2 cup sugar
>   3 tablespoons lemon juice
>   3 eggs, separated
>   2 cups hot mashed sweet potatoes
>   1/2 cup evaporated milk

Cream butter until soft, add salt and sugar and continue creaming until sugar is well blended. Add lemon juice, beaten egg yolks, potatoes and milk. Mix thoroughly. Pour into greased baking dish. Beat egg whites until stiff and spread over pudding. Bake in moderate oven (325° F.) until browned. Serves 6.

From the Military Meals at Home Cookbook, 1943.

Mrs. Truman's Punch
>   4 quarts grape juice
>   3 quarts ginger ale
>   1 quart lemon juice
>   3 gallons water
>   Sugar to taste

Keep cool by using a 2 quart brick of Lemon Ice in the punch bowl. Yield: 5 gallons

Harry S. Truman Library & Museum.

Mrs. Truman's Fruit Punch
>   1 pint lemon juice
>   3 quarts orange juice
>   2 quarts ginger ale
>   2 quarts White Rock
>   1 gallon water
>   1 pint white grape juice
>   Sugar to taste
>   Yield: 3 gallons

Harry S. Truman Library & Museum.

CHAPTER TEN

The Spice Pack

One of the rations developed during World War Two was the Spice Pack. This ration was actually a combination of actual spices and other items packed together as a supplement to the other rations that had been developed during the war. The main use of the Spice Pack was with larger units, bases and facilities that would have had a larger field kitchen or even a stationary kitchen such as those found in hospitals. It could be said that the spice pack was a combination of a lot of smaller things that did not fit neatly into other rations or packaging.

This chapter is named the Spice Rack for the same reasons. In this chapter you will find a lot of small bits of information on many topics. Some topics could be related to others, some could be pieces of standalone information and some have absolutely nothing to do with Chow.

Navy Food Notes
- "Active men need large amounts of energy, 3500 to 4500 calories per day. In a well balanced diet it is estimated that approximately 10 to 15 per cent of the calories should be derived from protein; 55 to 70 per cent from carbohydrates and 20 to 30 per cent from fat"
- "Dessert has a definite place in the menu because it gives a feeling of satisfaction. Many people crave sweets and are accustomed to having them after a meal."
- Coffee is a delicate and perishable product and requires careful handling. Navy coffee has been expertly blended and roasted."

Source—The Cookbook of the United States Navy, 1944.

WWII Food Notes

- **Puffed Corn & Soybeans**—Before the end of the war, and for a period of time after it, cereal manufactures used ground puffed corn as a substitute for almost 20% of wheat based cereals due to a shortage of baking flour. There was also an increase the production of soy flour. It was a cost effective solution to shortages and use increase in everything from commercial foods to ingredients for military rations.
- **Last Ration Standing**—The last rationed item to be removed from the official ration list was meat. It was taken off the ration list in the United Kingdom in 1954. Sugar was removed in 1953.
  Frozen Foods—Frozen foods made huge advancements prior to and during World War Two. However, the number of people in the United States that had a proper refrigerator with freezer able to properly store frozen foods increased dramatically only after the war was over.
- **Nutritional Benefits of Rationing**—In Britain it is often noted that there were some benefits to food and goods rationing as more and more people—rich or poor—were forced to eat the same diet without many extras and which was rich in vegetables. People walked more due to limitations on fuel, people worked in gardens and many jobs were more labor intensive due to the war effort.

Pabst Blue Ribbon Goes Camouflaged

During World War II rationing affected Pabst Brewing Company just as it did everyone else. Tin was one of the items the military needed and it was also used to make cans for Pabst Blue Ribbon beer. Most of the Pabst domestic packaging switched to bottles. But the familiar PBR can in blue; cream and silver did still remain in limited use. The majority of PBR bottled in cans during the war was shipped to military men, mostly in the Pacific. One of the more legendary beers in the Pacific was PBR in a green can, or according to Pabst officials—the Camo-can . . . or camouflage can.

Tin cans had a reflective surface so it had to be altered so it would not become a target. Many veterans will tell you that the cans were simply printed in green ink. But, instead of changing the whole production process to handle two versions of the can, one for civilian use and one for

*Photos and information courtesy of
Pabst Blue Ribbon and
Schlitz Brewing Co.*

PABST IN PICTURES

Pacific Veteran
Returns to Pabst

A veteran of the Pacific Theater of Operations is this Pabst Blue Ribbon can sent by Leonard Recla to Guest Relations Director Walter Kessler at the Milwaukee Plant. According to Lenny's letter, his shipmates "didn't all drink from the enclosed can, but it is symbolic of afternoons we won't soon forget. The can—when it reaches you—will have traveled a great distance. The fellows have eagerly affixed their names in the hope that Pabst will be found no matter what the island or country . . . In short, they wanted to join me in thanking you for the part you have splendidly contributed to making Pabst available so far from home." Lenny formerly worked at Pabst Depot in Milwaukee. His wife, Helen, is employed in the Milwaukee Employment Office.

military, Pabst went the extra step. The cans were produced one way and then the cans heading to the front were coated with a transparent dark green glaze. The reflective properties of the can were eliminated but the guys drinking the PBR could still see the label.

There can be something depressing about drinking out of a generic green can with "beer" printed on the side. Seeing the brand name and logo of a product from home nay have made a few GI's feel like they were getting a taste of home, even if it was in the Pacific.

Source—Pabst Blue Ribbon.

Saluting Quartermaster Numbers
- At the height of the World War Two the Quartermasters were providing more than 24 million meals every day and 70,000 different supply items.
- When the war was over, the Quartermaster Corps had recovered and buried nearly a quarter of a million soldiers. During the conflict a total of 4,943 Quartermaster soldiers lost their lives.
- By June of 1940 the Army was ready to start procurement of D ration bars. Initial production started 200,000 bars in September of 1941 but increased an amazing amount to ten million bars only a year later. By 1943 so many D ration bars had been ordered, manufactured and stored that none were ordered in 1943. A final procurement of D ration bars was made in 1944.
- In volume, approximately one billion special rations, costing about 675 millions of dollars, were procured between 1941 and 1945. More than 23 different rations and ration supplements were developed during the war by the United State military alone. This does not include rations developed by other Allied nations.
- The majority of standard recipes used during World War II by cooks and bakers were developed by 1941. Recipes were developed, tested and approved by soldiers acting as taste testers. These taste testers evaluated rations and cooked meals in various settings from inside to outdoors on maneuvers to simulate real life situations. Improvements to recipes and rations continued as the war progressed and different needs were addressed.

Source—Fort Lee Quartermaster Museum.

More Flavors

Besides the well known planting of assorted vegetables in Victory Gardens, planters also increased the use of easily grown spices and herbs such as thyme, mint, sage, marjoram and more.

A Few Notable Quotes From The Army Cook
- "Coffee is the most important beverage served in the Army."
- "Meat that has spoiled usually has an unmistakable odor."
- "Good cooking is recognized the world over as a fine art, and a

good cook always commands respect. Cooks who perfect themselves in their art are always in demand, and many acquire wealth and fame."

- "A good cook takes pride in serving appetizing meals, in keeping himself and the kitchen clean and sanitary, and preventing waste. When he takes interest in his duties and constantly turns out the best possible meals, it will promote health, contentment, and pride of organization in each soldier. On the other hand, poorly cooked meals will do more to make soldiers discontented than any other factor."

- "A good cook takes pride in serving appetizing meals, in keeping himself and the kitchen clean and sanitary, and preventing waste. When he takes interest in his duties and constantly turns out the best possible meals, it will promote health, contentment, and pride of organization in each soldier. On the other hand, poorly cooked meals will do more to make soldiers discontented than any other factor."

- "The soldier enjoys variety, not only in the food themselves but in methods of preparing them. He wants foods that appeal to his eyes and his sense of taste and smell; he wants to eat in pleasant surroundings. His food should be wholesome and good to eat."

Source—The Army Cook Training Manual, TM 10-405, April 24, 1942

Important QM History Notes

- The Quartermaster Department was established by Congress on June 16, 1775. The First Quartermaster General was Major (later Major General) Thomas Mifflin. He was appointed by General George Washington, commander of the Continental Army on August 14, 1775. It was not until 1912, when consolidation of the Quartermaster Department, made food a Quartermaster responsibility.

- The Civil war was the first place canned goods were used as a method to store and deliver rations and to feed troops. Use was limited by today's standards but many brands are still familiar to consumers today. Condensed milk, invented by Gail Borden, and pork and beans produced by Van Camp were sometimes enjoyed by troops and Tabasco brand hot sauce was already a military staple during the War Between the States.

- Military cooking standardization started in 1896. A cooking manual for Army cooks was developed and published by the Commissary General of the U.S. Subsistence Department Each recipe served 100 men. Many modern day military recipes still follow the 100 man rule. During World War II more precise ingredient measurements were developed, still following the 100 portion rule.

Source—Fort Lee Quartermaster Museum.

No Sliced Bread

During the war bakers in the United States had to stop selling sliced bread. Only whole loaves were made available to the public. Many factors were cited for the ban including a shortage of wax paper for wrapping, needed metal for blades should be used in the war effort. But many bakeries already had blades. These were ordered to stop slicing loaves because it gave an unfair advantage to them as compared to bakeries that did not have a slicer. The ban was largely ineffective and lifted in 1943.

Getting the Food there—Merchant Marine Facts

- The Merchant Marine was called the "Fourth Arm of Defense" by President Roosevelt and some argue the Allies would have lost had there not have existed the means to carry the food, rations, personnel, additional supplies, and equipment needed to defeat the Axis powers. According the USMM It took 7 to 15 tons of supplies to support one soldier for one year.
- The United States Merchant Marine prewar total of 55,000 experienced mariners was increased to over 215,000 through U.S. Maritime Service training programs.
- Merchant ships faced danger from not only from submarines but also mines, armed raiders and destroyers, aircraft, "kamikaze," and bad weather. About 8,300 mariners were killed at sea, 12,000 wounded of whom at least 1,100 died from their wounds, and 663 men and women were taken prisoner.
- 1 in 26 mariners serving aboard merchant ships in World WW II

died in the line of duty, suffering a greater percentage of war-related deaths than all other U.S. services. Casualties were kept secret during the War to keep information about their success from the enemy.

- The Merchant Marine took part in every invasion of World War II. Many Liberty Ships, and other types, had temporary accommodations for up to 200 troops.

Source—American Merchant Marine at War, www.usmm.org

Coke Goes To War

- According to the Coke Cola company 64 bottling plants were set up around the world to supply troops during the war. This followed an urgent request for bottling equipment and materials from General Eisenhower's base in North Africa. Many of these war-time plants were later converted to civilian use.
- A cablegram from General Dwight Eisenhower's Allied Headquarters in North Africa. Dated June 29, 1943, requested a shipment of materials and equipment for building 10 bottling plants overseas as well as 3 million filled bottles of Coca-Cola. Within six months, a Company engineer had flown to Algiers and opened the first plant, the forerunner of 64 bottling plants shipped abroad during World War II. The plants were set up as close as possible to combat areas in Europe and the Pacific.
- More than 5 billion bottles of Coke were consumed by military service personnel during World War Two, in addition to countless servings through dispensers and mobile, self-contained units in battle areas.

Source—Coca-Cola Co.

Baskin-Robins

Burton "Burt" Baskin was a Lieutenant in the U.S. Navy and was known produced ice cream for his fellow troops. When the war was over he opened up his own small chain of ice cream shops. He later teamed up with his brother-in-law, Irvine "Irv" Robbins, who also owned a group of ice cream parlors. Irv, also a WWII veteran, and grew up learning the ice cream business while working in his father's store. The new joint company was named Baskin-Robbins.   *Source—Baskin-Robins Co.*

301

Beer is the Issue?

The following quote is from the article "Rock" Morale written by Lt Col. C.L. Banks which appeared in the Marine Corps Gazette in February of 1946. The article dealt with ways morale could be kept up as the fighting ended in the Pacific and more and more men were shipped home as many stayed. Morale seemed to be a problem with troops.

"Probably one of the greatest morale factors on an isolated island is the beer issue. It is not only important that the men receive their beer but it is just as important that it be issued cold and as regular as the supply will permit. A beer garden or "slop chute" should be made available. This should be in a place that will induce the men to "drink it here" rather than in their tents. The cola issue is as important as the beer issue as the number of non-beer drinkers in the service is large."

Source—Courtesy of the Marine Corps History Division.

Adapting

Marines suffering from supply issues in Guadalcanal quickly adapted by supplementing their diets with items captured from Japanese supply dumps. At the start of the operation (Operation Order 6-42) called for ten days C rations, ten days D rations and 60 days B rations.

Source—Courtesy of the Marine Corps History Division.

Army Catering Corps

- "Food is a vital weapon, both in war and peace. The scale of issue to a soldier ensures that each individual receives a balanced ration that will keep him healthy. The preparation and cooking, therefore, of that ration is vital so that none of its value is wasted."

- "Rations, when issued, pass through many hands, and no efforts, however small, by anyone concerned in their preparation can be considered wasted if it enables wholesome and varied food to be served in an appetizing form and in surroundings of reasonable comfort. Waste should never be permitted."

- The main Army Catering Corps cooking school was located in Aldershot England. During the war the school trained cooks, instructors, messing sergeants, mess stewards, commanding officers and more. The school featured kitchens, field kitchen training areas, pantries, class rooms, mess halls and more. There was also space dedicated to improving food and rations and developing better methods of cooking and testing new equipment.

• The Army Catering Corps also had several smaller cooking schools available dotted around the country and in other countries. These were for smaller class sizes, or for more specialized training or just temporary facilities used when needed to train cooks. Some trained at the Messing Officers' Training Centre.

• Courses included a Commanding Officers Course, Messing Officers Course, Serjeant (Sergeant) Cooks Course, Corporal Cooks Course, Officers Mess Cooks Course, Potential Tradesmen Cooks Course, Senior NCO Hospital Cooks Course, Hospital Course, Instructors Course, Butchers Course and more.

Source—1945 Army Catering Corps Manual.

Childs Play

Before becoming a famous chef and author Julia Child worked secretly in the spy fold of the OSS, Office of Strategic Services, during the war. Classified material released in 2008 shows that the OSS, an early forerunner to the CIA, utilized the services of Miss Child as well as the sons of Teddy Roosevelt—Quentin and Kermit, John Hemingway—Ernest Hemingway's son, Supreme Court Justice Author Goldberg, Chicago White Sox catcher Moe Berg as well as many other civilians, actors, writers and more.

Source—*BBC News.*

Coast Guard WWII Facts

• During World War Two 241,093 Coast Guardsmen served with 1,917 killed in action or by other means.

• During the war in both the Pacific and during D-day, many of the invasion troops were transported to shore by Coast Guard manned ships and landing craft. During action in the Gilbert Islands the Coast Guard boat-crews continued their grueling and dangerous jobs for hours and days on end. They unloaded their craft of men and supplies on the beaches while providing cover fire and taking on fire. The crews worked for several days on end without getting off their small craft even to eat or sleep. Supplies, such as coffee, were lowered to them by rope and buckets from transports. The crews would sleep at night while anchored offshore.

- During the war the U.S. Navy credited Coast Guard forces with sinking or assisting in the sinking of thirteen U-boats and one Japanese submarine. Coast Guardsmen also captured two Nazi surface vessels including one, U-234, that was bound for Japan transporting a cargo of uranium and the latest German rocket and jet technology.

- The cutters, the U.S.S. Icarus, C.G., sank the U-352 and then rescued the surviving crewman off North Carolina in 1942 and have the distinction of being the first U.S. servicemen to capture German prisoners of war in World War II.

- The U.S.S. Spencer, C.G., one of the 327-foot Treasury Class cutters, attacked and sank the U-175 in the open Atlantic and two combat photographers caught the battle on film. Some of the Spencer's crew actually boarded the stricken submarine, becoming the first U.S. servicemen to board an enemy warship that was under way at sea since the War of 1812.

- The SPARs were established in 1942. LCDR Dorothy Stratton transferred from the Navy to serve as the director of the SPARs. More than 11,000 SPARs served during World War II. (The Coast Guard Academy was the first military service academy to admit women.)

- One of the most famous Coast Guard WWII veterans was a dog by the name of Sinbad who actually had a rank of K9C (Chief Petty Officer, Dog.) Sinbad was known for his "Favorite Bars" in port. Sinbad served on the Combat Cutter Campbell and did see combat in several cases.

- Some famous names that served in the Coast Guard During World War Two include Cesar Romero, Sid Caesar, Buddy Epsen, Arthur Godfrey, Otto Graham, Rudy Vallee and Tom Blake—Legendary surfer and pioneer in the invention and refinement of surfing and lifesaving equipment. His inventions include the hollow surfboard, paddleboard, rescue torpedo, ring buoy or life ring, sailboard (windsurfer), surfboard fin, and waterproof camera housing. And we can't forget . . . Donald Duck.

Source—United States Coast Guard Historians offfice.

Carrots & Eyesight Equals Radar

In Britain the government needed a way to get the public to eat more carrots. It was one food staple that was rarely in short supply. Not only did a very slick ad campaign using carrots for ingredients in many recipes gain quick success, the planted story of British night fighters developing better eyesight due to eating lots of carrots was also a success in covering up a huge advancement in radar technology. The story of Aircrews having a diet rich in carrots which helped them see enemy bombers better was placed in media outlets as a way to cover up the fact that better radar was in use. The story was needed to explain increases in down enemy planes during night raids without alerting German forces to advanced radar capabilities. The campaign was a huge success and covered up the new radar from the Germans. Also, carrot testing for better eyesight did take place for pilots during 1940.

Source—World Carrot Museum.

Krystal Hamburgers & WWII

The small square hamburgers served up by the growing Krystal Company, based in Chattanooga, Tennessee were becoming very popular since the chain started in 1932. As World War II began, the nation started to face food rationing on many items including beef. To keep up with business demands, Krystal introduces chicken and egg sandwiches. After the war, Krystal returns to selling its signature burger.

Source—The Krystal Co.

Spam Facts

- In 1943 Hormel hired 448 women to help replace men during the war effort. By 1944 over 1,300 women worked on the production lines.

  Source—Hormel Foods.

- By April 1945 over 100 million pounds of SPAM® Luncheon meat was shipped abroad. The SPAM® product had been available to the public since 1937. Sixty five percent to eighty percent of all Hormel products were produced for Uncle Sam in efforts to feed troops in both the Pacific and in Europe.

- During the war years SPAM® kept pace with the patriotic effort. In 1943 Hormel® used black and white printed cans to help reduce printing cost which helped keep consumer costs down. By 1945 the "Hormel® Girls" were touring the country performing for war rallies and talking up Hormel® products and SPAM®.
- During World War II, SPAM® was a Lend-Lease commodity and was used to help feed countless allied civilians and armed forces. A 12-ounce can of SPAM® was produced for civilian use and a large 6-pound version was made for use in military shipments.
- Edward R. Murrow, famous broadcaster for the U.S., commented on the air during a 1942 broadcast, "This is London. Although the Christmas table will not be lavish, there will be SPAM® luncheon meat for everyone."
- When the United States entered World War Two, Hormel adapted the security measures that were required of all war related facilities. All employees not only photographed for official ID tags, but they were also finger printed and required to wear identification badges when coming to work.

Source—Hormel Foods

- The Hormel Girls started as a simple promotion but grew into a collective group of talented women who not only spread the message of Hormel products, including SPAM, but also entertained listeners during war time radio broadcasts across the country. The Hormel Girls continued their message past the war years.

Source—Hormel Foods.

Here Comes Hershey

- The Hershey Chocolate Corporation provided milk chocolate bars to American doughboys in the first war. When World War II started the company produced a survival ration bar for military use. By the end of the war, more than a billion of these Ration D bars had been manufactured. Hershey's earned no less than five Army-Navy "E" Production Awards for its exceptional contributions to the war effort.

- According to the Hershey Company the military did not want the ration bars produced by the candy maker to taste too good! The thought was that if it tasted too delicious the soldiers would be tempted to eat it before they needed it and would not have it in an emergency. It's hard to ask a company that prides itself on quality products and taste to make something that does not taste good but the Hershey chocolate technologists came up with something that passed all tests. The specifications for the ration bar stated that it could only weighed about four ounces and that it would not melt at high temperatures. Of course it had to be high in food energy value as well.

- Hershey's Chocolate Corporation used its machine shop to help build parts for the Navy's antiaircraft guns.

- To The Moon!—The ration bars developed by the Hershey Company included several versions including the Field Ration D, that was so successful that by the end of 1945 approximately 24 million bars were being produced every week. More successful still was HERSHEY'S Tropical Chocolate Bar, a heat resistant bar with an improved flavor developed in 1943. In 1971, this bar even went to the moon with Apollo 15.

Source—The Hershey Co.

Guam & Pacific Memories

This information from the National Park Service relates food memories from the Pacific during World War Two.

- You ate until you could not eat anymore so you threw the food away. When the boxes would break open and food would fall out all over the place. . . . the Americans said, "You all eat these things. This is our food. Let's all eat while we are all still alive."
Isaac Gafu, a laborer from Malaita working on Guadalcanal, remembers food given out by American troops.

- "Our engineers found them using hand-grenades to kill fish, and then cooking them in an oven made out of belly-tanks jettisoned from airplanes. But the great shock of our "wilderness-expedition" was when the natives used to motion them to sit down at about 6 a.m. and 6 p.m. every day pull out a book and start conducting religious ceremonies . . . one of the favorite tunes was clearly "Onward Christian soldiers."

Notes from former U.S. Senator James M. Mead, Tell the Folks Back Home, talking about Pacific islanders.

- Food moved in both directions. Military rations were dispersed to Islanders while locally produced foods were given, bartered or sold to soldiers. A man from Nguna, Vanuatu remembers by stating; "Americans needed bananas, pineapple, sugarcane, chicken, and everything. We brought many things for them, and gave them to them. We were happy that we were able to help them with every-thing of the land."

Source—National Park Service, Pacific Encounters.

Getting To Know Your PT Boat

This information comes from an official booklet given to sailors coming aboard PT boats to serve. These notes are pulled from the section about living areas. Take note of the tip given to new sailors about the attitude of PT Boat Cooks.

- **Head.**—Use it right. Pumps are difficult to get. Be sure the valve is shut after the bowl is flushed or else you will start to ship water. An open-head pump underway is-like having a hole in your bottom. This space is also a good spot in which to stow canned goods and your spare anchor, as well as spare soap and toilet tissue.
- **Crew's Quarters.**—This will be your home. Take care of it. A well-painted deck usually will keep it dry. Don't forget to look under the lower deck plates. You may be carrying an aquarium around and not know it except that your boat will be slow and loggy.
- **Charthouse.**—Within the charthouse are the vitals of the boat. From here the movement of the boat is directed, hence it is the brains of the boat. The equipment it contains need not be listed here. The RM and QM should be well acquainted with their tools and so should the rest of the crew. A few points will be made here as to the use of some items. Like any engine, machine, or appara-tus, the equipment in the charthouse was made to be operated. Hence, it must be used to give efficient operation. If it is not used (like a man who doesn't take exercise) it gets sluggish and func-

tions poorly, if at all. Remember that a PT is exposed to moisture from both the sea and the atmosphere. All equipment should be run at least 15 minutes a day. This exercising will limber up the parts and dry them as well. To combat moisture from spray, watertight overhead and bulkheads cannot be allowed to wear or leak. Patch cracks and ruptures in the fabric promptly.

- **Galley.**—Here is where the "cook" heats up the cans. A PT galley is much more than that. It can and has turned out American, Italian, French, Chinese, and even Japanese cuisine. Pies, cookies, and cakes flow from this modernistic kitchen if you've got a happy cook. Your refrigerator can make ice cream, ice cubes, and frozen delights (especially good is frozen fruit cup). Once a Jap bullet punctured a refrigerator unit and drained it of all its freon. Several of the boats then decided to put armor plate about the refrigerator. So you see it's really very important, for it contributes to the living comforts which are all too few in the Area. Your refrigerator pump and motor need servicing. Don't let them wear down or overheat. To keep meat, your refrigerator must be in top shape. It is rare to have fresh meat and when issued it comes in 100-pound quantities. Hence the necessity for a good freeze or reefer. Have a drip pan properly placed or the meat juices will leak into the bilges and in a week you'll be accused of carrying a dead Jap around in your bilges.

- A bit of advice about the cook. He's likely to be temperamental and have his moods. He needs help at meal time. So keep him in good humor by mess cooking without griping and helping him get supplies. He may serve you breakfast in bed some morning. Generally, he's a good gunner, too. You'll learn to count on "cookie."

- The galley stove with all its attachments and source of power must be known by everyone. Above all, remember to have your generator running and galley switch "on", when the stove is operated. Also bear in mind that finding and destroying the enemy is more important than a hot pot of Joe. So don't gripe if the galley must be secured to give the needed juice to the radio equipment. In temperate zones and especially in the Tropics any food particles left about will attract insects and bugs.

309

- **Cockroach** races are swell to watch but not when the race course is your bread box. Aerosol bombs are used to fumigate the galley effectively.
- **Garbage** disposal appears to be a simple procedure on a PT but there are rules. Don't clutter up the beaches near your anchorage with tin cans. Punch holes in them. The best method is to dump garbage overboard at sea, taking care that cans are punctured. Guard against the loss of your garbage can. It's usually allowed to hang over the side to soak out. Don't forget to pick it up when your boat gets underway.
- **Day Room.**—A large place which can accommodate four bunks easily, and another sack set up in the center temporarily. A half—dozen army-style cots should be carried to accommodate sleepers topside. The day room is usually taken over by the engineers. They often make it into an ideal clubhouse except that smoking is absolutely prohibited in the day room.

Source—Know Your PT Boat booklet, 1945, *Navy Department Bureau of Ships.*

GI Slang

This is a very small selection of colorful slang terms for common war time items related to food . . . or chow. The interesting thing is the longevity of military slang. Some carry from conflict to conflict and generation to generation. Some have even made it into everyday use. Most of these are based on food, or food terms that are used to describe something else. An example would be when the word "cabbage" is used as a term for money.

- Army Chicken—Franks and beans.
- Armored Cow / Canned Cow/Sea Cow, canned milk or condensed milk, WWI & WWII.
- Bamboo juice—wine or alcohol in the Pacific.
- Battery Acid—Powdered lemonade or powdered juice.
- Blood / Red Eye—Ketchup and sometimes any sauce.
- Bug / Bug Wagon—Supply truck.
- Cabbage—A term for money.
- Canned Willie/Corned Willie—Several variations of this term

from the British for canned corned beef hash or canned hash or stew.

- Chicken—Colonels silver eagles.
- Chook, Scrambled Chook, Powdered Chook—Eggs of any variety, fresh or powdered.
- Chow—Any type of food or meal.
- Chow Down—Eating a meal, eating chow.
- Chow Hall—Mess hall or dining area.
- Cookhouse—Kitchen of any type
- Cookie—Cook, trained or even anyone in a unit that could "sling hash."
- Dixie, Dixie Basher, Dixie Bashing—A small pot, Washing dishes
- Dog Food or Goo—Corned beef hash, hash.
- Fly Light / Flying Light—Missing a meal or missing several meals.
- Gedunk—Sweets, ice cream, deserts—mostly Navy
- Grease / Axel Grease / Marge—Butter or Margarine
- Hard Tack / Tack / Dog Biscuit—Hard bread ration or cracker
- Hash Burner—cook
- Hooch—Hard liquor.
- Joe /Java/Mud—coffee
- Joe Pot—A coffee pot.
- Meat Hound—A guy that loves food.
- Mess / Mess Hall—Food or chow and dining area.
- Oranges—Vitamin C pills or tablets.
- Reefers — Often a Navy term for large refrigerators on ships.
- Scrambled Eggs—Gold braid on high ranking officers.
- Sea Gull / Sea Bird—Canned chicken or chicken
- Serum / Wank / Whallop—Whisky, beer, alcohol.
- Sewer Trout—Whitefish.
- Shot Up—Drunk
- Shrubbery—Sauerkraut or cooked cabbage.
- Slum / Slum Burner—Meat Stew & Cook or Rolling Kitchen.
- SOS—Shit on a Shingle—Chipped or Creamed beef on toast.
- Spam Can—B24 Liberator.
- Strawberries / Army Strawberries—Prunes.
- Tire Patch—Pancake (hoecake—made with cornmeal).

- Torpedo Juice—Homemade alcohol often made on PT boats.
- The Trots, Jungle Guts, Gallops—Many variations describing dysentery.
- Wad—Cake, scone, sandwich of any type.
- Weevils—Rice.

List compiled from interviews and museums and is in no way complete. WWII Slang words varied from country to country, from service to service and even from unit to unit.

Acknowledgement

Special thanks to Luther Hanson and the staff at Fort Lee Quartermaster Museum. And thanks to the many curators, staff, volunteers and directors of multiple museums and libraries who contributed to this book and to every military cook, baker, food service specialist and chow slinger who contributed their comments.

Museum List

An amazing number of museums, collectors, historians and history buffs helped out with this effort. Following is a listing of museums that submitted information, stories, pictures and more to this book. This is the most updated information at the time of printing, but I would urge anyone planning a visit to any of these museums

Air Force Historical Studies Office
The AFHSO has multiple locations around the Washington D.C area including some on Bolling Air Force Base. The best way to contact the AFHSO for research, and other information, is to visit them online. They have a complete contact page for all departments.
www.airforcehistory.hq.af.mil

American Merchant Marine Museum
United States Merchant Marine Academy
300 Steamboat Road
Kings Point, NY 11024
(516) 773-5515
http://www.usmma.edu/about/Museum

Army Historical Foundation
(Museum scheduled to open 2013)
www.armyhistory.org

Battleship North Carolina
1 Battleship Rd
Wilmington, NC 28401-2577
(910) 251-5797
www.battleshippnc.com

Camp Gordon Johnston Museum
1001 Gray Avenue
Carrabelle City Complex
Carrabelle, Florida 32322
850-697-8575
www.campgordonjohnston.com

Center For Military History
U.S. Army Center of Military History
Fort Lesley J. McNair, Washington, DC 20319-5058
www.history.army.mil/

Harry S. Truman Library & Museum
500 W. US Hwy. 24
Independence MO 64050
Phone: 816-268-8200
1-800-833-1225
www.trumanlibrary.org

Harold M. Freund American Museum of Baking
Supported by the American Institute of Baking
AIB International
1213 Bakers Way
Manhattan Kansas
66505-3999
1-785-537-4750
1-800-633-5137
https://museum.aibonline.org

MacArthur Memorial
MacArthur Square,
Norfolk, Virginia 23510
(757) 441-2965
http://www.macarthurmemorial.org/

National Air Force Museum of Canada
220 Rcaf Rd
Trenton, ON K0K 3W0, Canada
(613) 965-7223
www.airforcemuseum.ca

National Infantry Musem
Fort Benning Georgia
3800 South Lumpkin Road
Columbus, GA 31903-4211

(706) 545-2958
www.nationalinfantrymuseum.com

National Medal of Honor Museum
Post Office Box 11467
Chattanooga, Tennessee 37401
Located Inside Northgate Mall
(TN Hwy 153 at Hixson Pike)
Exhibit: (423) 394-0710
Archives: (423) 698-4511
www.mohm.org

National Museum of the Marine Corps
18900 Jefferson Davis Highway
Triangle, VA 22172
1-877-635-1775
www.usmcmuseum.com

National Museum of the U.S. Air Force
1100 Spaatz Street
Wright-Patterson AFB OH 45433
(937) 255-3286
www.nationalmuseum.af.mil

Naval Historical Society of Australia
The Boatshed, Building 25
Garden Island NSW 2011
Within Australia: (02) 9359 2372
Overseas: +61 2 9359 2372
www.navyhistory.org.au

Naval History & Heritage Command
805 Kidder Breese Street SE
Washington Navy Yard, DC
20374-5060
www.history.navy.mil

Quarter Ton & Military
Historic Military Vehicle Restoration

6654 Lafayette Road
Chickamauga, Georgia 30707

Royal Air Force Museum London
Grahame Park Way
London NW9, United Kingdom
020 8205 2266
www.rafmuseum.org.uk

The Royal Logistic Corps Museum
The Princess Royal Barracks
Deepcut
Surrey
GU16 6RW
Telephone: 01252 833371
www.rlcmuseum.co.uk

St. Mary's Submarine Museum
102 St. Marys Street West
Saint Marys, Ga. 31558-4945
912-882-2782
www.stmaryssubmuseum.com

San Francisco Maritime National Historical Park
USS Pampanito At Pier 45 Fisherman's Wharf
NOTE: The Maritime Museum offers several ships, displays and more at
several locations all near each other. Please call for hours of operation and
tour times for various ships etc.
San Francisco, CA 94123
415-775-1943
www.maritime.org

Sixth Cavalry Museum
6 Barnhardt Cir
Fort Oglethorpe, GA 30742-3646
(706) 861-2860
www.6thcavalrymuseum.com

The Dwight D. Eisenhower Presidential Library and Museum
200 S.E. 4th Street
Abilene, KS 67410
Tel: 785-263-6700
Toll free: 877 RING IKE
www.eisenhower.archives.gov

The History Shop
South Eastern Veterans Museum
6652 Lafayette Road
Chickamauga, Georgia 30707
706-375-1860
www.thehistorycompany.net

The Military Museums
(of Canada)
Naval Museum of Alberta
Army Museum of Alberta
Air Force Museum of Alberta
4520 Crowchild Trail SW
Calgary, AB T2T 5J4
www.themilitarymuseums.com

The National World War II Museum
504/ 528-1944
fax: 504/ 527-6088
945 Magazine Street
New Orleans, LA 70130
www.ddaymuseum.org

USS Alabama
Battleship Memorial Park
Battleship Parkway, Mobile Bay
P.O. Box 65
Mobile, AL 36601-0065
(251)433-2703
www.ussalabama.com

U.S. Army Quartermaster Museum
1201 22nd Street
Fort Lee, VA 23801
Phone: (804) 734-4203
www.qmmuseum.lee.army.mil

U.S. Coast Guard Museum
U.S. Coast Guard Academy
Waesche Hall
15 Mohegan Avenue
New London, CT 06320-8511
(860) 444-8511
www.uscg.mil/hq/cg092/museum

Veterans of All Wars Museum
71 Red Belt Road
Chickamauga, GA 30707

War in the Pacific National Park
135 Murray Boulevard, Suite 100
Hagåtña, GU 96910
Phone (671) 333-4050 or 333-4051
Fax (671) 477-7281
www.nps.gov/wapa

World Carrot Museum
Online Museum based in the UK
www.carrotmuseum.co.uk

Eisenhower's
Salad Dressing, 268
Salmon
  Cakes, 251-252
  Hash, 252
  Patties, Campbell's, 250
salt, shortages of, 32
Sandwich Pack, 54
Saturday Evening Post, 28
Sausage Rice Cake, 241
Savory Bean Stew, 239-240
Scalloped Asparagus and Spaghetti, 256
Schack, William A., 202
Schlitz Brewing Company, 297
Schollhamer, Franz, 123
schools, xx, 23, 38, 81, 84. *See also* U.S. Army Training School for Advanced Bakers
Scones, Potato Griddle, 291
scurvy, 181-182
Seabees, 130-131, 155, 175
783rd Military Police Battalion, 96
Sharpe, Henry G., 82
Shirey, Llewellyn E. "Lou", 180
shortages, 74, 145, 153, 165-166. *See also* rationing
Sifford, Herbert M., 119
Silver Star, 21, 22
Simmered Dry Beans, 259
Sinbad, 137, 304
Sisco, Herbert L., 199
6th Calvary Museum, 38, 40
sky trains, 18
slang, 310-312
Slaughter, John Robert, 132
Sleap Field, 98
S.O.S., 171, 175, 205, 238-239
soup. See Meats and Main Dishes
soybeans, 296
Spaghetti, Scalloped Asparagus and, 256
Spaghetti Italian Style, 244-245
Spam, 23, 108, 149, 178, 179, 190, 192, 197, 199, 200, 205, 226, 305-306

Spam recipes
  Fried Hot, 253
  and Potatoes, 253
  and Scrambled Eggs, 234
Spanish American War, 35-36, 81
Spanish Cream, 13
Spanish Rice, 266-267
SPARS, xiv, 29
Spice Pack, 58, 295
Spicer, Chrystopher J., 22
Spinach Loaf, 256
spoilage, 32, 35, 36, 163
Squash Flavored with Meat, 240
Stalin, Joseph, 9
Stanton, James J., 107
Stanton, Jim, 107
Stew, Savory Bean, 239-240
Stewart, James "Jimmy", 18-20
Stewed Okra and Tomatoes, 257
stews. *See* Meats and Main Dishes
storage, 44, 84, 179
Stratton, Dorothy, 304
submarines, 109-112, 161, 177, 212-213, 215-216
Subsistence Department, 33
subsistence noncommissioned officer, 86
Succotash, 266
sugar beets, 165-166
Sugar Cookies, Mamie's, 290
Sugarless Frosting, 281
supplies
  delivery of, 16-18
  reappropriation of, 165, 170, 193-194
supply lines
  improvements to, 39
  Normandy invasion and, 134-135
  PT boats and, 108
sutlers, 33, 34
Sweet Potato(es)
  Candied, 262-263
  Pudding, 294
Sweet-Sour Green Beans, 260

Tabasco Sauce, 1, 149, 300